THIRD EDITION

TOP NOTCH 3

ENGLISH FOR TODAY'S WORLD

JOAN SASLOW
ALLEN ASCHER

D1737074

With *Top Notch Pop* Songs and Karaoke
by Rob Morsberger

Top Notch: English for Today's World   Level 3, Third Edition

Copyright © 2015 by Pearson Education, Inc.

Pearson Education, 10 Bank Street, White Plains, NY 10606 USA

Staff credits: The people who made up the *Top Notch* team representing editorial, production, design, manufacturing, and marketing are Peter Benson, Kimberly Casey, Jennifer Castro, Tracey Munz Cataldo, Rosa Chapinal, Aerin Csigay, Dave Dickey, Gina DiLillo, Nancy Flaggman, Irene Frankel, Shelley Gazes, Christopher Leonowicz, Julie Molnar, Laurie Neaman, Sherri Pemberton, Rebecca Pitke, Jennifer Raspiller, Charlene Straub, and Kenneth Volcjak.

Cover credit: Sprint/Corbis

Text composition: TSI Graphics

Library of Congress Cataloging-in-Publication Data

Saslow, Joan M.
  Top Notch : English for today's world. Fundamentals / Joan Saslow, Allen Ascher ; With Top Notch Pop Songs
  and Karaoke by Rob Morsberger. — Third Edition.
      pages cm
  Includes biographical references.
  ISBN 978-0-13-354275-2 — ISBN 978-0-13-339348-4 — ISBN 978-0-13-354277-6 — ISBN 978-0-13-354278-3   1. English language—
  Textbooks for foreign speakers. 2. English language—Problems, exercises, etc. 3. English language—Sound recordings for foreign speakers.
  I. Ascher, Allen. II. Morsberger, Robert Eustis, 1929- III. Title. IV. Title: English for today's world.
  PE1128.S2757 2015
  428.2'4--dc23
                            2013044020

Printed in the United States of America
ISBN-10: 0-13-392821-7   ISBN-10: 0-13-354278-5 (with MyEnglishLab)
ISBN-13: 978-0-13-392821-1   ISBN-13: 978-0-13-354278-3 (with MyEnglishLab)
2 3 4 5 6 7 8 9 10—V003—19 18 17 16 15   2 3 4 5 6 7 8 9 10—V003—19 18 17 16 15

pearsonelt.com/topnotch3e

In Memoriam

Rob Morsberger (1959–2013)

The authors wish to acknowledge their memory of and gratitude to **Rob Morsberger**, the gifted composer and songwriter of the *Top Notch Pop* Songs and Karaoke that have provided learners both language practice and pleasure.

ABOUT THE AUTHORS

Joan Saslow

Joan Saslow has taught in a variety of programs in South America and the United States. She is author or coauthor of a number of widely used courses, some of which are *Ready to Go, Workplace Plus, Literacy Plus,* and *Summit.* She is also author of *English in Context,* a series for reading science and technology. Ms. Saslow was the series director of *True Colors* and *True Voices.* She has participated in the English Language Specialist Program in the U.S. Department of State's Bureau of Educational and Cultural Affairs.

Allen Ascher

Allen Ascher has been a teacher and teacher trainer in China and the United States, as well as academic director of the intensive English program at Hunter College. Mr. Ascher has also been an ELT publisher and was responsible for publication and expansion of numerous well-known courses including *True Colors, NorthStar,* the *Longman TOEFL Preparation Series,* and the *Longman Academic Writing Series.* He is coauthor of *Summit,* and he wrote the "Teaching Speaking" module of *Teacher Development Interactive,* an online multimedia teacher-training program.

Ms. Saslow and Mr. Ascher are frequent presenters at professional conferences and have been coauthoring courses for teens, adults, and young adults since 2002.

AUTHORS' ACKNOWLEDGMENTS

The authors are indebted to these reviewers, who provided extensive and detailed feedback and suggestions for *Top Notch,* as well as the hundreds of teachers who completed surveys and participated in focus groups.

Manuel Wilson Alvarado Miles, Quito, Ecuador • **Shirley Ando,** Otemae University, Hyogo, Japan • **Vanessa de Andrade,** CCBEU Inter Americano, Curitiba, Brazil • **Miguel Arrazola,** CBA, Santa Cruz, Bolivia • **Mark Barta,** Proficiency School of English, São Paulo, Brazil • **Edwin Bello,** PROULEX, Guadalajara, Mexico • **Mary Blum,** CBA, Cochabamba, Bolivia • **María Elizabeth Boccia,** Proficiency School of English, São Paulo, Brazil • **Pamela Cristina Borja Baltán,** Quito, Ecuador • **Eliana Anabel L. Buccia,** AMICANA, Mendoza, Argentina • **José Humberto Calderón Díaz,** CALUSAC, Guatemala City, Guatemala • **María Teresa Calienes Csirke,** Idiomas Católica, Lima, Peru • **Esther María Carbo Morales,** Quito, Ecuador • **Jorge Washington Cárdenas Castillo,** Quito, Ecuador • **Eréndira Yadira Carrera García,** UVM Chapultepec, Mexico City, Mexico • **Viviane de Cássia Santos Carlini,** Spectrum Line, Pouso Alegre, Brazil • **Centro Colombo Americano,** Bogota, Colombia • **Guven Ciftci,** Fatih University, Istanbul, Turkey • **Diego Cisneros,** CBA, Tarija, Bolivia • **Paul Crook,** Meisei University, Tokyo, Japan • **Alejandra Díaz Loo,** El Cultural, Arequipa, Peru • **Jesús G. Díaz Osío,** Florida National College, Miami, USA • **María Eid Ceneviva,** CBA, Bolivia • **Amalia Elvira Rodríguez Espinoza De Los Monteros,** Guayaquil, Ecuador • **María Argelia Estrada Vásquez,** CALUSAC, Guatemala City, Guatemala • **John Fieldeldy,** College of Engineering, Nihon University, Aizuwakamatsu-shi, Japan • **Marleni Humbelina Flores Urízar,** CALUSAC, Guatemala City, Guatemala • **Gonzalo Fortune,** CBA, Sucre, Bolivia • **Andrea Fredricks,** Embassy CES, San Francisco, USA • **Irma Gallegos Peláez,** UVM Tlalpan, Mexico City, Mexico • **Alberto Gamarra,** CBA, Santa Cruz, Bolivia • **María Amparo García Peña,** ICPNA Cusco, Peru • **Amanda Gillis-Furutaka,** Kyoto Sangyo University, Kyoto, Japan • **Martha Angelina González Párraga,** Guayaquil, Ecuador • **Octavio Garduño Ruiz,** Business Training Consultant, Mexico City, Mexico • **Ralph Grayson,** Idiomas Católica, Lima, Peru • **Murat Gultekin,** Fatih University, Istanbul, Turkey • **Oswaldo Gutiérrez,** PROULEX, Guadalajara, Mexico • **Ayaka Hashinishi,** Otemae University, Hyogo, Japan • **Alma Lorena Hernández de Armas,** CALUSAC, Guatemala City, Guatemala • **Kent Hill,** Seigakuin University, Saitama-ken, Japan • **Kayoko Hirao,** Nichii Gakkan Company, COCO Juku, Japan • **Jesse Huang,** National Central University, Taoyuan, Taiwan • **Eric Charles Jones,** Seoul University of Technology, Seoul, South Korea • **Jun-Chen Kuo,** Tajen University, Pingtung , Taiwan • **Susan Krieger,** Embassy CES, San Francisco, USA • **Ana María de la Torre Ugarte,** ICPNA Chiclayo, Peru • **Erin Lemaistre,** Chung-Ang University, Seoul, South Korea • **Eleanor S. Leu,** Soochow University, Taipei, Taiwan • **Yihui Li (Stella Li),** Fooyin University, Kaohsiung, Taiwan • **Chin-Fan Lin,** Shih Hsin University, Taipei, Taiwan • **Linda Lin,** Tatung Institute of Technology, Taiwan • **Kristen Lindblom,** Embassy CES, San Francisco, USA • **Patricio David López Logacho,** Quito, Ecuador • **Diego López Tasara,** Idiomas Católica, Lima, Peru • **Neil Macleod,** Kansai Gaidai University, Osaka, Japan • **Adriana Marcés,** Idiomas Católica, Lima, Peru • **Robyn McMurray,** Pusan National University, Busan, South Korea • **Paula Medina,** London Language Institute, London, Canada • **Juan Carlos Muñoz,** American School Way, Bogota, Colombia • **Noriko Mori,** Otemae University, Hyogo, Japan • **Adrián Esteban Narváez Pacheco,** Cuenca, Ecuador • **Tim Newfields,** Tokyo University Faculty of Economics, Tokyo, Japan • **Ana Cristina Ochoa,** CCBEU Inter Americano, Curitiba, Brazil • **Tania Elizabeth Ortega Santacruz,** Cuenca, Ecuador • **Martha Patricia Páez,** Quito, Ecuador • **María de Lourdes Pérez Valdespino,** Universidad del Valle de México, Mexico • **Wahrena Elizabeth Pfeister,** University of Suwon, Gyeonggi-Do, South Korea • **Wayne Allen Pfeister,** University of Suwon, Gyeonggi-Do, South Korea • **Andrea Rebonato,** CCBEU Inter Americano, Curitiba, Brazil • **Thomas Robb,** Kyoto Sangyo University, Kyoto, Japan • **Mehran Sabet,** Seigakuin University, Saitama-ken, Japan • **Majid Safadaran Mosazadeh,** ICPNA Chiclayo, Peru • **Timothy Samuelson,** BridgeEnglish, Denver, USA • **Héctor Sánchez,** PROULEX, Guadalajara, Mexico • **Mónica Alexandra Sánchez Escalante,** Quito, Ecuador • **Jorge Mauricio Sánchez Montalván,** Quito, Universidad Politécnica Salesiana (UPS), Ecuador • **Letícia Santos,** ICBEU Ibiá, Brazil • **Elena Sapp,** INTO Oregon State University, Corvallis, USA • **Robert Sheridan,** Otemae University, Hyogo, Japan • **John Eric Sherman,** Hong Ik University, Seoul, South Korea • **Brooks Slaybaugh,** Asia University, Tokyo, Japan • **João Vitor Soares,** NACC, São Paulo, Brazil • **Silvia Solares,** CBA, Sucre, Bolivia • **Chayawan Sonchaeng,** Delaware County Community College, Media, PA • **María Julia Suárez,** CBA, Cochabamba, Bolivia • **Elena Sudakova,** English Language Center, Kiev, Ukraine • **Richard Swingle,** Kansai Gaidai College, Osaka, Japan • **Blanca Luz Terrazas Zamora,** ICPNA Cusco, Peru • **Sandrine Ting,** St. John's University, New Taipei City, Taiwan • **Christian Juan Torres Medina,** Guayaquil, Ecuador • **Raquel Torrico,** CBA, Sucre, Bolivia • **Jessica Ueno,** Otemae University, Hyogo, Japan • **Ximena Vacaflor C.,** CBA, Tarija, Bolivia • **René Valdivia Pereira,** CBA, Santa Cruz, Bolivia • **Solange Lopes Vinagre Costa,** SENAC, São Paulo, Brazil • **Magno Alejandro Vivar Hurtado,** Cuenca, Ecuador • **Dr. Wen-hsien Yang,** National Kaohsiung Hospitality College, Kaohsiung, Taiwan • **Juan Zárate,** El Cultural, Arequipa, Peru

LEARNING OBJECTIVES

	COMMUNICATION GOALS	VOCABULARY	GRAMMAR
UNIT 1 **Make Small Talk** PAGE 2	• Make small talk • Describe a busy schedule • Develop your cultural awareness • Discuss how culture changes over time	• Asking about proper address • Intensifiers • Manners and etiquette	• Tag questions: use, form, and common errors • The past perfect: Statements **GRAMMAR BOOSTER** • Tag questions: short answers • Verb usage: present and past: overview
UNIT 2 **Health Matters** PAGE 14	• Show concern and offer help • Make a medical or dental appointment • Discuss types of treatments • Talk about medications	• Dental emergencies • Describing symptoms • Medical procedures • Types of medical treatments • Medications	• Drawing conclusions with <u>must</u> • <u>Will be able to</u>; Modals <u>may</u> and <u>might</u> **GRAMMAR BOOSTER** • Other ways to draw conclusions: <u>probably</u> and <u>most likely</u> • Expressing possibility with <u>maybe</u>
UNIT 3 **Getting Things Done** PAGE 26	• Offer a solution • Discuss how long a service will take • Evaluate the quality of service • Plan an event	• Ways to indicate acceptance • Services • Planning and running an event	• The causative • The passive causative **GRAMMAR BOOSTER** • Causative <u>make</u> to indicate obligation • <u>Let</u> to indicate permission • Causative <u>have</u>: common errors • The passive causative: the <u>by</u> phrase

UNIT 4
Reading for Pleasure
PAGE 38
	• Recommend a book
	• Ask about an article
	• Describe your reading habits
	• Discuss online reading
		• Genres of books
		• Ways to describe a book
		• Some ways to enjoy reading
			• Noun clauses: usage, form, and common errors
			• Noun clauses: Embedded questions
			  ∘ Form and common errors
			
			GRAMMAR BOOSTER
			• Verbs that can be followed by clauses with <u>that</u>
			• Adjectives that can be followed by clauses with <u>that</u>
			• Embedded questions
			  ∘ with whether
			  ∘ usage and common errors
			  ∘ punctuation

UNIT 5 **Natural Disasters** PAGE 50	• Convey a message • Tell someone about the news • Describe natural disasters • Prepare for an emergency	• Severe weather and other natural disasters • Reactions to news • Adjectives of severity • Emergency preparations and supplies	• Indirect speech: Imperatives • Indirect speech: <u>Say</u> and <u>tell</u>—tense changes **GRAMMAR BOOSTER** • Direct speech: punctuation rules • Indirect speech: optional tense changes

CONVERSATION STRATEGIES	LISTENING / PRONUNCIATION	READING	WRITING
• Talk about the weather to begin a conversation with someone you don't know • Use question tags to encourage someone to make small talk • Ask about how someone wants to be addressed • Answer a <u>Do you mind</u> question with <u>Absolutely not</u> to indicate agreement • Say <u>That was nothing!</u> to indicate that something even more surprising happened • Use <u>Wow!</u> to indicate that you are impressed	**Listening Skills** • Listen for main ideas • Listen to summarize • Confirm the correct paraphrases **Pronunciation** • Intonation of tag questions	**Texts** • A business meeting e-mail and agenda • An online article about formal dinner etiquette of the past • A survey about culture change • A photo story **Skills/Strategies** • Apply prior knowledge • Draw conclusions • Understand from context	**Task** • Write a formal and an informal e-mail message **WRITING BOOSTER** • Formal e-mail etiquette
• Introduce disappointing information with <u>I'm sorry, but . . .</u> • Show concern with <u>Is there anything wrong?</u> and <u>That must be awful</u> • Begin a question of possibility with <u>I wonder if . . .</u> • Use <u>Let's see . . .</u> to indicate you are checking for something • Confirm an appointment with <u>I'll / We'll see you then</u> • Express emphatic thanks with <u>I really appreciate it</u>	**Listening Skills** • Listen to activate vocabulary • Listen for details • Auditory discrimination **Pronunciation** • Intonation of lists	**Texts** • A travel tips website about dental emergencies • A brochure about choices in medical treatments • A medicine label • A patient information form • A photo story **Skills/Strategies** • Understand from context • Relate to personal experience • Draw conclusions	**Task** • Write an essay comparing two types of medical treatments **WRITING BOOSTER** • Comparisons and contrasts
• Use <u>I'm sorry, but . . .</u> and an excuse to politely turn down a request • Indicate acceptance of someone's excuse with <u>No problem.</u> • Suggest an alternative with <u>Maybe you could . . .</u> • Soften an almost certain <u>no</u> with <u>That might be difficult</u> • Use <u>Well, . . .</u> to indicate willingness to reconsider	**Listening Skills** • Listen to confirm • Listen for main ideas • Listen to summarize **Pronunciation** • Emphatic stress to express enthusiasm	**Texts** • A survey about procrastination • A business article about how to keep customers happy • A photo story **Skills/Strategies** • Infer point of view • Activate language from a text	**Task** • Write an essay expressing a point of view about procrastination **WRITING BOOSTER** • Supporting an opinion with personal examples
• Use <u>Actually</u> to show appreciation for someone's interest in a topic • Soften a question with <u>Could you tell me . . . ?</u> • Indicate disappointment with <u>Too bad</u> • Use <u>I'm dying to . . .</u> to indicate extreme interest • Say <u>Are you sure?</u> to confirm someone's willingness to do something	**Listening Skills** • Listen to take notes • Listen to infer a speaker's point of view and support your opinion **Pronunciation** • Sentence stress in short answers with <u>so</u>	**Texts** • An online bookstore website • A questionnaire about reading habits • A magazine article about the Internet's influence on our habits • A photo story **Skills/Strategies** • Recognize point of view • Understand meaning from context	**Task** • Write a summary and review of something you've read **WRITING BOOSTER** • Summarizing
• Use <u>I would, but . . .</u> to politely turn down an offer • Say <u>Will do</u> to agree to a request for action • Use <u>Well</u> to begin providing requested information • Say <u>What a shame</u> to show empathy for a misfortune • Introduce reassuring contrasting information with <u>But, . . .</u> • Say <u>Thank goodness for that</u> to indicate relief	**Listening Skills** • Listen for main ideas • Listen for details • Paraphrase • Listen to infer meaning **Pronunciation** • Direct and indirect speech: Rhythm	**Texts** • News headlines • A textbook article about earthquakes • Statistical charts • A photo story **Skills/Strategies** • Paraphrase • Confirm facts • Identify cause and effect • Interpret data from a chart	**Task** • Write a procedure for how to prepare for an emergency **WRITING BOOSTER** • Organizing detail statements by order of importance

	COMMUNICATION GOALS	VOCABULARY	GRAMMAR

UNIT 6
Life Plans
PAGE 62
	• Explain a change of intentions and plans
	• Express regrets about past actions
	• Discuss skills, abilities, and qualifications
	• Discuss factors that promote success
		• Reasons for changing plans
		• Qualifications for work or study
			• Expressing intentions and plans that changed: <u>Was / were going to</u> and <u>would</u>
			• Perfect modals
			
			GRAMMAR BOOSTER
			• Expressing the future: review
			• The future with <u>will</u> and <u>be going to</u>: review
			• Regrets about the past:
			  ◦ <u>Wish</u> + the past perfect
			  ◦ <u>Should have</u> and <u>ought to have</u>

UNIT 7
Holidays and Traditions
PAGE 74
	• Wish someone a good holiday
	• Ask about local customs
	• Exchange information about holidays
	• Explain wedding traditions
		• Types of holidays
		• Ways to commemorate a holiday
		• Some ways to exchange good wishes on holidays
		• Getting married: events and people
			• Adjective clauses with subject relative pronouns <u>who</u> and <u>that</u>
			  ◦ Usage, form, and common errors
			• Adjective clauses with object relative pronouns <u>who</u>, <u>whom</u>, and <u>that</u>
			  ◦ Form and common errors
			
			GRAMMAR BOOSTER
			• Adjective clauses: common errors
			• Reflexive pronouns
			• <u>By</u> + reflexive pronouns
			• Reciprocal pronouns: <u>each other</u> and <u>one another</u>
			• Adjective clauses: <u>who</u> and <u>whom</u> in formal English

UNIT 8 **Inventions and Discoveries** PAGE 86	• Describe technology • Take responsibility for a mistake • Describe new inventions • Discuss the impact of inventions / discoveries	• Describing manufactured products • Descriptive adjectives	• The unreal conditional: Review and expansion • The past unreal conditional ◦ Usage, form, and common errors **GRAMMAR BOOSTER** • Real and unreal conditionals: review • Clauses after <u>wish</u> • <u>Unless</u> in conditional sentences • The unreal conditional: variety of forms

UNIT 9
Controversial Issues
PAGE 98
	• Talk about politics
	• Discuss controversial issues politely
	• Propose solutions to global problems
	• Debate the pros and cons of issues
		• Political terminology
		• A continuum of political and social beliefs
		• Some controversial issues
		• Ways to agree or disagree
		• How to debate an issue politely
			• Non-count nouns that represent abstract ideas
			• Verbs followed by objects and infinitives
			
			GRAMMAR BOOSTER
			• Count and non-count nouns: review and extension
			• Gerunds and infinitives:
			  ◦ form and usage
			  ◦ usage after certain verbs

UNIT 10 **Beautiful World** PAGE 110	• Describe a geographical location • Warn about a possible risk • Describe a natural setting • Discuss solutions to global warming	• Geographical features • Compass directions • Ways to recommend or criticize a place • Ways to describe risks • Dangerous animals and insects • Geographic nouns and adjectives • Describing natural features • Energy and the environment	• Prepositional phrases of geographical places • <u>Too</u> + adjective and infinitive **GRAMMAR BOOSTER** • Prepositions of place: more usage • Proper nouns: capitalization • Proper nouns: use of <u>the</u> • Infinitives with <u>enough</u>

CONVERSATION STRATEGIES	LISTENING / PRONUNCIATION	READING	WRITING
• Say <u>No kidding!</u> to indicate delight or surprise • Say <u>How come?</u> to ask for a reason • Express a regret with <u>I should have . . .</u> • Use <u>You never know . . .</u> to reassure someone • Accept another's reassurance with <u>True</u>	**Listening Skills** • Listen for details • Listen to classify information • Listen to infer a speaker's motives **Pronunciation** • Reduction of <u>have</u> in perfect modals	**Texts** • Career and skills inventories • A magazine article with tips for effective work habits • A photo story **Skills/Strategies** • Understand from context • Confirm content	**Task** • Write a short autobiography **WRITING BOOSTER** • Dividing an essay into topics
• Show friendliness by wishing someone a good holiday • Reciprocate good wishes with <u>Thanks! Same to you!</u> • Preface a potentially sensitive question with <u>Do you mind if I ask you . . .</u> • Ask about socially appropriate behavior in order to avoid embarrassment • Express appreciation with <u>Thanks. That's really helpful</u>	**Listening Skills** • Listen for main ideas • Listen for details • Infer information **Pronunciation** • "Thought groups"	**Texts** • Factoids on holidays • A magazine article about holidays around the world • Proverbs about weddings • A photo story **Skills/Strategies** • Scan for facts • Compare and contrast • Relate to personal experience	**Task** • Write a detailed description of two holidays **WRITING BOOSTER** • Descriptive details
• Congratulate someone for a major new purchase • Apologize for lateness and provide an explanation • Indicate regret for a mistake by beginning an explanation with <u>I'm ashamed to say . . .</u> • Reduce another's self-blame with <u>That can happen to anyone</u> and <u>No harm done</u>	**Listening Skills** • Listen to draw conclusions • Listen to summarize • Listen to infer meaning • Infer the correct adjective **Pronunciation** • Contractions with <u>'d</u> in spoken English	**Texts** • Case studies of poor purchasing decisions • A book excerpt about antibiotics • Factoids on famous inventions • A photo story **Skills/Strategies** • Find supporting details • Understand from context	**Task** • Write an essay about the historical impact of an important invention or discovery **WRITING BOOSTER** • Summary statements
• Ask for permission when bringing up a topic that might be controversial • Use <u>So . . .</u> to begin a question clarifying someone's statement • Politely indicate unwillingness with <u>No offense, but . . .</u> • Apologize for refusing with <u>I hope you don't mind</u> • Use <u>How do you feel about . . .</u> to invite someone's opinion • Offer an explanation for one's opinion. • Use <u>Actually, . . .</u> to introduce a different point of view	**Listening Skills** • Infer a speaker's political and social beliefs • Infer a speaker's point of view • Listen to summarize • Auditory discrimination **Pronunciation** • Stress to emphasize meaning	**Texts** • A self-test of political literacy • A textbook introduction to global problems • A photo story **Skills/Strategies** • Activate language from a text • Critical thinking	**Task** • Write an essay presenting the two sides of a controversial issue **WRITING BOOSTER** • Contrasting ideas
• Show interest in someone's plans by asking follow-up questions • Indicate possible intention with <u>I've been thinking about it</u> • Qualify a positive response with <u>Sure, but . . .</u> • Elaborate further information using <u>Well, . . .</u> • Express gratitude for a warning	**Listening Skills** • Listen for main ideas • Listen to summarize • Listen for details • Infer a speaker's point of view **Pronunciation** • Voiced and voiceless <u>th</u>	**Texts** • Maps • An online article about ways to curb global warming • A photo story **Skills/Strategies** • Interpret maps • Understand from context • Critical thinking • Summarize	**Task** • Write a geographic description of your country, state, or province **WRITING BOOSTER** • Organizing by spatial relations

TO THE TEACHER

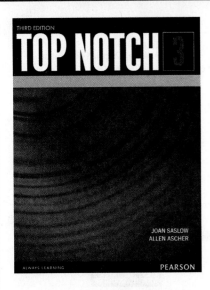

The goal of *Top Notch* is to make English unforgettable through:

- Multiple exposures to new language
- Numerous opportunities to practice it
- Deliberate and intensive recycling

The *Top Notch* course has two beginning levels—*Top Notch Fundamentals* for true beginners and *Top Notch 1* for false beginners. *Top Notch* is benchmarked to the Global Scale of English and is tightly correlated to the Can-do Statements of the Common European Framework of Reference.

Each full level of *Top Notch* contains material for 60–90 hours of classroom instruction. In addition, the entire course can be tailored to blended learning with an integrated online component, *MyEnglishLab*.

NEW This third edition of *Top Notch* includes these new features: Extra Grammar Exercises, digital full-color Vocabulary Flash Cards, Conversation Activator videos, and Pronunciation Coach videos.

* Summit 1 and Summit 2 are the titles of the 5th and 6th levels of the Top Notch course.

Award-Winning Instructional Design*

Daily confirmation of progress

Each easy-to-follow two-page lesson begins with a clearly stated practical communication goal closely aligned to the Common European Framework's Can-do Statements. All activities are integrated with the goal, giving vocabulary and grammar meaning and purpose. *Now You Can* activities ensure that students achieve each goal and confirm their progress in every class session.

Explicit vocabulary and grammar

Clear captioned picture-dictionary illustrations with accompanying audio take the guesswork out of meaning and pronunciation. Grammar presentations containing both rules and examples clarify form, meaning, and use. The unique *Recycle this Language* feature continually puts known words and grammar in front of students' eyes as they communicate, to make sure language remains active.

High-frequency social language

Twenty memorable conversation models provide appealing natural social language that students can carry "in their pockets" for use in real life. Rigorous controlled and free discussion activities systematically stimulate recycling of social language, ensuring that it's not forgotten.

Linguistic and cultural fluency

Top Notch equips students to interact with people from different language backgrounds by including authentic accents on the audio. Conversation Models, Photo Stories, and cultural fluency activities prepare students for social interactions in English with people from unfamiliar cultures.

Active listening syllabus

All Vocabulary presentations, Pronunciation presentations, Conversation Models, Photo Stories, Listening Comprehension exercises, and Readings are recorded on the audio to help students develop good pronunciation, intonation, and auditory memory. In addition, approximately fifty carefully developed listening tasks at each level of *Top Notch* develop crucial listening comprehension skills such as listen for details, listen for main ideas, listen to activate vocabulary, listen to activate grammar, and listen to confirm information.

*We wish you and your students enjoyment and success with **Top Notch 3**.*
We wrote it for you.

Joan Saslow and Allen Ascher

** **Top Notch** is the recipient of the Association of Educational Publishers' Distinguished Achievement Award.*

ActiveTeach

Maximize the impact of your *Top Notch* lessons. This digital tool provides an interactive classroom experience that can be used with or without an interactive whiteboard (IWB). It includes a full array of digital and printable features.

For class presentation . . .

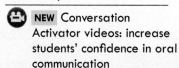 **NEW** Conversation Activator videos: increase students' confidence in oral communication

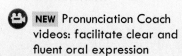 **NEW** Pronunciation Coach videos: facilitate clear and fluent oral expression

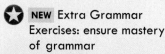 **NEW** Extra Grammar Exercises: ensure mastery of grammar

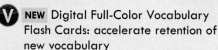 **NEW** Digital Full-Color Vocabulary Flash Cards: accelerate retention of new vocabulary

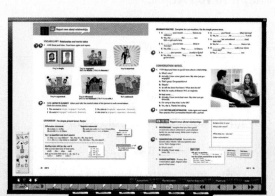

PLUS

- ▶ Clickable Audio: instant access to the complete classroom audio program
- *Top Notch TV* Video Program: a hilarious sitcom and authentic on-the-street interviews
- *Top Notch Pop* Songs and Karaoke: original songs for additional language practice

For planning . . .

- A *Methods Handbook* for a communicative classroom
- Detailed timed lesson plans for each two-page lesson
- *Top Notch TV* teaching notes
- Complete answer keys, audio scripts, and video scripts

For extra support . . .

- Hundreds of extra printable activities, with teaching notes
- *Top Notch Pop* language exercises
- *Top Notch TV* activity worksheets

For assessment . . .

- Ready-made unit and review achievement tests with options to edit, add, or delete items.

MyEnglishLab

An optional online learning tool

- **NEW** Grammar Coach videos, plus the Pronunciation Coach videos, and Digital Vocabulary Flash Cards
- **NEW** Immediate and meaningful feedback on wrong answers
- **NEW** Remedial grammar exercises
- Interactive practice of all material presented in the course
- Grade reports that display performance and time on task
- Auto-graded achievement tests

Workbook

Lesson-by-lesson written exercises to accompany the Student's Book

Full-Course Placement Tests

Choose printable or online version

Classroom Audio Program

- A set of Audio CDs, as an alternative to the clickable audio in the ActiveTeach
- Contains a variety of authentic regional and non-native accents to build comprehension of diverse English speakers
- **NEW** The entire audio program is available for students at www.english.com/topnotch3e. The mobile app *Top Notch Go* allows access anytime, anywhere and lets students practice at their own pace.

Teacher's Edition and Lesson Planner

- Detailed interleaved lesson plans, language and culture notes, answer keys, and more
- Also accessible in digital form in the ActiveTeach

For more information: www.pearsonelt.com/topnotch3e

Grammar Readiness
SELF-CHECK

The Grammar Readiness Self-Check is optional. Complete the exercises to confirm that you know this grammar previously taught in *Top Notch*.

QUANTIFIERS FOR INDEFINITE QUANTITIES AND AMOUNTS

A PRACTICE Circle the correct quantifiers.

1 There isn't (much / many / some) milk in the fridge.

2 There are (much / many / any) beautiful figures in the Gold Museum.

3 We need to go shopping. We don't have (much / many / some) shampoo for the trip.

4 She doesn't use (many / a lot of / some) toothpaste when she brushes her teeth.

5 I'm on a diet. I just want to have (much / any / some) soup for lunch.

6 There aren't (much / many / some) calories in a salad.

B USE THE GRAMMAR Complete each statement with real information. Use an affirmative or negative form of <u>there is</u> / <u>there are</u> and the quantifiers <u>some</u>, <u>any</u>, <u>a lot of</u>, <u>many</u>, or <u>much</u>.

1 In my bathroom, ... right now, but ....

2 In my fridge, ... right now, but ....

THE REAL CONDITIONAL

A PRACTICE Complete the statements and questions with the simple present tense or the future with <u>will</u>.

1 If .... me tomorrow morning, ... you the information you need.

　　you / call　　　　　　　　　　　　　I / give

2 .... open if .... after 6:00 P.M.?

　the hotel gift shop / be　　　　　I / arrive

3 If .... , ... open.

　　you / not / hurry　　　　　the fitness center / not / be

4 .... the express train if .... at the station after 4:00?

　we / miss　　　　　　　　　　we / arrive

5 If .... on the scroll bar, ... up and down.

　　you / click　　　　　　　the screen / move

B USE THE GRAMMAR Complete each statement, using the real conditional.

1 If I go on a trip to New York, I ....

2 I .... if it rains tomorrow.

THE UNREAL CONDITIONAL

A PRACTICE Choose the correct way to complete each unreal conditional sentence.

1 If you .... something in a store, would you pay for it?

a would break　　**b** broke　　　　**c** break

2 What .... if your computer crashed?

a would you do　　**b** were you doing　　**c** did you do

3 If I found someone's wallet in a restaurant, I .... the server.
  a would tell   **b** will tell   **c** told

4 I would go to Sam's Electronics if I .... to get a great deal on a new tablet.
  a would want   **b** want   **c** wanted

5 How .... if your husband got cosmetic surgery?
  a do you feel   **b** would you feel   **c** will you feel

6 If I .... to New York, I would go to the top of the Empire State Building.
  a go   **b** went   **c** would go

B **USE THE GRAMMAR** Complete these unreal conditional statements in your own words.

1 If I had a lot of money, ...

2 I would stop studying English if ....

COMPARISON WITH AS . . . AS

A **PRACTICE** Combine each pair of statements, using comparisons with as . . . as and the adverb in parentheses.

1 London is exciting. Rome is exciting too.

  (just) ....

2 The ceramic vase is beautiful. The glass vase is much more beautiful.

  (not / nearly) ....

3 I'm very rebellious. My sister is much more rebellious.

  (not / quite) ....

4 The Green Hotel is expensive. The Chelton Hotel is a little more expensive.

  (almost) ....

5 The movie *Kill Bill* was violent. *War of the Worlds* was violent too.

  (just) ....

B **USE THE GRAMMAR** Write statements with comparisons with as . . . as.

1 Compare two people in your family.

  ....

2 Compare two products, such as cars or electronics.

  ....

GERUNDS AND INFINITIVES

A PRACTICE Complete the advice by choosing a gerund or infinitive form of each verb.

Are you an introvert? Are you afraid of (1 speaking / to speak) in front of a group of people? Are you tired of (2 worrying / to worry) about what other people think? Let me give you some tips for (3 changing / to change) how you feel. First of all, enjoy (4 being / to be) who you are. There's nothing wrong with (5 getting / to get) nervous in social situations. If you want (6 feeling / to feel) comfortable in those situations, you can learn how. Finally, learn (7 accepting / to accept) that you have unique strengths.

B USE THE GRAMMAR Complete each personal statement with a gerund or infinitive phrase.

1 After I finish my English studies, I hope ....

2 I dislike .... , but I really don't mind ....

THE PASSIVE VOICE

A PRACTICE Change each sentence from active voice to passive voice. Use a <u>by</u>-phrase if it is important to mention who performs the action.

1 Gabriel García Márquez wrote *One Hundred Years of Solitude* in 1967.

....

2 People eat fried cheese balls for lunch or snacks.

....

3 The Spanish artist Diego Velázquez painted *Las Meninas* in 1656.

....

4 People turn down the beds every night at the Gates Hotel.

....

5 They grow mangos in many countries around the world.

....

B USE THE GRAMMAR Write two facts about your city or country, using the passive voice. For example: *In my country, fish is usually served with rice.*

1 ....

2 ....

THE PAST CONTINUOUS

A PRACTICE Complete the paragraph with the past continuous or the simple past tense.

I .... a problem yesterday. While I .... some information on the Internet,
_{1 have}   _{2 look up}

I .... a great website with some cool applications. So I .... to download one of
_{3 find}   _{4 decide}

them. While I .... that, my computer .... I .... restarting,
_5 do_ _6 crash_ _7 try_
but nothing happened. While I .... to solve the problem, the phone .... It
8 try _9 ring_
was my friend Mark. He .... that the website I found had a virus.
10 say

B **USE THE GRAMMAR** Complete the statements, using the past continuous or the simple past tense.

1 While I was leaving home for class today, ...

2 Someone called me while ....

USE TO / USED TO

A **PRACTICE** Complete each sentence with the correct affirmative or negative form of <u>use to</u> or <u>used to</u>.

1 I (like) .... to eat seafood, but now I do.

2 My school (be) .... near the mall, but it moved to another location.

3 .... you (go) .... to the beach a lot when you were a kid?

4 My brother (have) .... a tattoo on his arm, but he went to a doctor and she removed it.

5 I (be) .... kind of an introvert, but now I like being with lots of people.

6 There (be) .... so many hotels on Bliss Street, but now there are lots of them.

B **USE THE GRAMMAR** Complete the statements with real information.

1 There didn't use to be .... in our city.

2 I used to .... when I was a kid.

3 I didn't use to like .... , but now I do.

THE PRESENT PERFECT

A **PRACTICE** Choose the present perfect or simple past tense verb phrase to complete each conversation.

1 **A:** I'm worried we're going to be late. Has Tom taken a shower yet?
B: No. Actually, he (hasn't gotten up / didn't get up) yet!

2 **A:** Did you get Mr. Bland's message this morning?
B: Yes, I did. But I (didn't have / haven't had) time to respond yet.

3 **A:** Have you seen DiCaprio's new movie?
B: Actually, I (saw / have seen) it last night. It wasn't great.

4 **A:** Have you stayed at the Greenvale Hotel before?
B: Not at the Greenvale. But I (stayed / 've stayed) at the Huntington next door twice.

B **USE THE GRAMMAR** Complete the statements about yourself.

1 I haven't .... yet, but I'd like to.

2 I've .... more than three times.

3 I've .... since ....

4 I haven't .... for ....

Make Small Talk

COMMUNICATION GOALS

1 Make small talk.
2 Describe a busy schedule.
3 Develop your cultural awareness.
4 Discuss how culture changes over time.

PREVIEW

Reply   Reply All   Forward   Delete

From: ROWAN PAPER INTERNATIONAL
Sent: January 2 22:20:56 PM GMT
To: All Affiliates
Subject: Annual Meeting: Bangkok, Thailand, March 24–27

Meeting Etiquette

Since we all come together from different traditions and cultures, here are some guidelines to make this meeting run smoothly:

- Please arrive promptly for meetings.
- Dress is business casual: no ties or jackets required. However, no denim or shorts, please. Women should feel free to wear slacks.
- Please refrain from making or taking calls, or texting during meetings. Put all phones on vibrate mode. If you have an urgent call, please step outside into the corridor.
- Note: Please treat everyone on a first-name basis.

  FYI: Food is international style. All meals will provide non-meat options. If you have a special dietary requirement, please speak with Ms. Parnthep at the front desk.

See attached meeting agenda for advance planning.

Bangkok agenda

ROWAN PAPER INTERNATIONAL

Agenda–March 24

8:30	Breakfast buffet	
9:15	Welcome and opening remarks Philippe Martin, President and CEO	Salon Bangkok
9:45	Fourth quarter results and discussion Angela de Groot, CFO	Ballroom
10:30	Coffee break	Ballroom
11:00	International outlook and integrated marketing plans Sergio Montenegro	
12:00	Luncheon	Ballroom
2:00	Regional marketing plans	Gallery
	• U.S. and Canada Group	
	• Mexico and Central America Group	Salon A
	• Caribbean Group	Salon B
	• South America (Southern Cone and Andes) Group	Salon C
	• Brazil	Salon D
		Salon E

A Read and summarize the etiquette guidelines for an international business meeting. Write four statements beginning with <u>Don't</u>.

B **DISCUSSION** Why do you think Rowan Paper International feels it's necessary to tell participants about the meeting etiquette? What could happen if the company didn't clarify expectations?

C ▶1:02 **PHOTO STORY** Read and listen to a conversation between two participants at the meeting in Bangkok.

ENGLISH FOR TODAY'S WORLD
Understand English speakers from different language backgrounds.
Teresa = Spanish speaker
Surat = Thai speaker

Teresa: Allow me to introduce myself. I am Teresa Segovia from the Santiago office. *Sawatdee-Kaa.*

Surat: Where did you learn the *wai**? You're Chilean, aren't you?

Teresa: Yes, I am. But I have a friend in Chile from Thailand.

Surat: Well, *Sawatdee-Khrab.* Nice to meet you, Ms. Segovia. I'm Surat Leekpai.

Teresa: No need to be so formal. Please call me Terri.

Surat: And please call me Surat.

Teresa: OK. Surat, do you mind my asking you a question about that, though?

Surat: Not at all.

Teresa: Is it customary in Thailand for people to be on a first-name basis?

Surat: Well, at company meetings in English, always. In other situations, though, people tend to be a little more formal. It's probably best to watch what others do. You know what they say: "When in Rome . . . "

Teresa: Mm-hmm . . . , "do as the Romans do!"

*Thais greet each other with a gesture called the <u>wai</u> and by saying "Sawatdee-Kaa" (women) / "Sawatdee-Khrab" (men).

D **THINK AND EXPLAIN** Answer the questions.

1 Why was Surat surprised about the way Teresa greeted him? How do you know he was surprised?

2 Why do you think Teresa decided to say "Sawatdee-Kaa"?

3 What did Teresa mean when she said, "No need to be so formal"?

4 What do you think the saying "When in Rome, do as the Romans do" means?

SPEAKING

A **PERSONALIZATION** If you took a business or pleasure trip to another country, how would you like to be addressed? Complete the chart. Then discuss and explain your reasons to a partner.

I'd like to be called . . .	Always	In some situations	Never
by my title and my family name.	☐	☐	☐
by my first name.	☐	☐	☐
by my nickname.	☐	☐	☐
I'd prefer to follow the local customs.	☐	☐	☐

B **DISCUSSION** Talk about the questions.

1 In your opinion, is it inappropriate for two people of very different status (such as a CEO and an assistant) to be on a first-name basis? Explain.

2 In general, when do you think people should use first names with each other? When should they use titles and last names? Explain your reasons.

GOAL Make small talk

CONVERSATION MODEL

A ▶1:03 Read and listen to two people meeting and making small talk.

A: Good morning. Beautiful day, isn't it?

B: It really is. By the way, I'm Kazuko Toshinaga.

A: I'm Jane Quitt. Nice to meet you.

B: Nice to meet you, too.

A: Do you mind if I call you Kazuko?

B: Absolutely not. Please do.

A: And please call me Jane.

> ▶1:05 **Asking about proper address**
> Do you mind if I call you [Kazuko]?
> Would it be rude to call you [Kazuko]?
> What would you like to be called?
> How do you prefer to be addressed?
> Do you use <u>Ms.</u> or <u>Mrs.</u>?

B ▶1:04 **RHYTHM AND INTONATION** Listen again and repeat. Then practice the Conversation Model with a partner.

WILDLIFE CENTER NATURE TOURS

GRAMMAR Tag questions: Use and form

Use tag questions to confirm information you already think is true or to encourage someone to make small talk with you.
It's a beautiful day, **isn't it?**

When the statement is affirmative, the tag is negative. When the statement is negative, the tag is affirmative. Use the same verb tense or modal in the tag question as in the main statement.

> **Be careful!**
> **Use <u>aren't I</u> for negative tag questions after <u>I am</u>.**
> I'm on time, **aren't I?** BUT I'm not late, **am I?**
> **Use pronouns, not names or other nouns, in tag questions.**
> Bangkok is in Thailand, isn't **it?**
> NOT ~~isn't Bangkok?~~

affirmative statements

You're Lee,	**aren't you?**
She speaks Thai,	**doesn't she?**
He's going to drive,	**isn't he?**
They'll be here later,	**won't they?**
There are a lot of rules,	**aren't there?**
There isn't any sugar,	**is there?**
You were there,	**weren't you?**
They left,	**didn't they?**
It's been a great day,	**hasn't it?**
Ann would like Quito,	**wouldn't she?**
They can hear me,	**can't they?**

negative statements

You're not Amy,	**are you?**
I don't know you,	**do I?**
We're not going to eat here,	**are we?**
It won't be long,	**will it?**
He wasn't driving,	**was he?**
We didn't know,	**did we?**
She hasn't been here long,	**has she?**
You wouldn't do that,	**would you?**
He can't speak Japanese,	**can he?**

> **GRAMMAR BOOSTER** p. 127
> • Tag questions: short answers

A **FIND THE GRAMMAR** Find and underline a tag question in the Photo Story on page 3.

B **GRAMMAR PRACTICE** Complete each statement with the correct tag question.

1 Rob is your manager, ... ?

2 I turned off the projector, ... ?

3 Tim is going to present next, ... ?

4 She won't be at the meeting before 2:00, ... ?

5 We haven't forgotten anything, ... ?

6 It was a great day, ... ?

7 The agenda can't be printed in the business center before 8:00 A.M., ... ?

8 They were explaining the meeting etiquette, ... ?

9 She wants to be addressed by her first name, ... ?

10 There was no one here from China, ... ?

PRONUNCIATION *Intonation of tag questions*

A ▶1:06 Rising intonation usually indicates that the speaker is confirming the correctness of information. Read and listen. Then listen again and repeat.

1 People use first names here, don't they?
2 That meeting was great, wasn't it?
3 It's a beautiful day for a walk, isn't it?

B ▶1:07 Falling intonation usually indicates that the speaker expects the listener to agree. Read and listen. Then listen again and repeat.

1 People use first names here, don't they?
2 That meeting was great, wasn't it?
3 It's a beautiful day for a walk, isn't it?

C **PAIR WORK.** Take turns reading the examples of tag questions in the Grammar chart on page 4. Read each with both rising and falling intonation. Listen to tracks 1:06 and 1:07 to check your intonation.

NOW YOU CAN Make small talk

A **CONVERSATION ACTIVATOR** With a partner, personalize the Conversation Model to greet a classmate. Make small talk. Ask each other about how you would like to be addressed. Then change partners.

A: Good .... , isn't it?
B: It really is. By the way, I'm ....
A: I'm ....

Ideas for tag questions
[Awful] weather, ...
Nice [afternoon], ...
Great [English class], ...
[Good] food, ...
The food is [terrible], ...

DON'T STOP!
• Continue making small talk.
• Get to know your new classmates.
• Ask about families, jobs, travel, etc.

Maria, hi! I'm Deborah. Your parents are from Italy, aren't they?

B **EXTENSION** Write your name and a few facts about yourself on a sheet of paper and put it on a table. Choose another classmate's paper, read it quickly, and put it back on the table. Then meet that person and confirm the information you read, using tag questions.

	Maria Carbone
	I grew up here, but my parents are from
	Italy. I started studying English when I was
	in primary school.

GOAL Describe a busy schedule

GRAMMAR *The past perfect: Statements*

Use the past perfect to describe an action that occurred before a specific time in the past. Look at the timeline to see the order of the actions. Form the past perfect with <u>had</u> + a past participle.

```
        11:00              12:00
 ─────────┼──────────────────┼──────────►
The meeting ended at 11:00.   We arrived.   =   The meeting had ended before we arrived.
```

Time markers <u>by</u>, <u>already</u>, and <u>yet</u> are often used with the past perfect.

By four o'clock the tour **had begun**.
They **had already eaten** when their friends called.
When the flight took off, the storm **hadn't started yet** (OR **hadn't yet started**).

Use the past perfect with the simple past tense or the past of <u>be</u> to clarify which of two past actions occurred first.

The meeting **had begun** late, so we **didn't have** lunch until 2:00.
    (First the meeting began; then we had lunch.)
By the time the tour **was over**, Ann **had** already **met** Kazuko.
    (First Ann and Kazuko met; then the tour was over.)

> **Note:** In informal speech, you can use the simple past instead of the past perfect when the words <u>by</u>, <u>before</u>, and <u>after</u> make the order of events clear.
>
> By April he **started** his new job.
> Before I got married, I **studied** marketing.
> After she **made** the presentation, they promoted her.

> **GRAMMAR BOOSTER** p. 128
> • Verb usage: present and past (overview)

A GRAMMAR PRACTICE Choose the correct meaning for each statement.

1 "Before they decided to have the meeting in Bangkok, I had already decided to take my vacation there."
   ☐ First they decided to have the meeting in Bangkok. Then I decided to take my vacation there.
   ☐ First I decided to take my vacation in Bangkok. Then they decided to have the meeting there.

2 "By the time she got to the meeting, she had already reviewed the agenda."
   ☐ First she reviewed the agenda. Then she got to the meeting.
   ☐ First she got to the meeting. Then she reviewed the agenda.

3 "They had already asked us to turn off our cell phones when the CEO began her presentation."
   ☐ First they asked us to turn off our cell phones. Then the CEO began her presentation.
   ☐ First the CEO began her presentation. Then they asked us to turn off our cell phones.

B It's now 7:00 P.M. Read Meg's to-do list and complete the statements, using the past perfect, <u>already</u>, and <u>yet</u>.

1 At 8:30 Meg .... her laundry, but
   she .... the cat to her mom's house.

2 By 10:45 she .... the cat to her mom's house,
   but she .... for the meeting.

3 By 12:15 she .... the sales binders at
   Office Solutions, but she .... lunch with Adam.

4 At 1:30 she .... lunch with Adam, but she
   .... the DVDs to FilmPix.

5 By 2:15 she .... the DVDs to FilmPix,
   but she .... the dentist.

6 At 5:55 she .... the dentist, but she
   .... a manicure.

Monday, January 4

8:00	Drop off the laundry at Minute Wash.
9:00	
10:00	Take the cat to Mom's house.
11:00	Pack for the meeting.
12:00	Pick up the sales binders at Office Solutions.
1:00	Lunch with Adam.
2:00	Return the DVDs to FilmPix.
3:00	
4:00	See dentist. ☹
5:00	5:30 Pick up the laundry from Minute Wash.
6:00	Get a manicure if there's time!
7:00	
8:00	

CONVERSATION MODEL

A ▶1:08 Read and listen to someone describing a busy schedule.

A: So how was your day?

B: Unbelievably busy. By 9:00 I had taken the placement test, registered for class, and bought my books.

A: That's a lot to do before 9:00!

B: That was nothing! At 10:00, I had a meeting across town, but by 1:00 I had already arrived back at school for my class.

A: What did you do about lunch?

B: Well, when I got to class, I hadn't eaten yet, so I just got a snack.

A: Wow! I'll bet you're pretty hungry now!

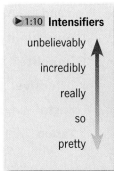

▶1:10 **Intensifiers**

unbelievably
incredibly
really
so
pretty

B ▶1:09 **RHYTHM AND INTONATION** Listen again and repeat. Then practice the Conversation Model with a partner.

NOW YOU CAN Describe a busy schedule

DIGITAL VIDEO

A **CONVERSATION ACTIVATOR** With a partner, change the Conversation Model to describe a busy day, morning, afternoon, evening, week, or any other period of time in the past. Use the past perfect. Then change roles.

A: So how was your .... ?
B: .... busy. By .... I ....
A: That's a lot to do before .... !
B: That was nothing! ....
A: What did you do about .... ?
B: Well, ...
A: Wow! I'll bet you .... !

DON'T STOP!

- Ask more questions about your partner's activities.
- Provide more details about the activities.

B **CHANGE PARTNERS** Practice the conversation again. Ask other classmates to describe their busy schedules.

BEFORE YOU LISTEN

DIGITAL
FLASH
CARDS

A ▶1:11 **VOCABULARY** • *Manners and etiquette* Read and listen. Then listen again and repeat.

etiquette rules for polite behavior in society or in a particular group

cultural literacy knowing about and respecting the culture of others

table manners rules for polite behavior when eating with other people

punctuality the habit of being on time

impolite not polite, rude

offensive extremely rude or impolite

customary usual or traditional in a particular culture

taboo not allowed because of very strong cultural or religious rules

B Complete each sentence with the correct word or phrase from the Vocabulary.

1 It's (taboo / impolite) to eat pork in some religions. No one would ever do it.

2 Many people believe that (cultural literacy / punctuality) is important and that being late is impolite.

3 In some cultures, it's (offensive / customary) to take pictures of people without permission, so few people do that.

4 Some people think that talking with a mouth full of food is an example of bad (cultural literacy / table manners).

5 In some cultures, it's (customary / offensive) to name children after a living relative, and most people observe that tradition.

6 Each culture has rules of (cultural literacy / etiquette) that are important for visitors to that country to know.

7 In more conservative cultures, it's slightly (impolite / taboo) to call someone by his or her first name without being invited to, but it isn't truly offensive.

8 The most successful global travelers today have developed their (punctuality / cultural literacy) so they are aware of differences in etiquette from culture to culture.

C **DISCUSSION** Discuss your opinions, using the Vocabulary.

1 What are some good ways to teach children etiquette? Give examples.

2 Do you know of any differences in etiquette between your culture and others? Give examples.

3 Why are table manners important in almost all cultures? How would people behave if there were no rules?

LISTENING COMPREHENSION

A ▶1:12 **LISTEN FOR MAIN IDEAS** Look at the subjects on the chart. Listen to three calls from a radio show. Check the subjects that are discussed during each call.

B ▶1:13 **LISTEN TO SUMMARIZE** Listen again. On a separate sheet of paper, take notes about the calls. Then, with a partner, write a summary of each call. Use the Vocabulary.

Subjects	1 Arturo / Jettrin	2 Hiroko / Nadia	3 Javier / Sujeet
table manners	☐	☐	☐
greetings	☐	☐	☐
dress and clothing	☐	☐	☐
male / female behavior	☐	☐	☐
taboos	☐	☐	☐
offensive behavior	☐	☐	☐
punctuality	☐	☐	☐
language	☐	☐	☐

A **FRAME YOUR IDEAS** With a partner, look at the questions about your culture on the notepad. Discuss each question and write answers.

How do people greet each other when they meet for the first time?

How do they greet each other when they already know each other?

Are greeting customs different for men and women? How?

When and how do you address people formally?

When and how do you address people informally?

What are some do's and don'ts for table manners?

Are certain foods or beverages taboo?

What are some taboo conversation topics?

What are the customs about punctuality?

What is a customary gift to bring on a visit to someone's home?

Are there any gift taboos (kinds of flowers, etc.)?

Are there places where certain clothes would be inappropriate?

Is there an important aspect of your culture that's not on this list?

Some people eat with chopsticks, and some eat with a spoon, a fork, and a knife.

C **GROUP WORK** Role-play a conversation with a visitor to your country. Tell the visitor about your culture. Use the answers to the questions on the notepad.

❝ It's bad table manners to pick up a soup bowl and drink soup from it. You have to use a spoon. ❞

❝ It's not customary for a man to extend his hand to shake hands with a woman. He should wait for the woman to do that. ❞

B **DISCUSSION** Combine classmates' notes on the board for the class to share. Does everyone agree? Discuss your differences of opinion.

GOAL Discuss how culture changes over time

BEFORE YOU READ

APPLY PRIOR KNOWLEDGE In what ways do you think table manners have changed since the days when your grandparents were children?

READING ▶ 1:14

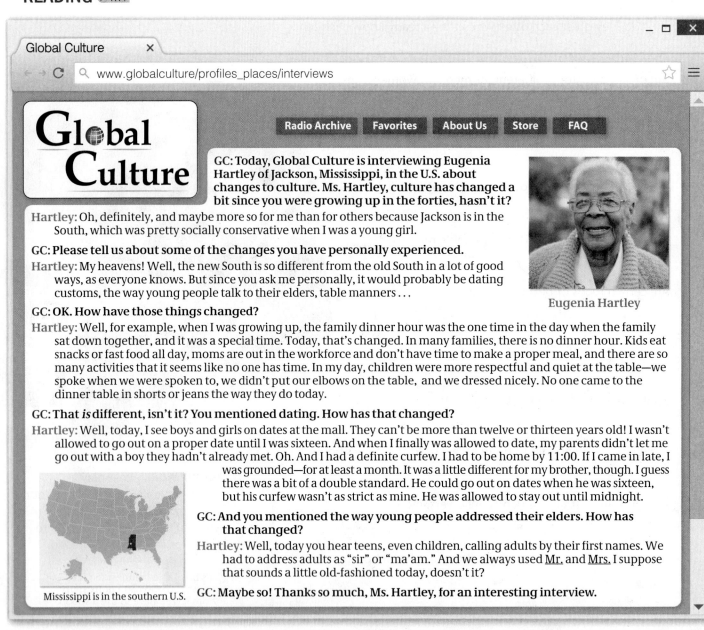

Global Culture ✕

C 🔍 www.globalculture/profiles_places/interviews ☆ ≡

Global Culture

Radio Archive | Favorites | About Us | Store | FAQ

GC: Today, Global Culture is interviewing Eugenia Hartley of Jackson, Mississippi, in the U.S. about changes to culture. Ms. Hartley, culture has changed a bit since you were growing up in the forties, hasn't it?

Eugenia Hartley

Hartley: Oh, definitely, and maybe more so for me than for others because Jackson is in the South, which was pretty socially conservative when I was a young girl.

GC: Please tell us about some of the changes you have personally experienced.

Hartley: My heavens! Well, the new South is so different from the old South in a lot of good ways, as everyone knows. But since you ask me personally, it would probably be dating customs, the way young people talk to their elders, table manners . . .

GC: OK. How have those things changed?

Hartley: Well, for example, when I was growing up, the family dinner hour was the one time in the day when the family sat down together, and it was a special time. Today, that's changed. In many families, there is no dinner hour. Kids eat snacks or fast food all day, moms are out in the workforce and don't have time to make a proper meal, and there are so many activities that it seems like no one has time. In my day, children were more respectful and quiet at the table—we spoke when we were spoken to, we didn't put our elbows on the table, and we dressed nicely. No one came to the dinner table in shorts or jeans the way they do today.

GC: That *is* different, isn't it? You mentioned dating. How has that changed?

Hartley: Well, today, I see boys and girls on dates at the mall. They can't be more than twelve or thirteen years old! I wasn't allowed to go out on a proper date until I was sixteen. And when I finally was allowed to date, my parents didn't let me go out with a boy they hadn't already met. Oh. And I had a definite curfew. I had to be home by 11:00. If I came in late, I was grounded—for at least a month. It was a little different for my brother, though. I guess there was a bit of a double standard. He could go out on dates when he was sixteen, but his curfew wasn't as strict as mine. He was allowed to stay out until midnight.

GC: And you mentioned the way young people addressed their elders. How has that changed?

Hartley: Well, today you hear teens, even children, calling adults by their first names. We had to address adults as "sir" or "ma'am." And we always used <u>Mr.</u> and <u>Mrs.</u> I suppose that sounds a little old-fashioned today, doesn't it?

Mississippi is in the southern U.S.

GC: Maybe so! Thanks so much, Ms. Hartley, for an interesting interview.

A **DRAW CONCLUSIONS** Answer the questions, based on the Reading. Explain the reasoning behind each of your answers.

1 How old do you estimate Ms. Hartley to be today?

2 Does Ms. Hartley prefer the culture of the past or the culture of the present?

3 What is Ms. Hartley's opinion of the change in the role of mothers?

4 Does Ms. Hartley approve of the differences in child and teen behavior that have taken place?

B UNDERSTAND FROM CONTEXT Find and underline each of the following words in the Reading. Then use your understanding of the words to write definitions.

elders	
workforce	
dating	
curfew	
grounded	

DIGITAL MORE EXERCISES

Discuss how culture changes over time

A FRAME YOUR IDEAS Think about how culture has changed since your parents or grandparents were your age. If necessary, ask your parents or grandparents for information. Complete the survey.

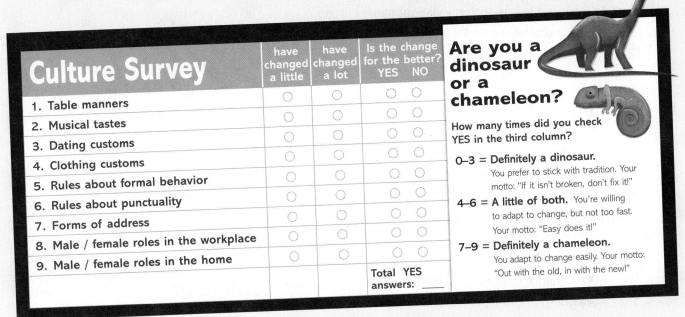

Culture Survey	have changed a little	have changed a lot	Is the change for the better? YES	NO
1. Table manners	○	○	○	○
2. Musical tastes	○	○	○	○
3. Dating customs	○	○	○	○
4. Clothing customs	○	○	○	○
5. Rules about formal behavior	○	○	○	○
6. Rules about punctuality	○	○	○	○
7. Forms of address	○	○	○	○
8. Male / female roles in the workplace	○	○	○	○
9. Male / female roles in the home	○	○	○	○
			Total YES answers: _____	

Are you a dinosaur or a chameleon?

How many times did you check YES in the third column?

0–3 = Definitely a dinosaur. You prefer to stick with tradition. Your motto: "If it isn't broken, don't fix it!"

4–6 = A little of both. You're willing to adapt to change, but not too fast. Your motto: "Easy does it!"

7–9 = Definitely a chameleon. You adapt to change easily. Your motto: "Out with the old, in with the new!"

B PAIR WORK Compare and discuss your answers. Provide specific examples of changes for each answer. Use the past perfect if you can.

C DISCUSSION Talk about how culture has changed. Include these topics in your discussion:

- Which changes do you think are good? Which changes are not good? Explain your reasons.

- How do you think older people feel about these changes?

- Do you think men and women differ in their feelings about cultural change? If so, how?

❝ I think clothing customs have become less modest. My mother wore a uniform to school. But by the time I started school, girls had stopped wearing them. Now girls can go to school in jeans and even shorts! ❞

Text-mining (optional)
Find and underline three words or phrases in the Reading that were new to you. Use them in your Discussion.
    For example: "strict."

RECYCLE THIS LANGUAGE.

Formality	Tag questions	Agreement / Disagreement
be on a first-name basis	[People don't __] as much,	I agree.
prefer to be addressed by __	do they?	I think you're right.
It's impolite to __.	[Customs] used to be __,	I disagree.
It's offensive to __.	didn't they?	Actually, I don't agree because __.
It's customary to __.		Really? I think __.
It isn't customary to __.		

A ▶1:15 Listen to the conversations between people introducing themselves. Check the statement that correctly paraphrases the main idea.

1 ☐ She'd like to be addressed by her title and family name.
☐ She'd like to be addressed by her first name.

2 ☐ She'd prefer to be called by her first name.
☐ She'd prefer to be called by her title and last name.

3 ☐ It's customary to call people by their first name there.
☐ It's not customary to call people by their first name there.

4 ☐ He's comfortable with the policy about names.
☐ He's not comfortable with the policy about names.

5 ☐ She prefers to use the title "Mrs."
☐ She prefers to use the title "Dr."

B Complete each sentence with a tag question.

1 You're not from around here, ... ?

2 You were in this class last year, ... ?

3 They haven't been here since yesterday, ... ?

4 Before the class, she hadn't yet told them how she wanted to be addressed, ... ?

5 I can bring flowers as a gift for the hosts, ... ?

6 You won't be back in time for dinner, ... ?

7 I met you on the tour in Nepal, ... ?

8 We'll have a chance to discuss this tomorrow, ... ?

9 They were going to dinner, ... ?

10 My friends are going to be surprised to see you, ... ?

C Complete each statement with a word from the Vocabulary on page 8.

1 Offending other people when eating a meal is an example of bad ....

2 Each country has customs and traditions about how to behave in social situations. The rules are sometimes called ....

3 Each culture has its own sense of .... It's important to understand people's ideas about lateness.

WRITING

Write two e-mail messages—one formal and one informal—telling someone about the cultural traditions in your country. Review the questionnaire about cultural traditions on page 9 for information to select from.

- For the formal e-mail, imagine you are writing to a businessperson who is coming to your country on a business trip.

- For the informal e-mail, imagine you are writing to a friend who is visiting your country as a tourist.

For additional language practice . . .

♫ **TOP NOTCH** POP • Lyrics p. 154
"It's a Great Day for Love"

DIGITAL SONG   DIGITAL KARAOKE

WRITING BOOSTER p. 146
- Formal e-mail etiquette
- Guidance for this writing exercise

ORAL REVIEW

TELL A STORY First, look at the pictures and tell the story of the Garzas and the Itos on June 10. Then look at the itineraries below and use the past perfect to talk about what they had done by June 6. Start like this:

By June 5, the Itos had been to . . .

PAIR WORK Create conversations.
1 Create a conversation for the two men in the first picture. Each man tells the other how he'd like to be addressed.
2 Create a conversation for the two women in the second picture. The women are making small talk.
3 Create a conversation for the people in the third picture. Ask and answer questions about their trips to Peru. Use the past perfect when possible.

JUNE 10, 10:00 A.M.

María and Antonio Garza

Haru and Kimi Ito

LATER THAT DAY

GetAway Travel, Inc.

María and Antonio Garza—Peru itinerary

May 30
Lima: María Angola Hotel
La Paz 610, Miraflores

June 3
Arequipa: Tierra Sur Hotel
Consuelo 210

June 6
Nasca: Brabant Hostel
Calle Juan Matta 978

June 9
Machu Picchu: Hanaq Pacha Hotel
(Aguas Calientes)

GLOBAL ADVENTURES, INC.

Haru and Kimi Ito—Peru Itinerary

May 29
Lima: María Angola Hotel
La Paz 610, Miraflores

May 31
Puno: Casa Andina Classic
Independencia 185, Plaza de Armas

June 4
Cusco: Novotel
San Agustín 239

June 9
Machu Picchu: Hanaq Pacha Hotel
(Aguas Calientes)

NOW I CAN

☐ Make small talk.
☐ Describe a busy schedule.
☐ Develop your cultural awareness.
☐ Discuss how culture changes over time.

Health Matters

COMMUNICATION GOALS

1 Show concern and offer help.
2 Make a medical or dental appointment.
3 Discuss types of treatments.
4 Talk about medications.

PREVIEW

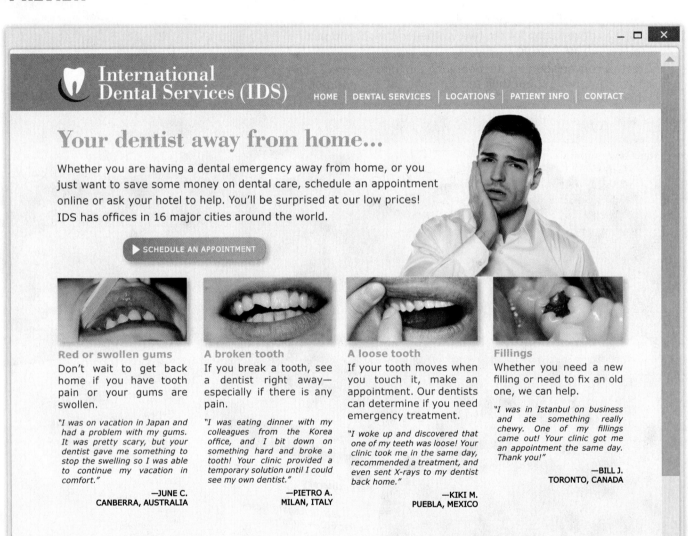

International Dental Services (IDS)

HOME | DENTAL SERVICES | LOCATIONS | PATIENT INFO | CONTACT

Your dentist away from home...

Whether you are having a dental emergency away from home, or you just want to save some money on dental care, schedule an appointment online or ask your hotel to help. You'll be surprised at our low prices! IDS has offices in 16 major cities around the world.

▶ SCHEDULE AN APPOINTMENT

Red or swollen gums
Don't wait to get back home if you have tooth pain or your gums are swollen.

"I was on vacation in Japan and had a problem with my gums. It was pretty scary, but your dentist gave me something to stop the swelling so I was able to continue my vacation in comfort."

—JUNE C.
CANBERRA, AUSTRALIA

A broken tooth
If you break a tooth, see a dentist right away— especially if there is any pain.

"I was eating dinner with my colleagues from the Korea office, and I bit down on something hard and broke a tooth! Your clinic provided a temporary solution until I could see my own dentist."

—PIETRO A.
MILAN, ITALY

A loose tooth
If your tooth moves when you touch it, make an appointment. Our dentists can determine if you need emergency treatment.

"I woke up and discovered that one of my teeth was loose! Your clinic took me in the same day, recommended a treatment, and even sent X-rays to my dentist back home."

—KIKI M.
PUEBLA, MEXICO

Fillings
Whether you need a new filling or need to fix an old one, we can help.

"I was in Istanbul on business and ate something really chewy. One of my fillings came out! Your clinic got me an appointment the same day. Thank you!"

—BILL J.
TORONTO, CANADA

A **DISCUSSION** Discuss each of the dental emergencies described on the website. What would you do if you were far from home? Consider these questions:

Would you . . .

- ignore the problem and just not do anything?
- make an appointment to see a local dentist right away?
- call or e-mail your own dentist for advice?

ENGLISH FOR TODAY'S WORLD
Understand English speakers from
different language backgrounds.
Guest / Patient = Spanish speaker
Clerk and Dentist = Russian speakers

B ▶1:18 **PHOTO STORY** Read and listen to someone with a dental emergency during a trip.

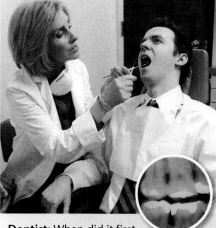

LATER

Guest: I need to see a dentist as soon as possible. I think it's an emergency. I was wondering if you might be able to recommend someone who speaks English.

Clerk: Let me check. Actually, there is one not far from here. Would you like me to make an appointment for you?

Guest: If you could. Thanks. I'm in a lot of pain.

Dentist: So I hear you're from overseas.

Patient: From Ecuador. Thanks for fitting me in.

Dentist: Luckily, I had a cancellation. So what brings you in today?

Patient: Well, this tooth is killing me.

Dentist: When did it first begin to hurt?

Patient: It's been bothering me since last night.

Dentist: Let's have a look. Open wide.

Patient: Ah . . .

Dentist: Well, let's take an X-ray and see what's going on.

C **FOCUS ON LANGUAGE** Find the following expressions in the Photo Story. Use the context to help you match the expressions and their meaning.

.... **1** I'll do it as soon as possible.

.... **2** I'll make an appointment.

.... **3** Thanks for fitting me in.

.... **4** It's killing me.

.... **5** Let's see what's going on.

a causing a lot of pain

b making time for an appointment

c arrange a time to come

d what the problem is

e right away

SPEAKING

A Have you—or someone you know—ever had an emergency that required dental or medical attention? Complete the chart.

Where did it happen?	When did it happen?	What happened?

B Tell your classmates about the emergency.

> ❝ Last year, I went skiing, and I broke my arm. I had to go to the emergency room at the hospital. ❞

VOCABULARY *Describing symptoms*

A ▶1:19 Read and listen. Then listen again and repeat.

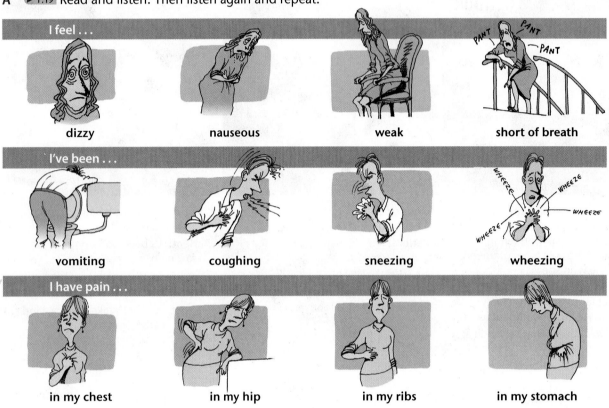

I feel . . .
dizzy	nauseous	weak	short of breath

I've been . . .
vomiting	coughing	sneezing	wheezing

I have pain . . .
in my chest	in my hip	in my ribs	in my stomach

B **PAIR WORK** Discuss what you would suggest to someone with some of the symptoms from the Vocabulary.

> ❝ If you feel dizzy, you should lie down. ❞

C ▶1:20 **LISTEN TO ACTIVATE VOCABULARY** Listen and check the symptoms each patient describes. Then listen again. If the patient has pain, write where it is.

	dizziness	nausea	weakness	vomiting	coughing	sneezing	wheezing	pain	If pain, where?
1	☐	☐	☐	☐	☐	☐	☐	☐	
2	☐	☐	☐	☐	☐	☐	☐	☐	
3	☐	☐	☐	☐	☐	☐	☐	☐	
4	☐	☐	☐	☐	☐	☐	☐	☐	
5	☐	☐	☐	☐	☐	☐	☐	☐	
6	☐	☐	☐	☐	☐	☐	☐	☐	

PRONUNCIATION *Intonation of lists*

A ▶1:21 Use rising intonation on each item before the last item in a list. Use falling intonation on the last item. Read and listen. Then listen again and repeat.

1 I feel weak and dizzy.
2 I've been sneezing, coughing, and wheezing.
3 I have pain in my neck, my shoulders, my back, and my hip.

B PAIR WORK Take turns using the Vocabulary to make lists of symptoms. Practice correct intonation for lists.

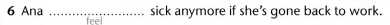
" I feel dizzy, weak, and short of breath. "

GRAMMAR *Drawing conclusions with* <u>must</u>

> **Remember:** <u>Can</u>, <u>could</u>, <u>should</u>, <u>will</u>, and <u>must</u> are modals. Modals don't change form. Always follow modals with a base form.

Use the modal <u>must</u> + the base form of a verb to draw a conclusion and indicate that you think something is probably true.

A: I think I just broke my tooth!
B: Oh, no. That **must hurt**.

A: The doctor said I should come in next week.
B: That's good. It **must not be** an emergency.

> **GRAMMAR BOOSTER** p. 129
> • Drawing conclusions with <u>probably</u> and <u>most likely</u>

GRAMMAR PRACTICE Complete the statements by drawing conclusions, using <u>must</u> or <u>must not</u>.

1 You look awful! You .... in a lot of pain.
   <u>be</u>

2 If your daughter feels nauseous, she .... to eat anything.
   <u>want</u>

3 The doctor said you're in perfect health! You .... really good.
   <u>feel</u>

4 If Gary has a headache, he .... to take a nap.
   <u>want</u>

5 I called the dentist's office, but no one answered. She .... in today.
   <u>be</u>

6 Ana .... sick anymore if she's gone back to work.
   <u>feel</u>

CONVERSATION MODEL

A ▶1:22 Read and listen to someone showing concern and offering help.

A: I'm sorry, but I don't think I can come to the meeting this morning.

B: Really? Is there anything wrong?

A: Well, actually, I don't feel very well. I've been coughing since last night, and I feel a little short of breath.

B: Oh, no. That must be awful. Would you like me to call a doctor?

A: That's really nice of you, but I'm sure I'll be fine.

B: Then call me later and let me know how you feel, OK?

A: I will. Thanks.

B ▶1:23 **RHYTHM AND INTONATION** Listen again and repeat. Then practice the Conversation Model with a partner.

NOW YOU CAN Show concern and offer help

A CONVERSATION ACTIVATOR With a partner, change the Conversation Model to describe other symptoms. Then change roles.

A: I'm sorry, but I don't think I can ....
B: Really? Is there anything wrong?
A: Well, actually, I don't feel very well. I ....
B: .... That must be .... Would you like me to .... ?
A: That's really nice of you, but I'm sure I'll be fine.
B: Then call me later and let me know how you feel, OK?
A: ....

B CHANGE PARTNERS Change the conversation again, using a different event or activity.

Other ways to offer to help
• make a doctor's appointment for someone
• drive someone to a hospital or a clinic
• pick up something from a pharmacy
• bring someone some soup or tea

RECYCLE THIS LANGUAGE.
Show concern
Oh, no. / I'm sorry to hear that.
That's [too bad / terrible / a shame].
You must feel [awful / terrible / horrible / pretty bad].

DON'T STOP!
• Describe more symptoms.
• Make other offers to help.

GOAL Make a medical or dental appointment

GRAMMAR *Will be able to; Modals may and might*

Will (OR **won't**) **be able to** + base form: future ability
The doctor **will be able to** see you tomorrow. (= The doctor can see you tomorrow.)
She **won't be able to** come to work this week. (= She can't come to work this week.)

May / **might** (OR **may not** / **might not**) + base form: possibility
The dentist **may** (OR **might**) arrive at the office a little late this morning.
You **may not** (OR **might not**) need to come in right away.

Note: You can use **be able to** with **may** and **might** for possibility or with **must** for drawing conclusions.
The doctor **may be able to**   see you today.
        I **might not be able to**   get there till 6:00.
    We **must be able to**   park here. See the sign?
    They **must not be able to**   cancel the appointment.

> **GRAMMAR BOOSTER** p. 130
> • Expressing possibility with **maybe**

GRAMMAR PRACTICE Complete each conversation. Use **might**, **might not**, **might be able to**, or **must not be able to** and the base form.

1 A: I'd like to see a dentist right away. I think it's an emergency.

   B: Well, I .... you an
   <u>get</u>
   appointment at 2:00. Would that be OK?

2 A: Is Dr. Lindt in this morning? I'm not feeling very well.

   B: She is, but she doesn't have any openings.

   However, she .... time
   <u>have</u>
   to see you this afternoon.

3 A: I think I .... a little sick this
   <u>be</u>
   morning. I feel nauseous, and I've been vomiting.

   B: Then you should see Dr. Anders. But he

   .... any openings today.
   <u>have</u>

4 A: I've been calling Mr. Reis for an hour. I know he's home, but no one's answering.

   B: That's strange. He ....
   <u>hear</u>
   the phone.

VOCABULARY *Medical procedures*

A ▶ 1:24 Read and listen. Then listen again and repeat.

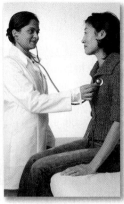
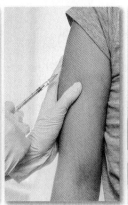
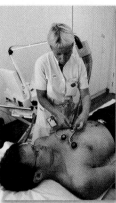
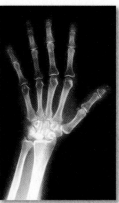

a checkup / an examination | a shot / an injection | an EKG / an electrocardiogram | an X-ray | a blood test

B **PAIR WORK** Discuss when a person might need each medical procedure from the Vocabulary.

> If you have pain in your arm, you might need an X-ray. 〞

CONVERSATION MODEL

A ▶1:25 Read and listen to someone making a medical appointment.

A: Hello. Doctor Star's office. Can I help you?

B: Hello. This is Ann Webb. I need to make an appointment for a blood test. I wonder if I might be able to come in early next week.

A: Let's see if I can fit you in. How about Tuesday?

B: Could I come in the morning?

A: Let me check . . . Would you be able to be here at 10:00?

B: That would be perfect.

A: We'll see you then.

B: Thanks! I really appreciate it.

B ▶1:26 **RHYTHM AND INTONATION** Listen again and repeat. Then practice the Conversation Model with a partner.

NOW YOU CAN Make a medical or dental appointment

DIGITAL VIDEO

A **CONVERSATION ACTIVATOR** With a partner, role-play making an appointment to see a doctor or dentist. Suggest a day and time. Write the appointment on the schedule. Then change roles.

A: Hello. Doctor .... 's office. Can I help you?

B: .... I need to make an appointment for .... I wonder if I might be able to come in ....

A: Let's see if I can fit you in. How about .... ?

B: Could I come in .... ?

A: Let me check . . . Would you be able to be here at .... ?

B: That would be perfect.

A: We'll see you ....

B: .... ! I really appreciate it.

DON'T STOP!

- Discuss other possible days and times.
- Ask for more information, such as name and phone number.

Ideas

How about . . .
- tomorrow?
- next week?
- early next week?
- at the end of next week?
- the week of [the 3rd]?

B **CHANGE PARTNERS** Make another appointment.

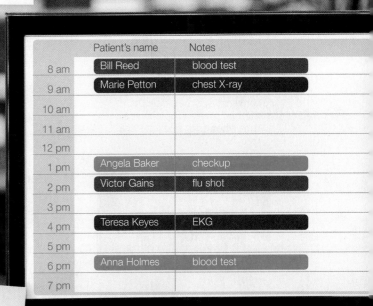

	Patient's name	Notes
8 am	Bill Reed	blood test
9 am	Marie Petton	chest X-ray
10 am		
11 am		
12 pm		
1 pm	Angela Baker	checkup
2 pm	Victor Gains	flu shot
3 pm		
4 pm	Teresa Keyes	EKG
5 pm		
6 pm	Anna Holmes	blood test
7 pm		

GOAL Discuss types of treatments

BEFORE YOU READ

WARM-UP What do you do when you get sick or you're in pain? Do you treat the problem yourself or see a doctor right away?

READING ▶ 1:27

Consider the Choices ...

Conventional Medicine

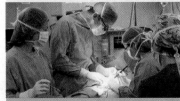

Surgical techniques have greatly improved over the last century.

The beginnings of conventional medicine can be traced back to the fifth century BCE in ancient Greece. It is based on the scientific study of the human body and illness.

In the last century, there has been great progress in what doctors have been able to do with modern surgery and new medications. These scientific advances have made conventional medicine the method many people choose first when they need medical treatments.

Homeopathy

Homeopathic remedies are popular in many countries.

Homeopathy was founded in the late eighteenth century in Germany. It is a low-cost system of natural medicine used by hundreds of millions of people worldwide.

In homeopathy, a patient's symptoms are treated with remedies that cause similar symptoms. The remedy is taken in very diluted form: one part remedy to one trillion (1,000,000,000,000) parts water.

Acupuncture

An acupuncturist inserts needles at certain points on the body.

Acupuncture originated in China over 5,000 years ago. Today, it is used worldwide for a variety of problems.

Acupuncture needles are inserted at certain points on the body to relieve pain and/or restore health. Many believe acupuncture may be effective in helping people stop smoking as well.

Spiritual Healing

Many believe meditation or prayer may help heal disease.

Also known as faith healing, or "mind and body connection," various forms of spiritual healing exist around the world. This is a form of healing that uses the mind or religious faith to treat illness.

A number of conventional doctors say that when they have not been able to help a patient, spiritual healing just may work.

Herbal Therapy

Herbs are used to treat many ailments.

Herbal medicine, often taken as teas or pills, has been practiced for thousands of years in almost all cultures around the world. In fact, many conventional medicines were discovered by scientists studying traditional uses of herbs for medical purposes.

The World Health Organization claims that 80% of the world's population uses herbal therapies for their regular health care.

A **UNDERSTAND FROM CONTEXT** Four of these words have similar meanings. Cross out the four words that don't belong. Look at the Reading again for help.

medications	treatments	symptoms	remedies
uses	purposes	therapies	illnesses

B **RELATE TO PERSONAL EXPERIENCE** Discuss the questions.

1 Which of the treatments in the Reading have you or your family tried?

2 Which treatments do you think are the most effective? Why?

C **DRAW CONCLUSIONS** Decide which treatment or treatments each patient would probably NOT want to try and which he or she might prefer. Explain your answers, using <u>might</u>, <u>might not</u>, <u>must</u>, or <u>must not</u>. (More than one therapy might be appropriate.)

1 **❝** I definitely want to see a doctor when I have a problem. But I want to avoid taking any strong medications or having surgery. **❞**

2 **❝** I believe you have to heal yourself. You can't just expect a doctor to do everything for you. **❞**

3 **❝** I think it would be silly to try a health care method that isn't strongly supported by scientific research. **❞**

DIGITAL
MORE
XERCISES

NOW YOU CAN Discuss types of treatments

A **NOTEPADDING** With a partner, discuss treatments and practitioners you prefer for each ailment. Write your views on the notebook.

Ailment	You	Your partner
a cold		
a headache		
nausea		
back pain		
a high fever		
a broken finger		

Practitioners
- a conventional doctor
- a homeopathic doctor
- an acupuncturist
- an herbal therapist
- a spiritual healer

B **DISCUSSION** Compare the kinds of treatments and practitioners you and your classmates would use. Say what you learned about your partner.

Text-mining (optional)
Find and underline three words or phrases in the Reading that were new to you. Use them in your Discussion.
For example: "low-cost."

❝ My partner has been to an acupuncturist a few times. It really helped for back pain. **❞**

❝ I would never try herbal therapy. I just don't think it works. My partner agrees. **❞**

❝ I see a homeopathic doctor regularly, but my partner doesn't believe in that. He prefers a conventional doctor. **❞**

GOAL Talk about medications

BEFORE YOU LISTEN

▶1:29 **Medicine label information**
Dosage: Take 1 tablet by mouth every day.
Warnings: Do not take while driving or operating machinery.
Side effects: May cause dizziness, nausea, or vomiting.

DIGITAL FLASH CARDS

A ▶1:28 VOCABULARY • *Medications* Read and listen. Then listen again and repeat.

a painkiller

cold tablets

a nasal spray / a decongestant

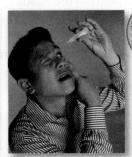

eye drops

an antihistamine

cough medicine

an antibiotic

an antacid

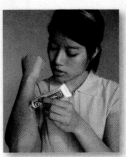

an ointment

vitamins

B PAIR WORK Discuss what you might use each medication for.

44 I might take an antacid for a stomachache. 77

LISTENING COMPREHENSION

A ▶1:30 LISTEN TO ACTIVATE VOCABULARY Listen to each conversation with a doctor Use the medications Vocabulary above and the symptoms Vocabulary from page 16 to complete the chart for each patient.

a prescription

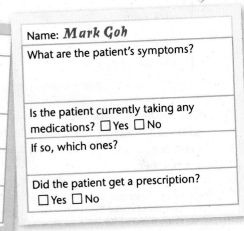

Name: Didem Yilmaz

What are the patient's symptoms?

Is the patient currently taking any medications? ☐ Yes ☐ No

If so, which ones?

Did the patient get a prescription?
☐ Yes ☐ No

Name: Lucy Fernández

What are the patient's symptoms?

Is the patient currently taking any medications? ☐ Yes ☐ No

If so, which ones?

Did the patient get a prescription?
☐ Yes ☐ No

Name: **Mark Goh**

What are the patient's symptoms?

Is the patient currently taking any medications? ☐ Yes ☐ No

If so, which ones?

Did the patient get a prescription?
☐ Yes ☐ No

B ▶1:31 **LISTEN FOR DETAILS** Listen again. Complete the information about each patient.

Mark Goh
Dosage: Apply ointment _____ a day
Side effects: ☐ Yes ☐ No
If so, what are they? _____
_____
_____

Didem Yilmaz
Dosage: One tablet _____ a day
Side effects: ☐ Yes ☐ No
If so, what are they? _____
_____

Lucy Fernández
Dosage: _____ a day
Side effects: ☐ Yes ☐ No
If so, what are they? _____
_____
_____

NOW YOU CAN Talk about medications

A **PREPARATION** Imagine you are visiting a doctor. Complete the patient information form.

B **GROUP WORK** With three other classmates, role-play a visit to a doctor. First, choose roles. Then role-play the three scenes below. Use the patient information form.

Roles
- a patient
- a friend, colleague, classmate, or relative
- a receptionist
- a doctor

Scene 1: The friend, colleague, classmate, or relative recommends a doctor.
Scene 2: The patient calls the receptionist to make an appointment.
Scene 3: The doctor asks the patient about the symptoms and recommends medication, etc.

Patient Information Form

Last name	First name

1. What are your symptoms?
☐ dizziness ☐ coughing ☐ nausea ☐ weakness
☐ sneezing ☐ vomiting ☐ shortness of breath
☐ wheezing ☐ pain (where?)
☐ other:

2. How long have you had these symptoms?

3. Are you currently taking any medications? ☐ Yes ☐ No
If so, which ones?

4. Are you allergic to any medications? ☐ Yes ☐ No
If so, which ones?

🔁 **RECYCLE THIS LANGUAGE.**

Scene 1
I've been [wheezing / coughing].
I feel [dizzy / nauseous].
I have pain in my [chest / ribs].

I think you should try ___.
Why don't you ___?
You may have to ___.
I hope you feel better soon.

Scene 2
I need to make an appointment for ___.
I wonder if I might be able to ___.
I really appreciate it.

Let me check.
Let's see if I can fit you in.
Would you be able to come [on / at] ___?

Scene 3
Thanks for fitting me in.
Are there any side effects?

Luckily, I had a cancellation.
Let's have a look.
Are you taking any medications?
Are you allergic to any medications?
Call me tomorrow and let me know how you feel.

C **PRESENTATION** Perform your role play for the class.

A ▶1:32 Listen to each conversation and complete the statements. Then listen again to check your answers.

1 The patient lost .... when she was eating ....

2 The patient has .... She needs to take ....

3 The patient needs .... of his ....

4 The patient would like to try .... for pain in her ....

B Suggest a medication for each person. (Answers will vary.)

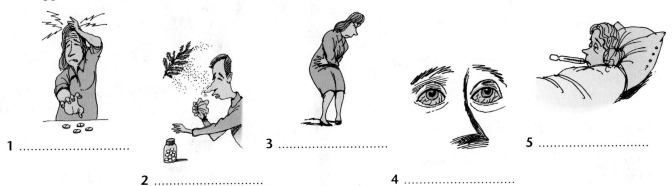

1 ....

2 ....

3 ....

4 ....

5 ....

C Complete each conversation by drawing your own conclusion with <u>must</u>.

1 A: I feel really nauseous. I've been vomiting all morning.
B: You *must feel terrible* ....

2 A: My dentist can't fit me in till next month.
B: Your dentist ....

3 A: My daughter was sick, but it wasn't anything serious, thank goodness.
B: You ....

4 A: My husband fell down and broke his ankle.
B: He .... !

D Rewrite each statement, using <u>may</u> (OR <u>might</u>) and <u>be able to</u>.

1 It's possible that the doctor can see you tomorrow.

2 It's possible that an acupuncturist can help you.

3 It's possible that the hotel can recommend a good dentist.

4 It's possible that she can't come to the office before 6:00.

5 It's possible that you can buy an antihistamine in the hotel gift shop.

> 1. The doctor might be able to see you tomorrow.

For additional language practice . . .

♫ TOP NOTCH **POP** • Lyrics p. 154
"X-ray of My Heart"

| DIGITAL SONG | DIGITAL KARAOKE |

WRITING

Compare two types of medical treatments. Use the Reading on page 20 and your own experiences and ideas. Consider the following questions:

- How are the two medical treatments similar or different?
- Which treatment do you think is more effective?
- Why might people choose each treatment?
- Which treatments do you—or people you now—use? Why?

WRITING BOOSTER p. 146
- Comparisons and contrasts
- Guidance for this writing exercise

ORAL REVIEW

PAIR WORK

1 Create a conversation for the women in the photo. Start like this:

I'm sorry, but I don't think I can . . .

2 Create a conversation between the receptionist in the doctor's office and the man on the phone in the pictures below. Make an appointment. Start like this:

A: Hello. Can I help you?
B: I wonder if I might be able to . . .

GAME Take turns with your classmates. Describe the doctor's office and draw conclusions, using <u>must</u> or <u>may</u> and <u>might</u>. (If a student can't say anything, he or she is out.) For example:

He's touching his arm. He must be in a lot of pain.

NOW I CAN

- ☐ Show concern and offer help.
- ☐ Make a medical or dental appointment.
- ☐ Discuss types of treatments.
- ☐ Talk about medications.

COMMUNICATION GOALS
1 Offer a solution.
2 Discuss how long a service will take.
3 Evaluate the quality of service.
4 Plan an event.

UNIT 3 Getting Things Done

PREVIEW

Are you a PROCRASTINATOR?

Take the survey.

1 At the beginning of every week, you ___.
- ☐ a. always make to-do lists for your calendar
- ☐ b. sometimes make to-do lists, but you often forget
- ☐ c. don't bother with planning and just let things happen

2 When you need to buy someone a gift, you ___.
- ☐ a. get something right away
- ☐ b. buy something a few days before you have to give it
- ☐ c. pick something up on the day you have to give it

3 When you have something that's broken, you ___.
- ☐ a. immediately take it in to be repaired
- ☐ b. wait for a convenient time to take it in
- ☐ c. never get around to taking it in

4 When you have a lot of things you need to do, you do ___.
- ☐ a. the hardest things first
- ☐ b. the easiest things first
- ☐ c. anything but what you need to do

5 When you need to get something done in a short amount of time, you ___.
- ☐ a. feel motivated to work even harder
- ☐ b. feel a little nervous, but you get to work
- ☐ c. have a hard time doing it

6 You ___ feel bad when there are things you haven't gotten done yet.
- ☐ a. always
- ☐ b. sometimes
- ☐ c. rarely

Your results

If you answered "c" four or more times:
You are a classic procrastinator! You tend to put things off.

If you answered "b" four or more times:
You are a bit of a procrastinator, but you try to get things done on time.

If you answered "a" four or more times:
You are organized and self-motivated. You never put off what you can get done now.

A PAIR WORK Compare responses on the survey with a partner. Does your score accurately describe the kind of person you are? Explain, using examples.

B DISCUSSION Based on the survey questions, what is a procrastinator? What do you think it means to be an "organized and self-motivated" person? What do you think are the advantages of being that type of person?

C ▶2:02 **PHOTO STORY**   Read and listen to some customers placing orders at a copy shop.

ENGLISH FOR TODAY'S WORLD
Understand English speakers from different language backgrounds.
Customer 2 = Chinese speaker

Manager: What can I do for you today, Ms. Krauss?

Customer 1: I need to have these documents copied a.s.a.p.* Do you think you could make 300 copies by 11:00?

Manager: I'm afraid that might be difficult. I've got a lot of orders to complete this morning.

Customer 1: Sorry. I know this is last minute. But it's really urgent.

Manager: Well, you're a good customer. I'll get someone to take care of it right away.

Customer 1: Thanks a million. You're a lifesaver!

Manager: Excuse me . . . Hello. Happy Copy.

Customer 2: Hi, Sam. Ken Li here.

Manager: Hi, Mr. Li. How can I help you today?

Customer 2: Well, I'm going through my to-do list, and I just realized I need to have fifty 30-page sales binders made up for our meeting next week. Any chance I could have them first thing tomorrow morning?

Manager: Tomorrow morning? No sweat. Can you bring the documents in before noon?

Customer 2: Absolutely. I owe you one, Sam!

Manager: Sorry to keep you waiting, Ms. Krauss.

Customer 1: Well, I see you've got a lot on your plate today. I won't keep you any longer.

Manager: Don't worry, Ms. Krauss. Your order will be ready on time.

Customer 1: Should I give you a call later?

Manager: No need for that. Come in at 11:00, and I'll have your documents ready.

Customer 1: Thanks, Sam.

*a.s.a.p. = as soon as possible

D   **FOCUS ON LANGUAGE**   Find an underlined expression in the Photo Story you might use for each of these situations. (Two of the expressions can be used for the same situation.)

1 You need something a.s.a.p.

2 You can see that someone is really busy.

3 There isn't a lot of time to do something.

4 You want to assure someone that a request is no problem for you.

5 You want to express gratitude for a favor.

6 You don't want to take too much of someone's time.

SPEAKING

Based on the survey on page 26, how would you describe each character in the Photo Story? Complete the chart and then compare opinions with your classmates. Which character are you the most like?

	Procrastinator?	Organized?	Explain
Sam	☐	☐	
Ms. Krauss	☐	☐	
Mr. Li	☐	☐	

GOAL Offer a solution

CONVERSATION MODEL

A ▶2:03 Read and listen to someone asking for a favor.

A: Do you think I could borrow your car this afternoon? Mine's at the repair shop, and I need to pick up my mom at the airport.

B: Gee, I'm sorry, but I'm going to need it. I have a doctor's appointment.

A: No problem. I'll think of something.

B: Hey. I have an idea. Maybe you could get Jack to lend you *his* car.

A: Good idea. I'll go ask him.

▶2:05 **Ways to indicate acceptance**
No problem.
I understand.
No worries.
Don't worry about it.

B ▶2:04 **RHYTHM AND INTONATION** Listen again and repeat. Then practice the Conversation Model with a partner.

GRAMMAR *The causative*

Use the causative to express the idea that one person persuades or "causes" another person to do something. Use <u>get</u> + an object and an infinitive.

	object	infinitive
I'll get	the waiter	to correct the check.
They got	him	to pay for dinner.
Did she get	her friends	to give money to the school?

You can also use <u>have</u> + an object and a base form as a causative. It expresses the idea that one person directs another to do something.

	object	base form
I'll **have**	my assistant	**call** your office.
We **had**	them	**bring** breakfast to our room.

GRAMMAR BOOSTER p. 130
• Causative <u>make</u> to indicate obligation
• <u>Let</u> to indicate permission
• Causative <u>have</u>: common errors

A **GRAMMAR PRACTICE** Complete each sentence with the causative <u>get</u>.

1 (give) Why don't you .... your assistant .... them a ride to the meeting?

2 (buy) I might be able to .... my brother .... us tickets to the game.

3 (pick up) Could you .... your friends .... some things for the party?

4 (make) You should .... someone .... hotel reservations for us.

5 (wash) Why don't you .... your kids .... the dishes after dinner?

6 (lend) I'm sure you can .... the restaurant .... you a tie.

B Now rewrite each sentence from Exercise A, using <u>have</u>.

1 ....

2 ....

3 ....

4 ....

5 ....

6 ....

C GRAMMAR PRACTICE Choose the correct forms in these sentences with the causatives <u>get</u> and <u>have</u>.

1 I'll have someone at the front desk (recommend / to recommend) a restaurant.

2 Will your friend get someone (go / to go) shopping for her?

3 Did you have the salesclerk (find / to find) you a larger size?

4 I'm going to get someone (clean / to clean) up this room.

5 They should have the waiter (bring / to bring) them the check.

D ▶ 2:06 **LISTEN TO ACTIVATE GRAMMAR** Listen to the conversations. Complete each statement, using the causative <u>get</u>.

1 She's going to .... the assistant .... to the post office.

2 They're going to .... Susan .... for the meal.

3 At the party, they tried to .... him .... for everyone.

4 He might try to .... his parents .... him some money.

5 She's going to .... her husband .... the kids.

6 They .... someone .... their picture.

DIGITAL
MORE
EXERCISES

NOW YOU CAN Offer a solution

DIGITAL
VIDEO

A CONVERSATION ACTIVATOR With a partner, change the Conversation Model. Change the request, the reason for turning it down, and the solution. Use the Ideas from the box or your own ideas. Then change roles.

A: Do you think .... ? ....
B: Gee, I'm sorry, but .... I ....
A: .... I'll think of something.
B: Hey. I have an idea. Maybe you could get .... to ....
A: Good idea. I'll go ask ....

DON'T STOP!

Make other suggestions.
What about __?
Why don't you ask __?

B CHANGE PARTNERS Make other requests. Offer other solutions.

Ideas for requests
• lend you [their laptop / some money]
• drive you to [the airport]
• pick up [some coffee / lunch] for you
• pick up someone from [the airport / the mall]

Some reasons to turn down a request
• You're late for an appointment.
• You have a meeting in an hour.
• You're expecting an important phone call.
• Your own reason: __

Do you think you could give me a ride to . . .

Do you think I could borrow your . . .

GOAL Discuss how long a service will take

GRAMMAR *The passive causative*

The passive causative focuses on the object rather than the subject of the sentence. Use a form of <u>have</u> + an object and a past participle.

> You can also form the passive causative with <u>get</u>, with no change in meaning.
> We **got** our picture **taken**.

	object	past participle
We **had**	our picture	taken after the meeting. (We had someone take it.)
They **plan to have**	the offices	painted next week. (They'll have someone paint them.)
Can she **have**	her X-rays	sent this morning? (Can she have someone send them?)

Remember: In the passive voice, a <u>by</u> phrase is used when the information is important.
We had the office painted last week. It looks great. (no <u>by</u> phrase)
We're having the office painted **by Royal Painting Services**. They're the best!

GRAMMAR BOOSTER p. 131
• The passive causative: the <u>by</u> phrase

A   FIND THE GRAMMAR   Look at the Photo Story on page 27. Find and underline two examples of the passive causative with <u>have</u>.

B   GRAMMAR PRACTICE   Write statements and questions, using the passive causative with <u>have</u>.

1 I'd like to make an appointment to / my teeth / clean.
....

2 could I / these two sweaters / gift-wrap?
....

3 where can I / my car / wash / in this neighborhood?
....

4 I need to / my luggage / bring / to my room.
....

5 yesterday / he / his hair / cut / very short.
....

6 we need to / these photos / upload / a.s.a.p.
....

DIGITAL MORE EXERCISES

DIGITAL FLASH CARDS

VOCABULARY *Services*

A   ▶ 2:07   Read and listen. Then listen again and repeat.

1 dry-clean a suit

2 repair shoes

3 frame a picture

4 deliver a package

5 lengthen / shorten a skirt

6 print a sign

7 copy a report

B **VOCABULARY / GRAMMAR PRACTICE** Name other things you can get the services on page 30 for. Use the passive causative.

> *You can also get sweaters or pants dry-cleaned.*

C ▶2:08 **LISTEN TO ACTIVATE VOCABULARY AND GRAMMAR** Listen to the conversations. Complete each statement with the item and the service. Use passive causatives.

1 She needs to have her ....

2 He needs to have the ....

3 She's thinking about having a ....

4 He needs to have his ....

5 She has to have her ....

6 He needs to have a .... this morning.

7 He wants to have his new ....

CONVERSATION MODEL

A ▶2:09 Read and listen to someone requesting express service.

A: Could I have this jacket dry-cleaned by tomorrow?

B: Tomorrow? That might be difficult.

A: I'm sorry, but it's pretty urgent. My friend is getting married this weekend.

B: Well, I'll see what I can do. But it won't be ready until after 4:00.

A: I really appreciate it. Thanks!

B ▶2:10 **RHYTHM AND INTONATION** Listen again and repeat. Then practice the Conversation Model with a partner.

NOW YOU CAN Discuss how long a service will take

DIGITAL VIDEO

A **CONVERSATION ACTIVATOR** With a partner, change the Conversation Model. Use the Ideas to request an express service and give a reason for why it's urgent. Then change roles.

A: Could I .... by .... ?
B: .... ? That might be difficult.
A: I'm sorry, but it's pretty urgent. ....
B: Well, I'll see what I can do. But it won't be ready until ....
A: .... ! **DON'T STOP!**

- Say you need to have the service completed earlier.
- Ask how much it will cost.

Ideas for express services
- frame [a photo / a painting / a drawing / a diploma]
- dry-clean [a suit / a dress / a sweater]
- lengthen or shorten [a dress / a skirt / pants]

Ideas for why it's urgent
- Someone is coming to visit.
- You're going on [a vacation / a business trip].
- There's going to be [a party / a meeting].
- Your own idea: __

🔄 **RECYCLE THIS LANGUAGE.**

I owe you one!	I know this is last minute.
Thanks a million.	I won't keep you any longer.
You're a lifesaver!	

B **CHANGE PARTNERS** Request other express services.

GOAL Evaluate the quality of service

BEFORE YOU READ

WARM-UP What are the best ways for a business to keep its customers coming back? Explain your reasons.

READING ▶ 2:11

How can I help you?

They say, "The customer is always right." That may not be completely true, but a smart business treats customers as though they are. Whether you work for a business or have your own, remember this secret: customers don't really buy services and products; they buy solutions and relationships. Here's how to keep them coming back:

Don't procrastinate! Make sure you get things done on time. Don't waste your customers' valuable time by making them wait for service. Giving customers what they want *now* is key to your success, and it should be at the top of your to-do list. The business that gets the job done efficiently and fast is the one that customers will come back to.

Be really reliable. If you say you are going to do something, do it. If a problem keeps you from doing it, apologize and promise to find a solution. However, avoid making promises you won't be able to keep. Treat customers right by being honest, and they will recommend you to their colleagues, friends, and family.

Stand by your products and services. The good workmanship and attention that go into your high quality product, excellent service, or reasonable prices will be appreciated. No one wants a product that falls apart or doesn't work. If that happens, take responsibility and arrange to repair it or replace it.

Be extremely friendly and courteous, as well as a good listener. Be sure your customers feel respected and heard. Pay attention to complaints as well as praise.

Always try to be helpful. Sometimes it's difficult to answer a customer's question or fulfill a request. Instead of "I don't know," say, "I may not have the answer right now, but I'll find out." Instead of "I don't have time right now," say, "I'll make time." A "can-do" attitude, even under stress, assures customers that you will treat them professionally and that you are ready and willing to help. Above all, make your customers feel important and valued, and always thank them for their business.

A INFER POINT OF VIEW Complete each statement, according to the point of view expressed in the Reading.

1 If you waste your customers' time, they .... come back.
   a will   **b** won't

2 If you don't do what you say you will do, your customers .... think you are reliable.
   a will   **b** won't

3 If you aren't courteous to your customers, they .... complain.
   a will   **b** won't

4 If your customers don't feel valued, they .... feel important.
   a will   **b** won't

5 If you don't have a "can-do" attitude, your customers .... think you're willing to help.
   a will   **b** won't

B **ACTIVATE LANGUAGE FROM A TEXT**
Find and underline these words in the
Reading on page 32. Complete the
descriptions, using the words.

| reliable | reasonable | workmanship | helpful | professional |

1 I find Portello's prices really .... compared to other places. I've shopped around, and I can't find another service with such low prices.

2 What I like about Link Copy Services is that they're so .... Even if the job is a bit unusual, they're willing to try.

3 Jamco Design is extremely .... You never have to worry about their doing anything less than an excellent job.

4 Dom's Auto Repair is incredibly .... If they promise to have a job ready in an hour, you can be sure that they will.

5 The .... at J&N is amazing. Their products are all hand-made, and they last for years.

DIGITAL
MORE
EXERCISES

DIGITAL
VIDEO
COACH

PRONUNCIATION *Emphatic stress to express enthusiasm*

▶ 2:12 Read and listen. Then listen again and repeat. Finally, read each
statement on your own, using emphatic stress.

1 They're **REAL**ly reliable.

2 They're in**CRED**ibly helpful.

3 They're ex**TREME**ly professional.

4 They're **SO** reasonable.

NOW YOU CAN Evaluate the quality of service

> **Reasons for choosing a business**
> - efficiency
> - helpfulness
> - location
> - professionalism
> - reasonable prices
> - reliability
> - workmanship
> - other: ___

A **FRAME YOUR IDEAS** Complete the chart with services you
or someone you know uses. Write the name of the business
and list the reasons why you use that business. Then compare
charts with a partner.

Service	Name of business	Reason
laundry / dry-cleaning		
repairs		
delivery		
haircuts		
copying		
other:		

B **DISCUSSION** Recommend local businesses from your chart. Explain why you
and their other customers use them. Use active and passive causatives.

> ❝ I always get my clothes dry-cleaned at Quick Clean. They're near my home and their prices are reasonable. ❞

> ❝ I rarely have my shoes repaired. But I hear that Al's Shoes is fast and reliable. ❞

> **Text-mining (optional)**
> Find and underline three words or phrases in the Reading
> that were new to you. Use them in your Discussion.
> For example: "treat them right."

GOAL Plan an event

BEFORE YOU LISTEN

A ▶2:13 **VOCABULARY** • *Planning and running an event* Read and listen. Then listen again and repeat.

1 send out the announcements

2 set up the room

Testing, testing, 1–2–3 . . .

6 a microphone / a mike

7 a handheld mike

8 a lapel mike

3 set up the projector

4 put up the signs

5 check the sound system

We'll start at 9:00. This is the agenda for the morning.

9 hand out the agenda

10 a handout

It's my pleasure to introduce . . .

11 introduce the speaker / the guest

12 — a podium

B **PAIR WORK** Which of the activities in the Vocabulary have you done yourself or seen someone do? Which activities would you volunteer to do?

LISTENING COMPREHENSION

A ▶2:14 **LISTEN TO CONFIRM** Listen to the conversations and check the items and equipment they mention.

☐ agendas ☐ coffee ☐ hand-held mikes ☐ lapel mikes ☐ projectors ☐ snacks
☐ announcements ☐ desks ☐ handouts ☐ podiums ☐ signs ☐ tickets

B ▶2:15 **LISTEN FOR MAIN IDEAS** Listen again. Use the Vocabulary and the causative to complete the statements.

Conversation 1

1 Brian's going to get his .... to .... before the event.

2 Brian will also try to get .... to .... the morning of the event.

Conversation 2

3 Myra's going to get her .... to .... in each room, and they'll make sure there's a choice of mikes for each speaker.

4 She's also going to get them to .... in each room.

Conversation 3

5 Lester's going to get people to .... with enough chairs for 30 to 40 people.

6 He's also going to get people to .... things and get someone to .... at the podium and introduce each speaker.

A **GROUP WORK** Plan an event for your class, school, or community. Fill out the form. Discuss each person's strengths and weaknesses and assign who will be responsible for each activity.

TYPE OF EVENT

LOCATION

DATE AND TIME

BEFORE EVENT	What do you need to get done before the event?	Who will get it done?

DURING EVENT	What do you need to get done at the event?	Who will get it done?

Some ideas
- a special meeting
- a talk or a speech
- an "English practice" day
- a *Top Notch TV* day
- a *Top Notch Pop* karaoke show

" Nathan's really organized. Why don't we get him to . . . "

" I'm not really good with technology, but I can get people to . . . "

B **DISCUSSION** Present your plans to your class. Be sure to use the causative with <u>get</u> and the passive causative with <u>have</u>. Then choose the best plan.

A ▶ 2:16 Listen to each conversation. Then complete the statements, using the passive causative with <u>have</u>. Listen again if necessary.

Example: He'd like to have his shoes repaired by tomorrow morning.

1 She'd like ....

2 He needs ....

3 He'd like ....

4 She'd like ....

B Complete each question or request, using the passive causative <u>have</u>.

1 (can I / my sweaters / dry-clean) .... by tomorrow?

2 (I'd like / this skirt / lengthen) ....

3 (where can I / these pants / shorten) .... ?

4 (could you / this document / copy) .... for me?

5 (where did she / her painting / frame) .... ?

6 (how much did he pay / his camera / repair) .... ?

7 (we'd like / some handouts / print) .... a.s.a.p.

8 (can I / this package / deliver) .... by Friday?

C Complete each causative statement in your own way, using the correct form of <u>get</u>. Remember to use the infinitive form of a verb.

1 After dinner last night, we .... the waiter ....

2 Last week, we .... our teacher ....

3 When I was young, my friends always .... me ....

4 When you arrive, you should .... the hotel ....

5 Don't forget to .... the doctor ....

6 I can never .... my friends ....

WRITING

Do you think being a procrastinator is a serious problem?
Explain your views by giving examples from personal experience.

Some possible examples
- getting things repaired
- having things cleaned
- paying bills
- making plans for a vacation
- keeping in touch with people

WRITING BOOSTER p. 148
- Supporting an opinion with personal examples
- Guidance for this writing exercise

For additional language practice . . .

♫ TOP NOTCH POP • Lyrics p. 154
"I'll Get Back to You"

DIGITAL SONG DIGITAL KARAOKE

ORAL REVIEW

Paul's Difficult Day

GAME Study the pictures for one minute, paying attention to the time in each picture. Then close your books. Ask and answer questions about the photos, using the causative. Start like this:

What does Paul need to have done at 2:00?

PAIR WORK Create a conversation for each situation. Start like this:

Do you think I could have this __ by __?

STORY Close your books. In a small group, tell the story of Paul's day. Start like this:

At 9:00, Paul needed to have __ . . .

NOW I CAN

☐ Offer a solution.
☐ Discuss how long a service will take.
☐ Evaluate the quality of service.
☐ Plan an event.

UNIT 4 Reading for Pleasure

COMMUNICATION GOALS

1 Recommend a book.
2 Ask about an article.
3 Describe your reading habits.
4 Discuss online reading.

PREVIEW

🔍 **Looking for a good classic?** Check our recommendations. Click on a category for more. ⌄

Fiction

see all >

NOVELS	MYSTERIES	THRILLERS	ROMANCE	SCIENCE FICTION	SHORT STORIES

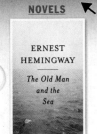 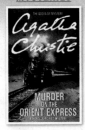   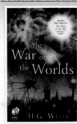 

Hemingway's masterpiece about a poor fisherman and the big fish he hopes will change his life.	Someone is killing people on Europe's most famous train. Can Inspector Poirot find the killer?	A thrilling contemporary story that will have you sitting on the edge of your seat!	A young doctor tries to forget his past. Will he find love again?	Strange beings from another planet try to conquer the planet Earth. Will they win?	A collection of thirty short stories by some of the world's most beloved writers.
print e-book audio	**print e-book audio**	**print e-book audio**	**print e-book audio**	**print e-book audio**	**print e-book audio**

Non-Fiction

see all >

BIOGRAPHIES	AUTOBIOGRAPHIES	TRAVEL	MEMOIRS	SELF-HELP

  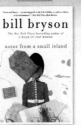  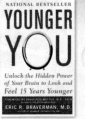

The true story of Nelson Mandela, the man who inspired millions.	In Nelson Mandela's own words—his unforgettable story.	A hilarious account of Bill Bryson's travels through the United Kingdom.	Author John Grogan remembers what life was like with his lovable pet dog, Marley.	Want to look and feel younger? Here are the secrets to a newer and better you!
print e-book audio	**print e-book audio**	**print e-book audio**	**print e-book audio**	

Credits appear on page 156.

A ▶2:19 **VOCABULARY • *Genres of books*** Read and listen. Then listen again and repeat.

Fiction		Non-Fiction	
a novel	a romance novel	a biography	a memoir
a mystery	a science fiction book	an autobiography	a self-help book
a thriller	a short story	a travel book	

B **DISCUSSION** Do you prefer fiction or non-fiction? What genres? Have you ever read a book in English? How about a magazine or a newspaper? If not, what would you like to read? Why?

C ▶2:20 **PHOTO STORY** Read and listen to a conversation between two friends at a bookstore.

Lynn: Hey, Sophie! I've never run into you here before!

Sophie: Lynn! Good to see you. Looking for anything special?

Lynn: No, I'm just browsing. How about you?

Sophie: I'm just picking up some gardening magazines for my mom. She can't get enough of them. . . . So, anything interesting?

Lynn: This one doesn't look bad. It's a biography of Helen Keller. What about you? Are you reading anything good these days?

Sophie: Well, I've got a new mystery on my night table, but I can't seem to get into it. I guess mysteries just aren't my thing.

Lynn: I know what you mean. They put me to sleep.

Sophie: Well, you're a big reader. I wonder if you could recommend something for me.

Lynn: Have you read the new John Grisham thriller?

Sophie: No, I haven't. I didn't know he had a new book out.

Lynn: Well, I can't put it down. It's a real page-turner.

Sophie: Thanks for the tip! Do you think I could borrow it when you're done with it?

Lynn: Of course. If you can wait till the end of the week, I'd be happy to lend it to you.

D **THINK AND EXPLAIN** Classify each of the six underlined expressions from the Photo Story by its meaning. Explain your choices.

Likes	Doesn't like
1	4
2	5
3	6

E **PARAPHRASE** Say each underlined verb in your *own* way.

1 I've never <u>run into</u> you here before.

2 I'm just <u>browsing</u>.

3 I'm <u>picking up</u> some gardening magazines for my mom.

4 Do you think I could <u>borrow</u> it when you're done with it?

5 I'd be happy to <u>lend</u> it to you.

SPEAKING

A What percentage of your total reading time do you spend on the reading materials in the chart? (Make sure it adds up to 100%!) Compare percentages with your classmates.

magazines		fiction	
newspapers		non-fiction	
websites		other	

B Tell a partner about what you read the most and the least, and why.

GOAL Recommend a book

VOCABULARY *Ways to describe a book*

A ▶2:21 Read and listen. Then listen again and repeat.

It's a **page-turner.** *It's so interesting that you want to keep reading it.*

It's a **cliff-hanger.** *It's so exciting that you can't wait to find out what happens next.*

It's a **best-seller.** *It's very popular, and everyone is buying copies.*

It's a **fast read.** *It's easy and enjoyable to read.*

It's **hard to follow.** *It's difficult to understand.*

It's **trash.** *It's very poor quality.*

Credits appear on page 156.

B **PAIR WORK** Discuss which types of books you find the most interesting. Use the Vocabulary from here and page 38.

> ❝ I prefer thrillers. A thriller is usually a pretty fast read. It helps pass the time. ❞

GRAMMAR *Noun clauses*

A noun clause functions as a noun, often as a direct object. A noun clause can be introduced by <u>that.</u>

	noun clause
I didn't know	**that he wrote this book.**
I think	**that Junot Díaz's novels are fantastic.**
Did you forget	**that her biography was 500 pages long?**

When a noun clause functions as a direct object, <u>that</u> may be omitted, especially in speaking.

I didn't know he wrote this book.

In short answers, use <u>so</u> to replace a noun clause after the verbs <u>think</u>, <u>believe</u>, <u>guess</u>, and <u>hope</u>.

A: Does Stephen King have a new book out?
B: I think so. / I believe so. / I guess so. / I hope so.
(<u>so</u> = that Stephen King has a new book out)

A noun clause can also be an adjective complement.

It's interesting **(that)** she wrote a new book.
I'm surprised **(that)** he hasn't written a new novel yet.

Noun clauses often follow these verbs and adjectives.

agree	hear	disappointed
think	see	happy
believe	understand	sad
feel	hope	sorry
suppose	forget	sure
doubt	remember	surprised
guess	know	

Be careful!
I don't think **so**. / I don't believe **so**.
BUT I guess **not**. / I hope **not**.
NOT I ~~don't guess so~~. / I ~~don't hope so~~.

GRAMMAR BOOSTER p. 131
• More verbs and adjectives that can be followed by clauses with <u>that</u>

A **FIND THE GRAMMAR** In the Photo Story on page 39, find three examples of noun clauses that omit <u>that</u>.

B **GRAMMAR PRACTICE** Write statements and questions with noun clauses using <u>that</u>.

1 I think / the author Paulo Coelho / be from / Brazil.

2 I believe / the novel *Juliet* / take place / in Italy.

3 I didn't know / U.K. author J.K. Rowling / write a new novel / in 2014.

4 Are you sure / Peruvian author Mario Vargas Llosa / write the novel *The Feast of the Goat* / in 1998?

5 Are you disappointed / U.S. author Stephen King / not win / the Nobel Prize for Literature yet?

6 I'm happy / the Chinese author Mo Yan / win / in 2012.

1. I think that the author Paulo Coelho is from Brazil.

C **GRAMMAR PRACTICE** Now rewrite each sentence from Exercise B, omitting <u>that</u>.

PRONUNCIATION *Sentence stress in short answers with so*

A ▶2:22 Read and listen. Notice the stress on the verb in short answers with <u>so</u>. Then listen again and repeat.

1 Are there a lot of characters in the story? I **THINK** so.
2 Has she read that book yet? I don't **THINK** so.
3 Do you think this thriller will be good? I **HOPE** so.
4 Does the story have a happy ending? I be**LIEVE** so.

B **PAIR WORK** Write five <u>yes</u> / <u>no</u> questions about your partner's future plans. Then read your questions aloud. Respond to your partner's questions with short answers, using <u>think</u>, <u>hope</u>, <u>believe</u>, or <u>guess</u>.

❝ Are you going to read anything this weekend? ❞

❝ I **THINK** so. ❞

CONVERSATION MODEL

A ▶2:23 Read and listen to someone recommending a book.

A: Have you read anything interesting lately?

B: Actually, I'm reading a thriller called *Don't Close Your Eyes*.

A: I've never heard of that one. Is it any good?

B: Oh, I think it's a great book. And it's a cliff-hanger. I highly recommend it.

A: Well, do you think I could borrow it when you're done? I love cliff-hangers.

B: Sure! I doubt I'll finish it before next week, though.

A: No problem. I can wait.

B ▶2:24 **RHYTHM AND INTONATION** Listen again and repeat. Then practice the Conversation Model with a partner.

NOW YOU CAN Recommend a book

A **NOTEPADDING** Write some notes about a book you've read, or choose one of the books on page 38. Use the Vocabulary from pages 38 and 40.

B **CONVERSATION ACTIVATOR** With a partner, personalize the Conversation Model. Recommend a book, using the notes on your notepad.

A: Have you read anything interesting lately?
B: Actually, I .... called ....
A: I've never heard of that one. Is it any good?
B: Oh, I think it's .... book. And it's a .... I highly recommend it.
A: Well, do you think I could borrow it when you're done? I love ....s.
B: Sure! I doubt I'll finish it before .... , though.
A: .... I can wait.

Genre of book:
Title:
Author:
What is it about?
Your description:

DON'T STOP!

Ask questions about the book.
What's it about?
Where does it take place?
Why did you decide to read it?

GOAL Ask about an article

CONVERSATION MODEL

A ▶2:25 Read and listen to someone asking about an article.

A: Is that this month's *Car Magazine*?

B: Yes, it is.

A: Could you tell me where you bought it? I can't find it anywhere.

B: At the newsstand across the street. But I think it's sold out.

A: Too bad. There's an article in there about SUVs. I'm dying to read it.

B: I can understand why. It was really interesting. Listen. Take *my* copy. I'm done with it.

A: Are you sure?

B: Definitely.

B ▶2:26 **RHYTHM AND INTONATION** Listen again and repeat. Then practice the Conversation Model with a partner.

GRAMMAR *Noun clauses: Embedded questions*

> **GRAMMAR BOOSTER** p. 132
> * Embedded questions:
>   ○ with <u>whether</u>
>   ○ usage and common errors
>   ○ punctuation

A question can be embedded in a noun clause. Use <u>if</u> to begin an embedded <u>yes</u> / <u>no</u> question.

<u>Yes</u> / <u>no</u> questions	Embedded <u>yes</u> / <u>no</u> questions
Is that magazine interesting?	Tell me **if that magazine is interesting.**
Did he like the article?	I'd like to know **if he liked the article.**
Have you finished that newspaper?	Could you tell me **if you've finished that newspaper?**

Use a question word to begin embedded information questions.

Information questions	Embedded information questions
What's the article about?	I can't remember **what the article's about.**
Why have you decided to read it?	I don't understand **why you've decided to read it.**
Who's the writer?	I wonder **who the writer is.**
Whose magazine is it?	I'm not sure **whose magazine it is.**
When was it written?	I don't know **when it was written.**
Where is the writer from?	Do you know **where the writer is from?**

Be careful!

Use normal word order (not question word order) in embedded questions.

Don't say: I wonder ~~who is~~ the writer. Do you know ~~where is~~ the writer from?

> **Punctuation**
> If an embedded question is . . .
> * within a statement, use a period.
> * with a question, use a question mark.

A **FIND THE GRAMMAR** Find and underline two embedded questions in the Photo Story on page 39.

B **GRAMMAR PRACTICE** Change the questions to embedded questions.

1 Does her daughter like to read?

I wonder ....

2 Where did you get that magazine?

Could you tell me .... ?

3 Is he a Bill Bryson fan?

I'd like to know ....

4 Why don't you read newspapers?

I don't understand ....

5 Who told her about your article?

I forgot ....

6 When did I see the new website?

I can't remember ....

C GRAMMAR PRACTICE Complete the chart. Look at a partner's chart. Use embedded questions to learn more about your partner's likes and dislikes.

> " Tell me why you like to read photography magazines. "

> " Could you tell me which sections of the newspaper you like to read online? "

My favorite magazines	My favorite sections of the newspaper
Some magazines I don't like	Newspaper sections I don't like

Newspaper sections
the international news section
the local news section
the sports section
the entertainment section
the business section
the food section
the travel section

DIGITAL
MORE
EXERCISES

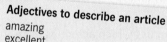

NOW YOU CAN Ask about an article

DIGITAL
VIDEO

A CONVERSATION ACTIVATOR With a partner, change the Conversation Model, using a magazine or newspaper you know. Use a different adjective. Then change roles.

A: Is that .... ?
B: Yes, it is.
A: Could you tell me where you bought it? I can't find it anywhere.
B: .... But I think it's sold out.
A: Too bad. There's an article in there about .... I'm dying to read it.
B: I can understand why. It was .... Listen. Take *my* copy. I'm done with it.
A: Are you sure?
B: ....

Adjectives to describe an article
amazing
excellent
exciting
fantastic
fascinating
funny
hilarious
inspiring
interesting
thought-provoking

DON'T STOP!
Ask more questions about the article.

B CHANGE PARTNERS Ask about another magazine or newspaper.

GOAL Describe your reading habits

BEFORE YOU LISTEN

A ▶2:27 **VOCABULARY** • *Some ways to enjoy reading* Read and listen. Then listen again and repeat.

curl up with [a book]

read aloud [to someone]

listen to audio books

do puzzles

read [articles] online

skim through [a newspaper]

read e-books / read electronic books

B **PAIR WORK** Discuss which activities from the Vocabulary match each situation below. Explain your reasons.

- Is convenient when you are driving
- Helps pass the time during a bus or train commute
- Is a good way to relax
- Is a way to keep up with the news

❝ I think doing puzzles is a great way to relax. ❞

LISTENING COMPREHENSION

▶2:28 **LISTEN TO TAKE NOTES** Listen and take notes to answer these questions about each speaker. Listen again if necessary.

1 What kinds of reading material does he or she like?

2 When does he or she like to read?

3 Where does he or she like to read?

Betty Song • Taiwan

Silvio Ferrante • Argentina

Melissa White • U.S.A.

A FRAME YOUR IDEAS Complete the questionnaire.

What are your reading habits?

1 Do you consider yourself to be a big reader? Why or why not?

_____
_____
_____

2 Do you spend a lot of time reading online? Why or why not?

_____
_____
_____

3 Do you listen to audio books? If so, when and where?

_____
_____
_____

4 When and where do you prefer to read the most?

_____
_____
_____

5 Do you have any favorite authors? Who are they?

_____
_____
_____

6 Do you prefer any particular genres of books? Which ones? Why?

_____
_____
_____

7 Are you a big newspaper reader? Why or why not?

_____
_____
_____

8 Do you read a lot of magazines? Why or why not? What kinds do you prefer?

_____
_____
_____

○ news ○ sports ○ travel
○ photography ○ politics ○ music
○ computers & electronics ○ finance
○ entertainment ○ fashion
○ health & fitness ○ business
○ science ○ food & cooking
○ other _____

9 Have you ever read aloud to someone? Has anyone ever read aloud to you? When?

_____
_____
_____

10 Is there anything else to add here about your reading habits?

_____
_____

B PAIR WORK Compare questionnaires with your partner. Discuss your reading habits. Ask and answer questions, and take notes about your partner's habits.

RECYCLE THIS LANGUAGE.

I [think / guess / believe / feel] that . . .
I [hear / understand / see] that . . .
It's [interesting / surprising] that . . .
I'm [sure / surprised] that
Could you tell me if . . . ?
I'd like to know if . . .

C GROUP WORK Now tell your classmates about your partner's reading habits.

❝ Ellen thinks the best place to read is in bed before she goes to sleep. She also likes . . . ❞

GOAL Discuss online reading

BEFORE YOU READ

WARM-UP In what ways do you think reading something online is different from reading in print?

READING ▶ 2:29

Reading Habits in Transition

Most experts agree that the Internet has fundamentally changed how we read, think, and remember things. However, whether this has had a positive or negative impact is still unknown.

How has the Internet changed the way we read?
There is evidence that we are reading fewer books, particularly non-fiction. Let's say you need medical advice, cooking instructions, or biographical information. Who wants to buy a 300-page book when you can find a 300-word article on the Internet about the same subject? It's easier to read, it's free, and it's a lot faster. However, we are, in fact, reading a lot more overall. In addition to our offline reading, we read online throughout the day as we check our smart phones, surf the Internet, visit social media sites, and catch up on our e-mail.

We also do a lot more skimming and scanning on the Internet than we do when we read physical books or periodicals, such as magazines and newspapers. As we surf the Internet, we skim quickly for topics that interest us and scan for the specific information we need. A search engine puts millions of possibilities at our fingertips.

How has the Internet changed how we think and remember?
Before there was an Internet, people spent a lot of time taking notes in libraries so they could remember and recall information easily. Today, when you can use a search engine to take you to what you're looking for in an instant, that kind of concentration isn't as necessary. You can simply bookmark any page and return to it easily. However, many argue that online information sources often contain errors and can't be trusted, so we need to be more careful when we use them.

Some wonder if the Internet has made it more difficult to concentrate on one task without getting distracted by other things. We are constantly interrupted by updates from social media sites and e-mail messages. We follow links to other websites where we find more links to other websites and jump from topic to topic. We are also bombarded with a lot of junk—for example, newsfeeds about celebrities, pop-up ads about products we don't want or need, and warnings about viruses.

Some consider what we read on the Internet to be trash compared to traditional offline reading, while others see many advantages in the reading we do on the Internet. Some argue that reading on the Internet is like exercise for the brain, making it easier for us to cope with distractions and think clearly as we learn to make choices that work for us. In a recent study, 81% of those surveyed agreed that our use of the Internet has actually made us smarter. If you are a digital native—that is, someone who grew up with the Internet—that's very good news, indeed.

A **RECOGNIZE POINT OF VIEW** The Reading mentions both positive and negative aspects of reading on the Internet. Summarize some of each in the chart.

Positive aspects	Negative aspects

B **UNDERSTAND MEANING FROM CONTEXT** Find and underline these words in the Reading. Use the context to match them with their meanings.

.... **1** skimming   **a** the ability to pay careful attention to one thing

.... **2** scanning   **b** reading quickly for a general understanding

.... **3** concentration   **c** made to see or read things continuously

.... **4** distracted   **d** reading quickly in search of specific information

.... **5** bombarded   **e** unable to focus because of interruptions

DIGITAL
MORE
EXERCISES

NOW YOU CAN Discuss reading online

A **NOTEPADDING** What do you read about on the Internet? Write some notes about your habits.

	Why?
What topics do you like to read about on the Internet?	
What websites do you visit regularly?	
What Internet content do you think is high quality?	
What Internet content do you think is "trash"?	

B **PAIR WORK** With a partner, compare what you wrote on your notepads and share your experiences with reading online. Do you think the Internet interferes with concentration, or do you think it makes you a better reader?

RECYCLE THIS LANGUAGE.

I think (that) . . .	I'm really into [social media].
I believe (that) . . .	I can't get enough of [celebrity newsfeeds].
I guess (that) . . .	[Blogs] aren't my thing.
In my opinion, . . .	[Online games] don't turn me on.
	[Celebrity websites] put me to sleep.

Text-mining (optional)
Find and underline three words or phrases in the Reading that were new to you. Use them in your Pair Work.
For example: "a positive or negative impact."

A ▶2:30 Listen to each conversation and write the type of book each person is discussing. Then listen again and decide if the person likes the book. Explain your answer.

Type of book	Likes it?	Explain your answer
1	Y N	
2	Y N	
3	Y N	
4	Y N	

B Write the name of each type of book.

1 A novel about people falling in love: ....

2 A book about a famous person: ....

3 A book that a famous person writes about his or her own life: ....

4 A very exciting novel with people in dangerous situations: ....

5 Books that are about factual information: ....

6 A strange fictional story about the future: ....

C Use the expressions in the box to change each question to an embedded question. (Use each expression once.) Use correct punctuation at the end of each one.

> I wonder . . .   Could you tell me . . .   I don't know . . .
> I can't remember . . .   Do you know . . .

1 Where does the story take place?

....

2 Who is the main character in the novel?

....

3 How much was that newspaper?

....

4 How do you say this in English?

....

5 What does this word mean?

....

For additional language practice . . .

♫ **TOP NOTCH** **POP** • Lyrics p. 154
"A True Life Story"

DIGITAL SONG .... **DIGITAL KARAOKE**

WRITING

Write a review of something you've read—a book or an article from a magazine, a newspaper, or the Internet.

WRITING BOOSTER p. 149
• Summarizing
• Guidance for this writing exercise

• Summarize what it was about.

• Make a recommendation to the reader.

ORAL REVIEW

GAME Close your books. Make an "I" statement about the reading habits of the man or woman. Your partner guesses if you're describing the man or woman. For example:

> *I like to do the puzzles in the newspaper.*

PAIR WORK

1 Create a conversation for the man and woman in which he asks about the book she is reading. She makes a recommendation. He asks if he can borrow the book. Start like this:

> *Are you reading anything interesting?*

2 Use the pictures to create a conversation in which the man and woman discuss their reading habits. For example:

> *I usually like to curl up in bed with a good book.*

✓ NOW I CAN

- ☐ Recommend a book.
- ☐ Ask about an article.
- ☐ Describe my reading habits.
- ☐ Discuss online reading.

Natural Disasters

COMMUNICATION GOALS
1 Convey a message.
2 Tell someone about the news.
3 Describe natural disasters.
4 Prepare for an emergency.

PREVIEW

HISTORIC DISASTERS

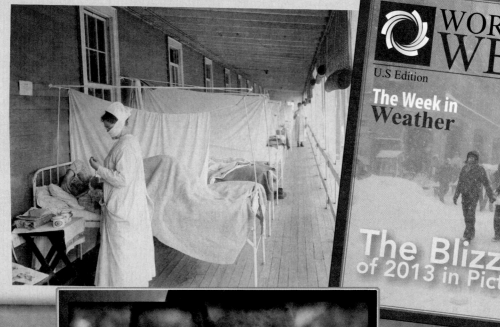

The influenza epidemic of 1918–1919 left an estimated 25 million people dead worldwide.

WORLD WEEK

U.S Edition

February 2013

The Week in Weather

The Blizzard of 2013 in Pictures

In February 2013, a major blizzard hit the Northeastern U.S. with heavy snowfall and high winds. Snowfall in some areas reached 100 cm, causing travel delays, school closures, and power outages.

Between 2010 and 2012, 260,000 people died in Somalia in one of the worst food shortages in modern history.

WORLD NEWS *Famine in Somalia*

A DISCUSSION Discuss one or more of the topics about the content of the news.

1 When stories about natural disasters such as epidemics, famines, and weather emergencies appear in the news, are you interested in knowing about them? Why or why not?

2 Why do newspapers often put stories like this on the front page?

3 Not all disasters are caused by nature. What are some other kinds of disasters? What are some of their causes?

B ▶ 3:02 **PHOTO STORY** Read and listen to a conversation about a natural disaster.

Rachel: Oh, my goodness. Take a look at this!

Tom: Why? What's going on?

Rachel: There's this enormous flood in Slovakia—look at these people on the roof! The water's up to the second floor. And look at these cars. I sure hope there was no one in them.

Tom: That sounds horrendous. Any word on casualties?

Rachel: It says, "No reports of deaths or injuries so far . . . ." But it's in the middle of a city, for goodness sake. The death toll could end up being huge.

Tom: And can you imagine the property damage?

Rachel: Well, they estimate almost 50% of the houses in town are under water already.

Tom: What a disaster!

Rachel: I wonder how this flood compares to the one they had in New Orleans a few years back. Remember that?

Tom: You bet I do. How could anyone forget? And that flooded almost half the city, too.

Rachel: Let's turn on CNN. They usually have breaking news about stuff like this.

C **FOCUS ON LANGUAGE** Complete each statement with words or phrases from the Photo Story.

1 Two words that mean very big are .... and ....

2 The number of .... indicates the number of people who are injured or killed in an event.

3 A two-word phrase that means the destruction of or harm to buildings, cars, and other things that belong to victims of an event is ....

4 A two-word expression that is used to describe the first news reports of an important event that is happening at the present is ....

SPEAKING

A Check your news sources and write an advantage and disadvantage for each one.

	Advantages	Disadvantages
☑ a newspaper	you can save an article	not as up-to-date as online news

	Advantages	Disadvantages
☐ a newspaper		
☐ Internet news sites		
☐ TV or radio newscasts		
☐ a weekly news magazine		
☐ word of mouth		

B **PAIR WORK** Compare opinions with your partner. Do you both use the same sources? Why or why not?

GOAL Convey a message

GRAMMAR *Indirect speech: Imperatives*

To report what someone said without quoting the exact words, use indirect speech.
Don't use quotation marks when you write indirect speech.

Direct speech: Peter said, "Be careful if you go out during the storm."
Indirect speech: Peter said to be careful if you go out during the storm.

An imperative in direct speech becomes an infinitive in indirect speech.

They said, "Read the weather report." → They said to read the weather report.
She says, "Don't go out without a full tank of gas." → She says not to go out without a full tank of gas.

Change the pronouns in indirect speech as necessary for logic.

Martin said, "Tell me as soon as you know." → Martin told me to tell him as soon as I know.
She told me, "Please call me when you get home." → She asked me to call her when I get home.

> Indirect speech is a kind of noun clause. It is the direct object of a reporting verb such as <u>say</u>, <u>tell</u>, or <u>ask</u>.

> **GRAMMAR BOOSTER** p. 133
> • Direct speech: punctuation rules

A GRAMMAR PRACTICE Rewrite each statement in indirect speech. Make necessary changes to the pronouns.

1 Martha told me, "Be home before the snowstorm."   *1. Martha told me to be home before the snowstorm.*

2 Everyone is saying, "Get ready for a big storm."

3 The radio says, "Get supplies of food and water in case the roads are closed."

4 They told her, "Don't be home too late this afternoon."

5 Maria always tells them, "Don't leave your doors open."

6 Carl told me, "Call me when you hear the news."

B PAIR WORK For each sentence, say what you think the speaker's original words were. Take turns.

1 He asked them to call him when it starts raining.   **❝** Please call me when it starts raining. **❞**

2 The newspaper said to leave a window or door open when there's going to be a severe storm.

3 She told his parents to read the emergency instructions in the newspaper.

4 Ray told Allison to look for the story about him in the paper on Tuesday.

5 She asked him to pick up some food for her on the way home.

6 They told me not to wait until the snow gets heavy.

DIGITAL MORE EXERCISES

DIGITAL VIDEO COACH

PRONUNCIATION *Direct and indirect speech: Rhythm*

A ▶ 3:03 Notice the rhythm of sentences in direct and indirect speech. Read and listen. Then listen again and repeat.

1 He said, [pause] "Be home before midnight." → He said to be home before midnight.

2 I told your parents, [pause] "Get a flu shot at the clinic." → I told your parents to get a flu shot at the clinic.

B PAIR WORK Take turns reading aloud the sentences in Exercise A Grammar Practice, above. Read both the original sentences and the sentences you wrote, using correct rhythm for direct and indirect speech.

CONVERSATION MODEL

A ▶3:04 Read and listen to someone conveying a message.

A: I'm on the phone with your parents. Would you like to say hello?

B: I would, but I'm running late.

A: Anything you'd like me to tell them?

B: Yes. Please tell them to turn on the TV. There's a storm on the way.

A: Will do.

B ▶3:05 **RHYTHM AND INTONATION** Listen again and repeat. Then practice the Conversation Model with a partner.

NOW YOU CAN Convey a message

A **NOTEPADDING** Read the possible excuses and messages. Then write one or two more excuses and messages.

> **Possible excuses**
> I'm running late.
> I have an appointment.
> I don't have time.

B **CONVERSATION ACTIVATOR** With a partner, change the Conversation Model. Role-play conveying a message. Choose messages and excuses from the lists in the boxes, or use your own. Then change roles.

> **Possible messages**
> [Watch / Listen to] the news. There's a story about __.
> Check the weather online. There's a bad storm on the way.
> Call me at the office.

A: I'm on the phone with ....
Would you like to say hello?

B: I would, but ....

A: Anything you'd like me to tell .... ?

B: Yes. Please tell .... to ....

A: ....

DON'T STOP!

Continue the conversation. Ask your partner:
what time he or she will be home.
to do you a favor.
to call you later.

C **CHANGE PARTNERS** Practice the conversation again. Use another message. Use another excuse.

VOCABULARY *Severe weather and other natural disasters*

A ▶3:06 Read and listen. Then listen again and repeat.

| a tornado | a hurricane / a typhoon | a flood | a landslide | a drought |

B ▶3:07 **LISTEN TO INFER** Listen to the news. Write the kind of event the report describes.

1 .... 2 .... 3 .... 4 ....

C ▶3:08 **LISTEN TO CONFIRM INFORMATION** Listen again. After each report, say if the statement is true or false. Explain your answers.

1 She said it hadn't rained in a month.

2 He said it hadn't rained for a week.

3 She said the storm had done a lot of damage.

4 He said the storm wouldn't do a lot of damage.

GRAMMAR *Indirect speech: Say and tell—tense changes*

> GRAMMAR BOOSTER p. 134
> • Indirect speech: optional tense changes

> Use <u>tell</u> when you mention the listener. Use <u>say</u> when you don't.
>
> Maggie told her parents to stay home. (listeners mentioned)
> Maggie said to stay home. (listeners not mentioned)
>
> When <u>say</u> and <u>tell</u> are in the past tense, the verbs in the indirect speech statement often change.
> Present becomes past. Past becomes past perfect. <u>Will</u> becomes <u>would</u>. <u>Can</u> becomes <u>could</u>.
>
> They said, "The weather is awful." → They said (that) the weather was awful.
> Dan said, "We all had the flu." → Dan said (that) they all had had the flu.
> They said, "There will be snow tonight." → They said there would be snow tonight.
> My husband said, "You can come with me." → My husband said I could come with him.

A **GRAMMAR PRACTICE** Circle the correct verbs for indirect speech.

My Great-Grandmother Meets Hurricane Cleo

Hurricane Cleo struck the United States in August, 1964. My great-grandmother, Ana, was traveling in Miami when the hurricane struck. She (1 said / told) me that she still remembers how scared everyone was. She (2 said / told) me that the hotel (3 has called / had called) her room one morning and had (4 said / told) her that a big storm (5 is / was) on the way. They (6 said / told) that all hotel guests (7 have to / had to) stay in the hotel until the weather service (8 tell / said) that it (9 is / was) safe to leave. She stayed in her room, and she didn't know what happened until the storm was over. When she turned on the TV, the reports (10 said / told) that a lot of people (11 have been / had been) injured and that all the roads (12 are / were) flooded. She always (13 says / said) that she still (14 feels / felt) lucky to have survived Hurricane Cleo.

B **GRAMMAR PRACTICE** Change each statement from direct speech to indirect speech, changing the verb tense in the indirect speech statement.

1 The TV reporter said, "The landslide is one of the worst in history."

> 1. The TV reporter said the landslide was one of the worst in history.

2 He also said, "It caused the destruction of half the houses in the town."

3 My sister called and said, "There is no electricity because of the hurricane."

4 The newspaper said, "There will be a typhoon in the next thirty-six hours."

5 The paper said, "The drought of 1999 was the worst natural disaster of the twentieth century."

6 After the great snowstorm in 1888, a New York newspaper reported, "The blizzard of '88 caused more damage than any previous storm."

DIGITAL
MORE
EXERCISES

CONVERSATION MODEL

A ▶ 3:09 Read and listen to a conversation about the news.

A: What's going on in the news today?

B: Well, the *Times* says there was a terrible storm in the South.

A: Really?

B: Yes. It says lots of houses were destroyed.

A: What a shame!

B: But there haven't been any deaths.

A: Thank goodness for that!

> **Reactions to news**
> ☹ What a shame!
> ☺ Thank goodness for that!

B ▶ 3:10 **RHYTHM AND INTONATION** Listen again and repeat. Then practice the Conversation Model with a partner.

NOW YOU CAN Tell someone about the news

A **NOTEPADDING** Read each headline. Then, on a separate sheet of paper, write what it said. Use indirect speech.

> The Daily Post Online says an earthquake killed 20,000 in Iran.

DIGITAL
VIDEO

B **CONVERSATION ACTIVATOR** Tell your partner what the news is, using the headlines. Then change roles and headlines.

A: What's going on in the news today?

B: Well, ... says ....

A: Really?

B: Yes. It says ....

A: .... !

DON'T STOP!
- Discuss other headlines.
- Express your reactions to the news.

> 🔄 **RECYCLE THIS LANGUAGE.**
> What a shame!
> Thank goodness for that!
> Oh, no!
> What a disaster!
> That's [enormous / gigantic / huge / horrendous]!

DAILY POST

20,000 killed in earthquake in Iran »

Over 100,000 homeless »

ASIA TIMES

Bird influenza epidemic causes 200 deaths in Mongolia
Doctors urge children and elderly to receive vaccinations

········ Digital ········
» NEWS Update

- People flee flooded river valley farms ›

- Animals die in worst flood in U.S. history ›

Load More

SPECIAL REPORT
The Weekly Mail

DROUGHT IN ETHIOPIA
causes widespread
FAMINE

THOUSANDS DIE
of **HUNGER**

Journal and Times
Mexicali hit by second huge storm this year
Less damage to cars, buildings this time

C **CHANGE PARTNERS** Practice the conversation again, using a different headline.

BEFORE YOU READ

mild	!
moderate	!!
severe	!!!
deadly	!!!!
catastrophic	!!!!

A ▶3:11 **VOCABULARY • *Adjectives of severity*** Read and listen. Then listen again and repeat.

DIGITAL FLASH CARDS

B **WARM-UP** Have you or someone you know experienced a natural disaster? What kind of disaster was it? How severe was it? Tell the class about it.

READING ▶3:12

EARTHQUAKES

Port-au-Prince, 2010

Earthquakes are among the deadliest natural disasters, causing the largest numbers of casualties, the highest death tolls, and the greatest destruction. In 1556 in China, the deadliest earthquake in history killed 830,000 people. But many other earthquakes have caused the deaths of more than 200,000 people, and it is not unusual, even in modern times, for an earthquake death toll to reach 20,000–30,000 people with hundreds of thousands left homeless and with countless injured. The floodwaters of the 2004 tsunami in Sumatra, which killed over 200,000 people, were caused by a catastrophic earthquake.

There are four factors that affect the casualty rate of earthquakes: magnitude, location, quality of construction of buildings, and timing.

MAGNITUDE
The magnitude, or strength, of an earthquake is measured on the Richter scale, ranging from 1 to 10, with 10 being the greatest. Earthquakes over 6 on the Richter scale are often deadly, and those over 8 are generally catastrophic, causing terrible damage.

LOCATION
A severe earthquake that is located far from population centers does not cause the same damage as a less severe one that occurs in the middle of a city. As an example, in 1960, the strongest earthquake ever recorded, 9.5 magnitude on the Richter scale, struck in the Pacific Ocean near the Chilean coastline, destroying buildings, killing over 2,000, and injuring another 3,000 in regional cities near the coast. The location of this earthquake, far away from a population center, however, prevented it from being catastrophic, with hundreds of thousands of deaths.

QUALITY OF CONSTRUCTION
Modern building construction techniques can lessen the death toll and economic impact of a moderate earthquake that would otherwise cause severe destruction of older-style buildings.

In 2010, a terrible earthquake in Port-au-Prince, the capital of Haiti, caused the destruction of a tremendous number of the city's buildings, mostly due to poor construction. In contrast, an even stronger earthquake later that year in Chile caused less destruction because of that country's use of earthquake-resistant construction.

TIMING
Finally, the time of occurrence of an earthquake can affect the number of deaths and casualties. Earthquakes that occur in the night, when people are indoors, usually cause a greater death toll than ones that occur when people are outdoors.

Ten Largest Earthquakes by Magnitude		
Year	Place	Magnitude
1960	Valdivia, Chile	9.5
1964	Alaska, U.S.	9.2
2004	Sumatra, Indonesia	9.1–9.3
1952	Kamchatka, Russia	9.0
2011	Tochuko region, Japan	9.0
1615	Arica, Chile	8.8
1833	Sumatra, Indonesia	8.7–9.2*
1906	Ecuador / Colombia	8.8
2010	Bio-Bio, Chile	8.8
1700	Pacific Ocean:U.S. / Canada	8.7–9.2*

* estimate

A **PARAPHRASE** Rewrite the statements in your own words, changing the underlined word or phrase.

1 The <u>magnitude</u> of an earthquake is measured by the Richter scale.

2 There are four <u>factors</u> that affect the casualty rate of an earthquake.

3 Good construction techniques can <u>lessen</u> the danger to people in buildings affected by an earthquake.

4 Damage is often <u>due to</u> poor construction.

5 If an earthquake occurs near a major <u>population center</u>, more people will be affected.

B **CONFIRM FACTS** Answer the questions, according to the information in the Reading. Use indirect speech.

   1 Where did the deadliest earthquake in history take place?

   2 Which earthquake had the highest recorded Richter-scale reading?

   3 How can location affect the death toll of an earthquake?

   4 What else can lessen the destruction and economic impact of an earthquake?

> *1. The article said the deadliest earthquake in history took place in . . .*

C **IDENTIFY CAUSE AND EFFECT** Discuss how magnitude and timing affect the casualty rate and economic impact of earthquakes. Explain your ideas by putting together information from the article.

NOW YOU CAN Describe natural disasters

A **PAIR WORK** Partner A, read the fact sheet about the Indonesia typhoon. Partner B, read the fact sheet about the Bangladesh earthquake. In your own words, tell your partner about the disaster.

> " A severe typhoon hit Indonesia on October 12. There were high winds and catastrophic property damage. "

INDONESIA TYPHOON

Date:	October 12
Place:	Indonesia and western Malaysia
Event:	Typhoon with highest winds ever recorded

Property damage: Catastrophic destruction

Casualties: 5,309 deaths with more than 1,740 missing; 8 million affected with many homeless

BANGLADESH EARTHQUAKE

Date:	September 20
Place:	Bangladesh
Event:	Earthquake

Property damage: At least 70% of homes (12,000) destroyed.

Casualties: 630 deaths and hundreds more injured

B **NOTEPADDING** Choose one of the historic disasters from the list. Find information about it on the Internet, at a library, or in a bookstore. (OR choose a disaster you are already familiar with.) Write details about the disaster on your notepad.

Some historic disasters
- The San Francisco earthquake of 1906 (U.S.)
- The Bam earthquake of 2003 (Iran)
- The tsunami of 2004 (Indian Ocean)
- Hurricane Katrina 2005 (New Orleans, U.S.)
- A natural disaster of your choice: __

Date:	
Place:	
Event:	
Property damage:	
Casualties:	

C **GROUP WORK** Make a news broadcast or presentation about the disaster you researched (OR one of the disasters in Exercise A above). Describe the natural disaster to your class.

RECYCLE THIS LANGUAGE.

Types of disasters	Adjectives	Features
earthquake	mild	casualties
epidemic	moderate	death toll
famine	severe	injuries
flood	deadly	property damage
landslide	catastrophic	
storm		

Text-mining (optional)
Find and underline three words or phrases in the Reading that were new to you. Use them in your Group Work.
   For example: "death toll."

GOAL Prepare for an emergency

BEFORE YOU LISTEN

A ▶ 3:13 **VOCABULARY** • *Emergency preparations and supplies* Read and listen. Then listen again and repeat.

evacuate to remove all people from an area that is too dangerous

an emergency a very dangerous situation that requires immediate action

a power outage an interruption in the flow of electrical power over a large area

a shelter a safe place where people may go when the area they live in has been evacuated

a first-aid kit a small box or package containing supplies to treat minor injuries and illnesses

a flashlight a portable, battery-operated light

non-perishable food food that doesn't need refrigeration, such as canned or dried food

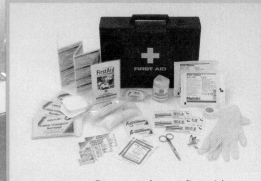

Be sure to have a first-aid kit with scissors and bandages.

A battery-operated flashlight is a must when there is a power outage.

In a power outage, candles can provide light.

Sometimes an evacuation is necessary in an emergency.

B **PAIR WORK** With a partner, write sentences using the Vocabulary words and phrases.

> They tried to evacuate the entire population of the city before the flood, but lots of people refused to go.

LISTENING COMPREHENSION

A ▶ 3:14 **LISTEN FOR MAIN IDEAS** Listen to an emergency radio broadcast. Write a sentence to describe the emergency the broadcaster is reporting.

B ▶ 3:15 **LISTEN FOR DETAILS** Listen again and correct each of the following false statements, using indirect speech.

Example: He said you should stand near windows during the storm.

> 66 No. He said *not* to stand near windows during the storm. 99

1 He said you should turn your refrigerator and freezer off.

2 He said that in case of a flood, you should put valuable papers on the lowest floor of your home.

3 He said you should read the newspapers for the location of shelters.

C PARAPHRASE What did the radio announcer say in the emergency radio broadcast? With a partner, discuss the questions and complete each statement, using indirect speech. Listen again if necessary.

1 What should you do to get your car ready for an evacuation?

He said to ....

2 What should you do with outdoor furniture?

He said to ....

3 What should you buy for flashlights and portable radios?

He said to ....

4 How should you prepare to have food and water in case you have to stay indoors for several days?

He said to ....

5 What should you listen to in case of an evacuation?

He said to ....

NOW YOU CAN Prepare for an emergency

Kinds of emergencies
- a flood
- a tornado
- a severe storm (blizzard, hurricane, typhoon)
- an epidemic
- a famine
- a drought
- a landslide
- an earthquake

A GROUP WORK Choose an emergency from the list. Write some plans for the emergency on the notepad. Provide a reason for each plan.

Plans	Reasons
Have 2 liters of water per person per day.	to have enough water in case the water is unsafe to drink

Type of emergency:	
Plans	Reasons

batteries

matches

bottled water

B Present your plans to the class. Compare your plans.

Our group prepared for a storm. We said to be sure cell phones were working. A power outage might occur.

A ▶3:16 Listen to the report. The reporter describes three kinds of disasters. Listen carefully and check the ones that fall into the categories she describes. Listen again if necessary.

		Disaster	Place	Year	Killed
	The 10 most deadly natural disasters of the 20th century				
☐	1	epidemic	worldwide	1917	20,000,000
☐	2	famine	Soviet Union	1932	5,000,000
☐	3	flood	China	1931	3,700,000
☐	4	drought	China	1928	3,000,000
☐	5	epidemic	worldwide	1914	3,000,000
☐	6	epidemic	Soviet Union	1917	2,500,000
☐	7	flood	China	1959	2,000,000
☐	8	epidemic	India	1920	2,000,000
☐	9	famine	Bangladesh	1943	1,900,000
☐	10	epidemic	China	1909	1,500,000

B Complete each statement with the name of the disaster or emergency.

1 In .... , mud and soil cover the houses and can bury entire towns.

2 A widespread event in which many people become sick with the same illness is ....

3 A storm with high winds and rain is ....

4 A .... is a natural event in which there is no rain for a long period of time.

5 In .... , there is not enough food and many people go hungry.

C Complete each indirect statement or question with <u>said</u> or <u>told</u>.

1 They .... me to call the office in the morning.

2 The students .... the test had been very difficult.

3 He .... the storm was awful.

4 Who .... us to get extra batteries?

D Rewrite the indirect speech statements in direct speech. Be sure to use correct punctuation.

1 She said she knew the reason there was so much property damage.

2 I said not to tell the children about the storm.

3 The radio announcer told the people to fill up their cars with gas before the storm.

4 He asked if the epidemic had been severe.

E Rewrite the direct speech statements in indirect speech.

1 Robert told Marie, "Don't wait for the evacuation order."

2 Sylvia said, "I think the earthquake occurred during the night."

3 The emergency broadcast said, "Buy bottled water before the hurricane."

4 They told Marlene, "Call us on Tuesday."

For additional language practice . . .

♫ TOP NOTCH **POP** • Lyrics p. 154
"Lucky to Be Alive"

| DIGITAL SONG | DIGITAL KARAOKE |

WRITING

Write about how to prepare for an emergency. Choose an emergency and include information on what to do, what supplies to have, and what preparations to make.

WRITING BOOSTER p. 150
• Organizing detail statements by order of importance
• Guidance for this writing exercise

TUESDAY

ORAL REVIEW

TELL A STORY Give the people names and relationships. Then tell the story of Tuesday and Wednesday in the pictures. For example:

On Tuesday, [Robert] called [his father] and told him to __.

PAIR WORK

1 Tell your partner what the TV announcer said on Tuesday. Then switch roles. Your partner tells you what the radio announcer said on Wednesday. Use indirect speech. For example:

The announcer said a tropical storm was coming . . .

2 Create a conversation between the two men on Tuesday. Start like this:

Hello, [Dad]. There's going to be a bad storm. They say . . .

WEDNESDAY

✔ NOW I CAN

- ☐ Convey a message.
- ☐ Tell someone about the news.
- ☐ Describe natural disasters.
- ☐ Prepare for an emergency.

COMMUNICATION GOALS
1 Explain a change of intentions or plans.
2 Express regrets about past actions.
3 Discuss skills, abilities, and qualifications.
4 Discuss factors that promote success.

PREVIEW

What's the best career for you?

Take the preference inventory to see which fields might be a good match for you. Check the activities you like (or would like) to do.

- ○ work on experiments in a science laboratory
- ○ write songs
- ○ manage a department of a large business corporation
- ○ repair furniture
- ○ be a doctor and care for sick people
- ○ design the stage scenery for a play
- ○ teach adults how to read
- ○ study a company's sales
- ○ restore antique cars
- ○ teach science to young people
- ○ help families with problems
- ○ manage a company's sales representatives
- ○ make clothes to sell
- ○ interpret X-rays and other medical tests
- ○ make paintings and sculptures
- ○ help couples with marriage problems
- ○ start my own business
- ○ build houses

Write the number of check marks you have by each color.

Field: ☐ BUSINESS ☐ SCIENCE ☐ CRAFTS ☐ SOCIAL WORK ☐ ARTS

A DISCUSSION Talk about the questions.

- Which field or fields did you have the most check marks in?
- Were you surprised by your results? Explain.
- What are some jobs or professions in that field?

B ▶ 3:19 **PHOTO STORY** Read and listen to a conversation about a career choice.

Charlotte: Dr. Miller, I wonder if I could pick your brain.

Dr. Miller: Sure, Charlotte. What's on your mind?

Charlotte: Well, I always thought I would go to engineering school, but now I'm not so sure anymore.

Dr. Miller: Well, it's not so unusual for a person your age to change her mind . . .

Dr. Miller: I must have changed mine ten times before I settled on medicine! Have you decided on something else?

Charlotte: Well, actually, I've developed an interest in the health field, and since you're a doctor . . .

Dr. Miller: Are you thinking of medicine?

Charlotte: Not specifically. Something related that doesn't take that long to study . . .

Charlotte: I know there are some good options, but I'm having trouble making up my mind.

Dr. Miller: Well, have you given any thought to becoming a physical therapist? It's a great field. You help people, and there's always a job available.

Charlotte: Hmm. Physical therapy. I should have thought of that. I'll keep that in mind.

C **FOCUS ON LANGUAGE** Find the following expressions in the Photo Story. Use the context to help you match the expressions and their meanings.

.... 1 make up one's mind
.... 2 keep something in mind
.... 3 be on one's mind
.... 4 settle on
.... 5 change one's mind
.... 6 pick someone's brain

a decide to do something else
b remember something
c think of something
d decide to do something after considering conflicting choices
e ask someone about something
f make a final decision that won't change

SPEAKING

A Have you ever changed your mind before settling on something? Check any areas in which you have changed your mind.

☐ a career or job choice
☐ a field of study
☐ a marriage
☐ a divorce
☐ the choice of a boyfriend or girlfriend
☐ other ....

B **DISCUSSION** Survey the class. How many classmates checked each box? Discuss the reasons why people changed their plans.

GOAL Explain a change of intentions or plans

CONVERSATION MODEL

A ▶3:20 Read and listen to a conversation about a change in plans.

A: So what are you doing these days?

B: Well, I'm in dental school.

A: No kidding! I thought you had other plans.

B: That's right. I was going to be an artist, but I changed my mind.

A: How come?

B: Well, it's hard to make a living as a painter!

B ▶3:21 **RHYTHM AND INTONATION** Listen again and repeat.
Then practice the Conversation Model with a partner.

GRAMMAR *Expressing intentions and plans that changed: Was / Were going to and would*

Express and ask about past intentions and plans that changed with was / were going to + a base form.

I was going to get married (but I didn't).   They were going to study art (but they didn't).
Was she going to take the course?   Were you going to study with Dr. Mellon?

Weren't you going to study law? (Yes, I was. / No, I wasn't.)
Where were they going to work? (In Kuala Lumpur.)
Who was going to teach this class? (My sister was.)

You can also use **would** (the past of **will**) + a base form to express plans and intentions that changed, but only in a noun clause following verbs such as **thought**, **believed**, or **said**.

She thought she would be a doctor (but she changed her mind).
We always believed they would get married (but they never did).
They said they would pay for their daughter's studies (but they didn't).

Note: You can also use **was / were going to** in a noun clause after **thought**, **believed**, or **said**.

They said they were going to arrive before noon (but they didn't).

Be careful!
Don't use **would** + a base form alone. It must be used in a noun clause. Use **was / were going to** instead.

She was going to be a doctor.
NOT She ~~would be~~ a doctor.

GRAMMAR BOOSTER p. 135
- Expressing the future: review
- The future with **will** and **be going to**: review

GRAMMAR PRACTICE Write what each person said he or she was going to do.

1
❝ I'm going to stop smoking. ❞

2
❝ I'm going to apply to law school. ❞

3
❝ I'm going to find a husband. ❞

4
❝ I'm going to marry Sylvia. ❞

1. He said he was going to . . .

VOCABULARY *Reasons for changing plans*

A ▶3:22 Read and listen. Then listen again and repeat.

I wanted to be a rock star, but **my tastes changed**.

I was going to be an artist, but **it's hard to make a living as** an artist.

I thought I would be a lawyer, but **I didn't pass the exam**.

I wanted to become a firefighter, but my family **talked me out of it**.

I was going to marry George, but **I changed my mind**.

B **VOCABULARY / GRAMMAR PRACTICE** Complete each sentence, using <u>would</u> and a reason from the Vocabulary. Then compare reasons with a partner.

1 Laura thought / be / a doctor, but . . .

2 I thought / become / an astronaut, but . . .

3 We were sure / Bill and Stella / get / a divorce, but . . .

4 Joe always believed / become / a writer, but . . .

C ▶3:23 **LISTEN TO ACTIVATE VOCABULARY** Listen to the conversations. Complete each statement about the decision each person made. Then listen again and use the Vocabulary to write the reason each person changed his or her mind.

1 She wanted to be a .... , but she changed her mind because ....

2 He was going to .... Jessica, but he didn't because ....

3 He always thought she would become a .... , but she didn't because ....

4 She was going to .... a Romanian named Andrei, but she didn't because ....

NOW YOU CAN Explain a change of intentions or plans

A **NOTEPADDING** On the notepad, write some intentions or plans you had in the past but changed your mind about. Write the reasons for the changes, using the Vocabulary or other reasons.

B **CONVERSATION ACTIVATOR** With a partner, change the Conversation Model, using the information on your notepad. Then change roles.

for my life:

for my studies:

for my career:

A: So what are you doing these days?
B: Well, ...
A: No kidding! I thought you had other plans.
B: That's right. I was going to .... , but ....
A: How come?
B: Well, ...

DON'T STOP!

- Ask more questions.
- Explain your choices and decisions.
- Discuss the future.

C **CHANGE PARTNERS** Practice the conversation again about other intentions or plans from your notepad.

GOAL Express regrets about past actions

GRAMMAR *Perfect modals*

Use perfect modals to express feelings and beliefs about past actions and events:

- **Regrets or judgments:** <u>should have</u> + past participle

  I **should have studied** medicine. (But unfortunately, I didn't.)
  She **shouldn't have divorced** Sam. (But unfortunately, she did.)

- **Possibility:** <u>may have</u> / <u>might have</u> + past participle

  I **may** (OR **might**) **have failed** the final exam. It was really hard.
  He **may** (OR **might**) **not have been** able to make a living as a painter.

- **Ability (OR possibility):** <u>could have</u> + past participle

  He was the driver. He **could have prevented** the accident.
  The museum was closed, but she **couldn't have known** that. It's usually
  open on Tuesdays.

- **Certainty:** <u>would have</u> + past participle

  You should have gone to Rio. You **would have loved** it.
  It's good he broke up with Anne. They **wouldn't have been** happy together.

- **Conclusions:** <u>must have</u> + past participle

  Beth isn't here. She **must have gone** home early.
    (I think that's what happened.)
  They didn't buy the house. The price **must not have been** acceptable.
    (I think that's the reason.)

> I should have studied medicine.

GRAMMAR BOOSTER p. 136

Regrets about the past: <u>wish</u> +
the past perfect; <u>should have</u> and
<u>ought to have</u>

A GRAMMAR PRACTICE Choose the modal that logically completes each sentence.
Write that modal and the verb in the perfect modal form.

1 I don't know why she married him. He .... the only man available.
                                               (must OR should) be

2 I .... architecture. I... really good at it.
      (should OR may) study   (must OR would) be

3 Jenna's not studying Chinese anymore. It... too hard to learn Chinese
                                         (should OR might) be
   and Japanese at the same time.

4 We didn't know we were going to have five children. We... such a small house.
                                           (could not OR should not) buy

5 Ella still loves Ben. She .... with him.
                 (must not OR should not) break up

6 When I was young, everyone thought I was a great singer. But I decided to become a lawyer instead.
   Looking back, I think I .... on the wrong career.
                 (may OR should) decide

B PAIR WORK Provide three possible reasons for each statement. Use <u>may</u> / <u>might have</u>,
<u>must have</u>, and <u>could have</u>. Follow the example.

Example: John is late for dinner.

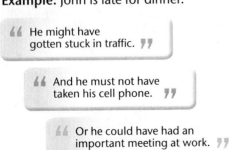

      ❝ He might have
      gotten stuck in traffic. **❞**

        ❝ And he must not have
        taken his cell phone. **❞**

          ❝ Or he could have had an
          important meeting at work. **❞**

1 My brother never got married.

2 All the classes were canceled today.

3 Michael is forty, and he just became a doctor.

4 Rachel grew up in New York, but now she lives in São Paulo.

5 They had one child, and then they adopted three more.

6 They had their honeymoon in the U.S. instead of in France.

DIGITAL
MORE
EXERCISES

PRONUNCIATION *Reduction of <u>have</u> in perfect modals*

A ▶3:24 Notice the reduction of <u>have</u> in perfect modals. Read and listen. Then listen again and repeat.

/ʃʊdəv/
1 I should ḥave married Marie.

/maɪtəv/
2 They might ḥave left.

/nɑtəv/
3 We may not ḥave seen it.

/kʊdəv/
4 She could ḥave been on time.

B **PAIR WORK** Take turns reading the sentences with perfect modals in Exercise A. Use correct reduction of <u>have</u>.

CONVERSATION MODEL

A ▶3:25 Read and listen to a conversation between two people discussing a regret about the past.

A: I should have married Steven.

B: Why do you think that?

A: Well, I might have had children by now.

B: Could be. But you never know. You might not have been happy.

A: True.

B ▶3:26 **RHYTHM AND INTONATION** Listen again and repeat. Then practice the Conversation Model with a partner.

NOW YOU CAN Express regrets about past actions

A **NOTEPADDING** Write about some regrets you have about past actions. Say how you think things might have been different in your life today.

Past action	Regret	How might things have been different?
a job / career choice	I didn't take the job at MacroTech.	I might have been CEO by now!

Past action	Regret	How might things have been different?
a job / career choice		
a field of study		
a marriage / divorce		
a boyfriend / girlfriend choice		
a breakup		

B **CONVERSATION ACTIVATOR** With a partner, personalize the Conversation Model. Discuss your regrets and speculate on how things might have been different. Use information from your notepad and perfect modals. Then change roles.

A: I should (OR I shouldn't) have ....
B: Why do you think that?
A: Well, I ....
B: Could be. But you never know. You might ....
A: ....

DON'T STOP!
• Ask your partner more questions about his or her regrets.
• Speculate about what happened.
• Offer advice.

RECYCLE THIS LANGUAGE.
Why did / didn't you ___?
Why don't you ___?
How about ___?

must (not) have ___
may / might (not) have ___
could have ___

GOAL Discuss skills, abilities, and qualifications

BEFORE YOU LISTEN

A ▶ 3:27 **VOCABULARY** • *Qualifications for work or study* Read and listen. Then listen again and repeat.

talents	abilities in art, music, mathematics, etc., that you are born with *She was born with <u>talents</u> in both mathematics and art.*
skills	abilities that you learn, such as cooking, speaking a foreign language, or driving *She has several publishing <u>skills</u>: writing, editing, and illustrating.*
experience	time spent working at a job *Martin has a lot of <u>experience</u> in sales. He has worked at three companies.*
knowledge	understanding of or familiarity with a subject gained from experience or study *James has extensive <u>knowledge</u> of the history of film. You can ask him which classics to see.*
qualifications	talents, skills, experience, and knowledge that make a person a good candidate for a job *I have two <u>qualifications</u> for the English teaching position: I have a teaching certificate, and I have taught English for two years.*

B **THINK AND EXPLAIN** Explain the following in your own words. Use examples from your life.

- the difference between a talent and a skill
- the difference between experience and knowledge

LISTENING COMPREHENSION

A ▶ 3:28 **LISTEN FOR DETAILS** Listen to nine people being interviewed at an international job fair. Stop after each interview and match the interviewee with his or her qualification for a job. Listen again if necessary.

Interviewee	Qualifications
...*h*... 1 Sonia Espinoza	**a** a good memory
.... 2 Silvano Lucastro	**b** artistic ability
.... 3 Ivan Martinovic	**c** mathematical ability
.... 4 Agnes Lukins	**d** logical thinking
.... 5 Elena Burgess	**e** compassion
.... 6 Karen Trent	**f** manual dexterity
.... 7 Ed Snodgrass	**g** common sense
.... 8 Akiko Uzawa	**h** athletic ability
.... 9 Mia Kim	**i** leadership skills

B **PAIR WORK** With a partner, classify each qualification from Exercise A. Do you agree on all the classifications? Discuss and explain your opinions.

a talent	a skill
athletic ability	

I think athletic ability is a talent. You're born with that.

I don't agree. I think if you train and work at it, you can develop into a great athlete. I think it's a skill.

A **FRAME YOUR IDEAS** Take the skills inventory.

Preparing for an Interview

Whether you're looking for a job or interviewing for a school, interviewers expect you to answer questions about your interests, talents, skills, and experience. Take this inventory to prepare yourself for those questions.

Interests
Check the fields that interest you:
- ☐ business   ☐ art
- ☐ science   ☐ manufacturing
- ☐ education ☐ other _____

Qualifications
Check the qualifications you believe you have:
- ☐ manual dexterity   ☐ artistic ability
- ☐ logical thinking   ☐ compassion
- ☐ mathematical ability   ☐ a good memory
- ☐ common sense   ☐ leadership skills
- ☐ athletic ability   ☐ other _____ (advanced computer skills, for example)

Experience
Briefly note information about your experience, skills, and any special knowledge you have.

Experience: _____

Skills: _____

Special knowledge: _____

B **NOTEPADDING** On your notepad, write specific examples of your qualifications. Then share and discuss your skills, abilities, and qualifications with a partner.

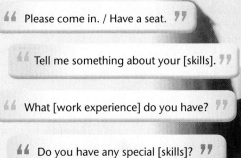

Qualification	Example
mathematical ability	I'm great at number puzzles.

Qualification	Example

C **PAIR WORK** Use the information on your notepad to do one of the following activities.

- Role-play an interview for a job.
- Role-play an interview for career advice.
- Role-play an interview for entry into a professional (or other kind of) school.

❝ Please come in. / Have a seat. ❞

❝ Tell me something about your [skills]. ❞

❝ What [work experience] do you have? ❞

❝ Do you have any special [skills]? ❞

♻ RECYCLE THIS LANGUAGE.
I have experience in [teaching].
I don't have much experience, but ___.
I'm good at [math].
I have three years of [French].

D **GROUP WORK** Tell your class what you learned about your partner in the interview.

❝ My partner has a lot of experience in . . . ❞

BEFORE YOU READ

A WARM-UP How important do you think the following factors are to career success? Number the factors in order of importance, making 1 the most important and 6 the least important.

☐ skills   ☐ talent   ☐ work habits
☐ prior experience   ☐ job knowledge   ☐ other
☐ physical appearance, dress, etc.

B DISCUSSION Explain the reasons for your most important and least important choices. Use concrete examples.

READING ▶ 3:29

The Five Most Effective Work Habits
Advice to new workers from a CEO

If you are new to the working world, you are eager to demonstrate your skills and knowledge. However, in addition to those, some basic work habits may be even more effective in promoting your success. Read the following advice to new workers, written by the head of a company.

1 **Volunteer for assignments** One of the best ways to signal that you are a keen learner and are not afraid of hard work is to volunteer for assignments. However, before volunteering for a task, be sure you have the skills and knowledge to accomplish it successfully.

2 **Be nice to people** Be nice to people regardless of their rank or position. When you are nice to people, they go out of their way to help you, and every new worker needs help in order to get ahead.

3 **Prioritize your work** We all love to start work on things that are close to our hearts. However, these may not be the most urgent and important in our list of tasks to do. Have a list of things to do according to their strategic importance to your company. When you prioritize your work,

you are more productive, and that increases your chances of career success.

4 **Stay positive** As someone new in the working world, you are not used to office culture. And there may be office politics that complicate things. Try to stay above politics and remain positive in the face of challenges. When you are positive, you stay focused on your goals. You make better decisions and, therefore, get more things done.

5 **Highlight a problem but bring solutions** Offer a solution each time you highlight a problem to your boss or management. You need to remember that when you bring problems and not solutions, people may think of you as a "complainer."

These five work habits, at first glance, may seem like common sense. However, in actual working environments, people tend to forget the basics. I counsel new workers in our company to internalize this behavior and consistently use it to increase their chances of career success.

Source: Adapted from www.career-success-for-newbies.com.

A **UNDERSTAND FROM CONTEXT** Find and underline the words below in the Reading. Use context to help you write a definition for each. Then compare definitions with a partner.

a habit	
a solution	
volunteer	
prioritize	

B **CONFIRM CONTENT** Answer the questions, according to what the CEO suggests.

1 Which may be most important in determining a new worker's success: knowledge, work habits, or skills?

2 Why should workers volunteer to do tasks?

3 Why is "being nice" a valuable habit to develop?

4 What is the value of prioritizing tasks?

5 How does staying positive help you be more productive?

6 What's wrong with stating a problem without proposing a solution?

DIGITAL
MORE
EXERCISES

NOW YOU CAN Discuss factors that promote success

A **NOTEPADDING** On your notepad, write some factors that have helped you be successful in your life, studies, or work, and some factors that have prevented you from being successful. (You can choose one, some, or all areas to comment on.) Then compare notepads with a partner.

Area	Factors that helped ☺	Factors that hurt ☹
my personal life	love, patience, common sense!	not listening to or paying attention to others

Area	Factors that helped ☺	Factors that hurt ☹
my personal life		
managing my home		
my studies / work		

B **DISCUSSION** Discuss factors that you think promote success and factors that don't. Use your notepad for support, but expand on it with specific examples from your life to illustrate each factor. Talk about plans that changed and any regrets you may have.

RECYCLE THIS LANGUAGE.

Factors	Changes in plans	Regrets
talents	I thought I would __, but __.	I should have __.
skills	I was going to __, but I changed	I could have __.
experience	my mind.	I might have __.
knowledge	__ talked me out of it.	I would have __.
common sense	It's hard to make a living as __.	
	My tastes changed.	

Text-mining (optional)
Find and underline three words or phrases in the Reading that were new to you. Use them in your Discussion.
For example: "prioritize your work."

A ▶3:30 Listen to the conversations between people talking about life changes. Write information on the notepad. Listen again if necessary.

	Why did the person change his or her mind?	Any regrets?
1		
2		
3		
4		

B Explain the meaning of each of the qualifications. Then write an occupation or course of study for a person with each qualification.

	Qualification	Definition	Occupation or Study
1	athletic ability		
2	artistic ability		
3	mathematical ability		
4	logical thinking ability		
5	a good memory		
6	leadership skills		

C Complete each statement of belief, using <u>would</u>.

1 When I was a child, I thought I ....

2 My parents believed ....

3 My teachers were sure ....

4 When I finished school, I didn't know ....

D Read each sentence. Complete the statement in parentheses, using a perfect modal.

1 Marie was very unhappy in her marriage. (She should . . .)

2 After Sylvia and David got separated, they discovered they were still in love. (They could . . .)

3 My parents were sorry they sold their country house. (They shouldn't . . .)

4 I can't understand how she learned to speak Italian so fast. (She might . . .)

5 Look at John's car. It's all smashed up. (He must . . .)

> *1. She should have tried to communicate*
> *more with her husband.*

For additional language practice . . .

🎵 TOP NOTCH POP • Lyrics p. 155
"I Should Have Married Her"

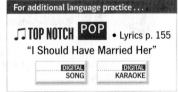

WRITING

Write a short autobiography. Include information about one or all of the topics below. If you have any regrets, express them, using perfect modals.

- your birth
- your childhood
- your studies
- other aspects of your life

> **WRITING BOOSTER** p. 150
> - Dividing an essay into topics
> - Guidance for this writing exercise

ORAL REVIEW

STORY IN PAIRS Choose one of the characters: Michael or Carlota. Look at the pictures for each of the three dates. Tell the story of your character to your partner. Then change partners and choose a different character.

Michael   **Carlota**

1980 Their parents' plans and dreams for them

1990 Their wishes and dreams for themselves

NOW Their actual choices and regrets

✓ NOW I CAN

- ☐ Explain a change of intentions or plans.
- ☐ Express regrets about past actions.
- ☐ Discuss skills, abilities, and qualifications.
- ☐ Discuss factors that promote success.

UNIT 7 Holidays and Traditions

COMMUNICATION GOALS

1 Wish someone a good holiday.
2 Ask about local customs.
3 Exchange information about holidays.
4 Explain wedding traditions.

PREVIEW

Japan

People picnicking and viewing the cherry blossoms at a *Hanami* party in Japan

United States

Thanksgiving dinner in the United States, featuring the traditional main dish of roast turkey

Mexico

Friends who have come together for *Quinceañera* to celebrate a girl's fifteenth birthday and her entry into adulthood in Mexico

Korea

A couple dressed in the traditional hanbok during the Korean holiday of *Chuseok*

Brazil

Dancers in the fantastic costumes of Brazil's world-famous yearly celebration of *Carnaval*

A Look at the photos. Which traditions are you already familiar with? Which ones would you like to know more about? Why?

B **DISCUSSION** Why do people keep traditions alive? Do you think it's important to learn about the customs of other cultures? Explain your reasons.

C ▶4:02 **PHOTO STORY**   Read and listen to a conversation about holiday traditions.

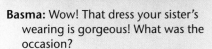

Basma: Wow! That dress your sister's wearing is gorgeous! What was the occasion?

Mi-Cha: Oh, that was for Chuseok. The dress is called a hanbok.

Basma: Did you say Chuseok? What's that—a holiday?

Mi-Cha: That's right. It's a traditional Korean holiday. It takes place in September or October each year to celebrate the harvest.

Basma: So does everyone dress up like that?

Mi-Cha: Some people do.

Basma: So what else does everyone do on Chuseok?

Mi-Cha: We get together with our relatives. And we eat a lot!

Basma: Well, that sounds nice.

Mi-Cha: Not only that, but we go to our hometowns and visit the graves of our ancestors.

Basma: So I suppose the airports and train stations are mobbed with people, right?

Mi-Cha: Totally. And the traffic is impossible. It takes hours to get anywhere.

Basma: I think every country's got at least one holiday like that!

Mi-Cha: What holiday comes to mind for you?

Basma: It reminds me of Eid al-Adha, a four-day religious holiday we celebrate where I come from.

Mi-Cha: In what way?

Basma: Well, people put on their best clothes, and we eat a ton of great food. We also travel to be with our relatives and visit the graves of our loved ones who have died.

Mi-Cha: How about that! Sounds just like our holiday.

D **PARAPHRASE**   Find each underlined expression in the Photo Story. Write each sentence in your own words.

1 "It takes place in September or October."

....

2 "We get together with our relatives."

....

3 "The train stations are mobbed with people."

....

4 "The traffic is impossible."

....

5 "It reminds me of Eid al-Adha."

....

E **FOCUS ON LANGUAGE**   Write five sentences about a holiday or a tradition in your country, using the underlined language from Exercise D.

| Songkran takes place in April.

SPEAKING

Complete the chart about traditions in your country. Present your information to the class.

A special type of clothing	Explain when it is worn.
A type of music	Explain when it is played.
A special dish	Explain when it is eaten.
A traditional dance	Explain when it is danced.
A special event	Explain what happens.

GOAL Wish someone a good holiday

CONVERSATION MODEL

A ▶4:03 Read and listen to a conversation about a holiday.

A: I heard there's going to be a holiday next week.

B: That's right. The Harvest Moon Festival.

A: What kind of holiday is it?

B: It's a seasonal holiday that takes place in autumn. People spend time with their families and eat moon cakes.

A: Well, have a great Harvest Moon Festival!

B: Thanks! Same to you!

B ▶4:04 **RHYTHM AND INTONATION** Listen again and repeat. Then practice the Conversation Model with a partner.

▶4:05 **Types of holidays**
seasonal
historical
religious

a moon cake

DIGITAL FLASH CARDS

VOCABULARY *Ways to commemorate a holiday*

A ▶4:06 Read and listen. Then listen again and repeat.

set off fireworks

march in parades

have picnics

pray

send cards

give gifts

wish each other well

remember the dead

wear costumes

B **PAIR WORK** Match the Vocabulary with holidays and celebrations you know.

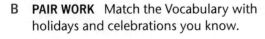
Everyone wears costumes on . . .

	Type of holiday	What people do to celebrate
Mardi Gras (U.S.)		
Bastille Day (France)		
Tsagaan Sar (Mongolia)		

GRAMMAR *Adjective clauses with subject relative pronouns* <u>who</u> *and* <u>that</u>

Adjective clauses identify or describe people or things. Introduce adjective clauses about people with the relative pronouns <u>who</u> or <u>that</u>.

A mariachi singer is someone	who (OR that) sings traditional Mexican music.
Carnaval is a great holiday for people	who (OR that) like parades.
Families	who (OR that) want to watch the fireworks go to the park.

Use <u>that</u>, not <u>who</u>, for adjective clauses that describe things.

Thanksgiving is a celebration	that takes place in November.
The parade	that commemorates Bastille Day is very exciting.

Be careful!
Don't use a subject pronoun after the relative pronouns <u>who</u> or <u>that</u>.
Don't say: Thanksgiving is a celebration that ~~it~~ takes place in November.

> **GRAMMAR BOOSTER** p. 136
> * Adjective clauses: common errors
> * Reflexive pronouns
> * <u>By</u> + reflexive pronouns
> * Reciprocal pronouns: <u>each other</u> and <u>one another</u>

A **UNDERSTAND THE GRAMMAR** Underline the adjective clauses and circle the relative pronouns. Then draw an arrow from the relative pronoun to the noun or pronoun it describes.

1 Ramadan is a religious tradition (that) begins on a different day every year.

2 Chuseok is a Korean seasonal holiday that celebrates the yearly harvest.

3 The woman who designed those amazing costumes for the parade is really talented.

4 The celebrations that take place in Brazil during Carnaval are really wild!

5 People who remember April Fool's Day every April 1st have a lot of fun.

6 The Dragon Boat Festival in China is a holiday that takes place in May or June.

B **GRAMMAR PRACTICE** On a separate sheet of paper, write five sentences with adjective clauses to describe some holidays and traditions in your country.

> . . . is a religious tradition that . . .
> . . . is a great holiday for people who . . .

NOW YOU CAN Wish someone a good holiday

A **CONVERSATION ACTIVATOR** Use your chart from page 75 to role-play the Conversation Model with a visitor to your country. Wish each other a good holiday. Then change roles.

A: I heard there's going to be a holiday next ....
B: That's right. ....
A: What kind of holiday is it?
B: It's a .... holiday that takes place .... People ....
A: Well, ... !
B: ....

Some ways to exchange good wishes on holidays
Have a [nice / great / happy] holiday!
Enjoy yourself on [Chuseok]!
You too! / Same to you!

DON'T STOP!
Ask and answer more questions. Use the Vocabulary.
What else do people do?
Do people [send cards]?
What kinds of [food do you eat / music do they play]?
Where do people [march in parades]?

B **CHANGE PARTNERS** Exchange wishes about other holidays.

People celebrate the Holi Festival in India by throwing colored powder and water on each other.

GOAL Ask about local customs

CONVERSATION MODEL

A ▶4:08 Read and listen to a conversation about local customs.

A: Do you mind if I ask you about something?

B: Of course not. What's up?

A: I'm not sure about the customs here. If someone invites you for dinner, should you bring the host a gift?

B: Yes. It's a good idea. But the gift that you bring should be inexpensive.

A: Would it be appropriate to bring flowers?

B: Definitely!

A: Thanks. That's really helpful.

B ▶4:09 **RHYTHM AND INTONATION** Listen again and repeat. Then practice the Conversation Model with a partner.

GRAMMAR *Adjective clauses with object relative pronouns* <u>who</u>, <u>whom</u>, *and* <u>that</u>

> **In some adjective clauses, the relative pronoun is the subject of the clause. In other adjective clauses, the relative pronoun is the object of the clause.**
>
> <u>who</u> as subject = (**The people** are the guests.)   <u>who</u> as object = (You invite **the people**.)
> The people who are the guests should bring gifts.   The people who you invite should bring gifts.
>
> **When a relative pronoun is an object of a clause, use <u>who</u>, <u>that</u>, or <u>whom</u> for people and <u>that</u> for things. The relative pronoun is often omitted, especially in speaking.** (Note: <u>whom</u> is very formal.)
>
> The people who (OR that / whom) you invite should bring gifts. / The people you invite should bring gifts.
> The gifts that you bring should be inexpensive. / The gifts you bring should be inexpensive.
>
> **Be careful!**
> **When the relative pronoun is the subject of the clause, it can NOT be omitted.**
> Don't say: ~~The people are the guests~~ should bring gifts.
>
> **Do not use an object pronoun after the verb.**
> Don't say: The people who you invite ~~them~~ should bring gifts.

> **GRAMMAR BOOSTER** p. 138
> • Adjective clauses: <u>who</u> and <u>whom</u> in formal English

A **UNDERSTAND THE GRAMMAR** Correct the error in the adjective clause in each sentence. Explain each correction.

   that
1 Putting butter on a child's nose is a birthday tradition ~~who~~ people observe on the Atlantic coast of Canada.

   66 Only use <u>who</u> for people. 99

2 On the Day of the Dead, Mexicans remember family members who they have died.

3 The tomatoes that people throw them at each other during La Tomatina in Buñol, Spain, make a terrible mess.

4 The performer sang that traditional holiday song is world-famous.

5 The fireworks people set them off during the summer festivals in Japan are very beautiful.

A **SCAN FOR FACTS** Complete the chart. Check the holidays on which each tradition is observed, according to the information in the Reading. Explain your answers.

On this holiday, people...	Ramadan	Chinese New Year	Bolívar's Birthday
give gifts.	○	○	○
wear costumes.	○	○	○
pray.	○	○	○
wish each other well.	○	○	○
get together with their families.	○	○	○
perform traditional dances.	○	○	○
decorate their homes.	○	○	○
celebrate for several days.	○	○	○
give away money.	○	○	○
have parades.	○	○	○
avoid eating during the day.	○	○	○

Which holiday is celebrated in more than one country?

○ Ramadan ○ Chinese New Year ○ Simón Bolívar's Birthday

B **COMPARE AND CONTRAST** Which holiday or tradition from the Reading do you find the most interesting? Why?

C **RELATE TO PERSONAL EXPERIENCE** Name one holiday you know for each tradition in the chart.

NOW YOU CAN Exchange information about holidays

A **NOTEPADDING** With a partner, choose three holidays in your country. Discuss the traditions of each holiday and write notes about them on your notepads.

	A historical holiday	A seasonal holiday	A religious holiday
name of holiday			
purpose			
typical food			
typical music			
typical clothing			
other traditions			

B **GROUP WORK** Choose a holiday from your notepad and present it to your class. Your classmates ask questions.

Text-mining (optional)
Find and underline three words or phrases in the Reading that were new to you. Use them in your Group Work.
For example: "a special occasion."

GOAL Explain wedding traditions

BEFORE YOU LISTEN

A ▶4:12 **VOCABULARY** • *Getting married* Read and listen. Then listen again and repeat.

THE EVENTS

an engagement an agreement to marry someone—**get engaged** *v.*

a (marriage) ceremony the set of actions that formally makes two single people become a married couple—**get married** *v.*

a wedding a formal marriage ceremony, especially one with a religious service

a reception a large formal party after a wedding ceremony

a honeymoon a vacation taken by two newlyweds after their wedding

THE PEOPLE

a fiancé a man who is engaged

a fiancée a woman who is engaged

a bride a woman at the time she gets married

a groom a man at the time he gets married

newlyweds the bride and groom immediately after the wedding

B **DISCUSSION** Read about wedding traditions in many English-speaking countries. How are these similar to or different from traditions practiced in your country?

The bride throws the bouquet after the wedding ceremony. The woman who catches it is believed to be the next to get married.

The newlyweds cut the cake together at the wedding reception.

The groom carries the bride "across the threshold," through the doorway to their new home. Soon after the wedding, they go on their honeymoon.

LISTENING COMPREHENSION

A ▶4:13 **LISTEN FOR MAIN IDEAS** Listen to Part 1 of a lecture about a traditional Indian wedding. Which of the statements best summarizes the information?

☐ **a** An Indian couple gets engaged long before the wedding.

☐ **b** There's a lot of preparation before an Indian wedding.

☐ **c** An Indian wedding lasts for days.

B ▶4:14 **LISTEN FOR DETAILS** Listen again to Part 1 and circle the best way to complete each statement.

1 A traditional Hindu wedding celebration can last for more than (two / five) days.

2 The bride's and groom's birthdates are used to choose the (engagement / wedding) date.

3 Before the wedding, musicians visit the (bride's / groom's) home.

4 The (bride / groom) is washed with oil.

5 An older relative offers the (bride / groom) money.

6 Relatives spend a lot of time painting the (bride's / groom's) skin.

C ▶4:15 **LISTEN FOR MAIN IDEAS** Now listen to Part 2 of the lecture. What is the information mainly about?

☐ **a** the wedding ceremony   ☐ **b** the honeymoon   ☐ **c** the reception after the wedding

D ▶4:16 **LISTEN FOR DETAILS** Listen again to Part 2 and check the statements that are true. Correct the statements that are false.

☐ **1** Relatives wash the bride's and groom's hands.

☐ **2** The bride is seated behind a cloth so the groom cannot see her.

☐ **3** Relatives throw rice grains at the bride and groom.

☐ **4** The couple gives each other rings made of flowers.

☐ **5** The groom places a flower necklace around the bride's neck.

NOW YOU CAN Explain wedding traditions

A **FRAME YOUR IDEAS** With a partner, read each saying or proverb about weddings and marriage. Discuss what you think each one means.

"The woman cries before the wedding and the man after."
Poland

"Marry off your son when you wish. Marry off your daughter when you can."
Italy

"Marriages are all happy. It's having breakfast together that causes all the trouble."
Ireland

"Marriage is just friendship if there are no children."
South Africa

Advice to the bride: "Wear something old and something new, something borrowed, and something blue."
United Kingdom

B **DISCUSSION** Do you find any of the sayings or proverbs offensive? Why or why not? What sayings or proverbs about weddings do you know in your own language?

C **NOTEPADDING** On your notepad, make a list of wedding traditions in your country. Compare your lists with those of other groups.

D **PAIR WORK** Role-play a conversation in which you describe local wedding traditions to a visitor to your country. Ask and answer questions about the details. Use the Vocabulary.

RECYCLE THIS LANGUAGE.

[a religious] tradition
[a huge] celebration
the bride / the groom / the newlyweds

take place in
spend time with [someone]

It's [customary / common / appropriate] to ___.

❝ Well, before they get engaged, they have to . . . ❞

❝ So how does a couple get engaged here? ❞

Before the wedding:
At the wedding ceremony:
After the wedding:

A ▶ 4:17 Listen to each conversation and circle the occasion or the people they are talking about. Then listen again and circle T if the statement is true or F if it is false. Correct any false statements. Listen again if necessary.

1 (an engagement / a reception / a honeymoon)   T F   The man who is speaking is the groom.

2 (an engagement / a reception / a honeymoon)   T F   The man who is speaking will be the groom.

3 (a bride / a groom / relatives)   T F   The woman who is speaking is the bride.

4 (a bride / a groom / relatives)   T F   The woman who is speaking is a guest.

B Complete each statement, using verbs from the unit Vocabulary. Then write the name of a holiday you know for each statement.

Name a holiday when people . . .	Examples
1 .... fireworks.	
2 .... in parades.	
3 .... picnics.	
4 .... time with their families.	
5 .... costumes.	
6 .... gifts.	
7 .... each other well.	

C Complete each sentence with an adjective clause. Find the information in this unit, if necessary.

1 A groom is a man *who has just gotten married* ....

2 Eid ul-Fitr is a religious holiday ....

3 A honeymoon is a vacation ....

4 A hanbok is a traditional dress ....

5 A wedding reception is a party ....

6 Chuseok is a holiday ....

D On a separate sheet of paper, complete each statement about local traditions in your country.

1 If someone invites you to his or her house for dinner, you should . . .

2 If someone gives you an expensive gift, you should . . .

3 If you are invited to a formal wedding, you should wear . . .

4 If a friend or colleague gets engaged, you should . . .

5 If someone wants to get married, he or she should . . .

> **For additional language practice . . .**
> 🎵 **TOP NOTCH** POP • Lyrics p. 155
> "Endless Holiday"
> DIGITAL SONG   DIGITAL KARAOKE

WRITING

Describe two different holidays that are celebrated in your country.
Include as many details as you can about each.

• What kind of holiday is it?

• When is it celebrated?

• How is it celebrated?

• What do people do / eat / say / wear, etc.?

> **WRITING BOOSTER** p. 151
> • Descriptive details
> • Guidance for this writing exercise

ORAL REVIEW

PAIR WORK CHALLENGE   For one minute, look at the Fact Sheet for one of the holidays. Your partner looks at the other Fact Sheet. Then close your books. Ask and answer questions about each other's holidays. For example:

Why do people celebrate Songkran?

PAIR WORK   Create conversations for the people.
1 Ask about one of the holidays. Start like this:

I heard there's going to be a holiday.

2 Ask about local customs during the holiday. Start like this:

Do you mind if I ask you something?

GROUP PRESENTATION   Choose one of the holidays and give a presentation to your group or class. Use adjective clauses.

Songkran is a seasonal holiday that . . .

FACT SHEET

Songkran Water Festival

Celebrated in Thailand. Lasts for three days.

Marks the . . .
• start of the Buddhist New Year.
• beginning of the farming season.

People . . .
• clean their homes.
• make offerings at temples.
• sing and dance in the street.
• throw lots of water at each other!

NOTE: Don't worry! It's customary for people to throw lots of water at complete strangers on this holiday.

FACT SHEET

Mexican Independence Day

Celebrated on September 15 and 16.

Commemorates . . .
• the beginning of the War of Independence.
• Mexico's independence from Spain.

People . . .
• march in parades.
• perform traditional music and dances.
• decorate with the colors of the Mexican flag (red, white, and green).
• set off fireworks.
• eat special dishes (sometimes red, white, and green).

NOTE: It's customary for people to shout, "Viva México!" Even if you are not Mexican, you can join in.

✓ NOW I CAN

☐ Wish someone a good holiday.
☐ Ask about local customs.
☐ Exchange information about holidays.
☐ Explain wedding traditions.

COMMUNICATION GOALS

1 Describe technology.
2 Take responsibility for a mistake.
3 Describe new inventions.
4 Discuss the impact of inventions / discoveries.

Inventions and Discoveries

The wheel

Penicillin:
the first "wonder drug"

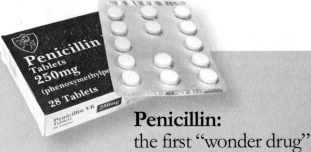

The 3-D printer

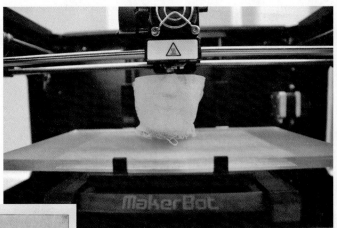

The mosquito net

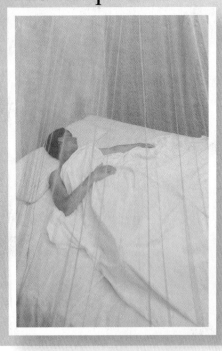

The X-ray

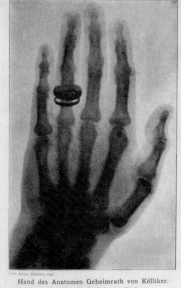

Hand des Anatomen Geheimrath von Kölliker.
Im Physikal. Institut der Universität Würzburg
mit X-Strahlen aufgenommen
von Professor Dr. W. C. Röntgen.

The television

A DISCUSSION Most of the pictures represent inventions. Do you know which one(s) resulted from a discovery? How would you explain the difference between an invention and a discovery? Provide some examples of inventions and discoveries.

B ▶4:20 **PHOTO STORY** Read and listen to a conversation about how an invention might have helped someone.

Leslie: This itching is driving me crazy!

Jody: Look at your arm! Are those mosquito bites?

Leslie: Yeah. Ben and I got eaten alive last weekend. We went away for a second honeymoon at this cute little bed and breakfast in the mountains, but the mosquitoes were brutal.

Jody: That doesn't sound very romantic. Didn't they have screens in the windows?

Leslie: Well, they did, but ours had a big hole, and we didn't realize it until the middle of the night. What a nightmare!

Jody: Too bad you didn't bring any insect repellent. There are tons of mosquitoes in the mountains this time of year. Hello!

Leslie: We actually *did* have some, but it just didn't work that well. You know how Ben is—everything has to be organic and natural and . . .

Jody: Well, with all due respect to Ben, you just have to bite the bullet once in a while and use the stuff that works. Whether you like it or not, the poison *is* effective.

Leslie: I agree, but Ben won't hear of it. You know, next time we go away for a romantic weekend, I'm packing one of those mosquito nets to hang over the bed.

C **PARAPHRASE** Say each of the underlined expressions from the Photo Story in your own way.

1 "Ben and I got eaten alive last weekend."

2 ". . . the mosquitoes were brutal."

3 "There are tons of mosquitoes in the mountains this time of year."

4 ". . . you just have to bite the bullet once in a while and use the stuff that works."

5 "Whether you like it or not, the poison *is* effective."

6 "I agree, but Ben won't hear of it."

D **THINK AND EXPLAIN** Answer the questions, according to the Photo Story.

1 What effect does a mosquito bite cause?

2 Where were Leslie and Ben when they got the mosquito bites?

3 How did mosquitoes get into their bedroom?

4 Why would Ben object to "the stuff that works"?

5 What is another preventive measure against mosquitoes?

SPEAKING

Read the list of important inventions and discoveries and add another important one to the list. Then rank them in order of importance from 1 (most important) to 10 (least important). With a partner compare rankings and explain your reasons for ranking one the most important.

Rank	Item	Rank	Item
	air travel		the printing press
	antibiotics		the Internet
	smart phones		vaccination
	insect repellents		water purification systems
	mosquito nets		other:

GOAL Describe technology

VOCABULARY *Describing manufactured products*

A ▶4:21 Read and listen. Then listen again and repeat.

Uses new technology		Offers high quality		Uses new ideas	
high-tech	OR	high-end	OR	innovative	OR
state-of-the-art	OR	top-of-the-line	OR	revolutionary	OR
cutting-edge		first-rate		novel	

B ▶4:22 **LISTEN TO ACTIVATE VOCABULARY** Listen to the ads and choose the correct word or phrase.

1 The Strawberry smart phone is (state-of-the-art / top-of-the-line).

2 The Blackstone is a (revolutionary / high-end) device.

3 The Micro scanner is a (high-end / cutting-edge) product.

4 The Digicon B1X Beta is a (novel / first-rate) camera.

5 The 17-inch LCD monitor is (innovative / top-of-the-line).

GRAMMAR *The unreal conditional: Review and expansion*

> **Contractions**
> I / you would → I'd / you'd
> he / she would → he'd / she'd
> we / they would → we'd / they'd

Remember: Unreal conditional sentences describe unreal conditions—conditions that don't exist.
Use the simple past tense or <u>were</u> in the <u>if</u> clause. Use <u>would</u> or <u>could</u> in the result clause.

if clause (unreal action or condition)	result clause (if it were true)
If I **wanted** a cutting-edge phone,	I'd **look** for one at TechnoWorld. (But I *don't* want one.)
If you **were** here,	we **could study** together. (But you are *not* here.)

The <u>if</u> clause can occur first or last. If the <u>if</u> clause comes first, use a comma.
If it weren't so expensive, they would buy it. OR They would buy it if it weren't so expensive.

> **Be careful!**
> Never use <u>would</u> in an <u>if</u> clause.
> Don't say: If you ~~would be~~ here . . .

Questions
If you **saw** a lighter laptop, **would** you **buy** it? (Yes, I would. / No, I wouldn't.)
Where **would** you **go** if there **were** an affordable cruise?
If your car **died** on the highway, who **would** you **call**?

> **GRAMMAR BOOSTER** p. 139
> • Real and unreal conditionals: review
> • Clauses after <u>wish</u>
> • <u>Unless</u> in conditional sentences

A **UNDERSTAND THE GRAMMAR** Check the statements that describe unreal conditions.

☐ 1 If they see something first-rate, they buy it.

☐ 2 If you turned off your phone in the theater, it wouldn't bother the other theatergoers.

☐ 3 I'll save a lot of money on gas if I rent the Alva.

☐ 4 She could show us how to use the Digicon remote keyboard if she were here.

B **GRAMMAR PRACTICE** Choose the correct forms to complete the unreal conditional sentences.

1 If the Teknicon 17-inch monitor (were / would be) on sale, I (will / would) buy it right away.

2 If they (would invent / invented) a safe way to text-message while driving, people (will / would) be happy.

3 If she (knew / would know) about the Pictopia camera watch, she (will / would) use it on her trip.

4 What (will / would) you do if your laptop (broke / would break)?

C Use the prompts to create unreal conditional sentences.

1 (Most people / buy) high-end products if (they / have) enough money.

2 If (there / be) an Internet connection in her room, (she / send) her office the report now?

3 (I / not / get) a Lunetti phone if (I / have) all the money in the world. They say it's cutting-edge, but I don't think it's first-rate.

4 If (you / go) to Airport Electronics, (you / pay) a lot less for a top-of-the-line tablet?

D **PAIR WORK** Complete the statements. Then share and explain your statements with your class.

1 If money were not a problem, . . .

2 People would stop getting infected with diseases if . . .

3 I would stay up all night tonight if . . .

DIGITAL
MORE
EXERCISES

CONVERSATION MODEL

A ▶4:23 Read and listen to a conversation about new technology.

A: I just got a new car.

B: No kidding! What kind?

A: The Alva 500. The 500 model is top-of-the-line. I thought I'd treat myself.

B: Well, congratulations! If I had the money, I'd get a new car myself.

B ▶4:24 **RHYTHM AND INTONATION** Listen again and repeat. Then practice the Conversation Model with a partner.

NOW YOU CAN Describe technology

A **NOTEPADDING** Write one product you've recently gotten (OR would like to have) for each category.

Quality	Product name	Adjective
Uses new technology:	the Whisper combination hairdryer / cell phone	state-of-the-art

Quality	Product name	Adjective
Uses new technology:		
Offers high quality:		
Uses new ideas:		

DIGITAL
VIDEO

B **CONVERSATION ACTIVATOR** With a partner, role-play a new conversation, changing the Conversation Model with one of the products and adjectives on your notepad. Use the unreal conditional. Then change roles.

A: I just got ....
B: No kidding! What kind?
A: .... It's .... I thought I'd treat myself.
B: Well, congratulations! If I .... , I'd ....

DON'T STOP!

Discuss another product and use other adjectives. Ask questions about it:
What does it look like?
How does it work?
How [fast / accurate / powerful] is it?
Does it work well?
Is it guaranteed?

C **CHANGE PARTNERS** Personalize the conversation again, using other products on your notepad.

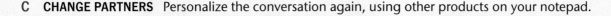

GOAL Take responsibility for a mistake

CONVERSATION MODEL

A ▶4:25 Read and listen to someone taking responsibility for a mistake.

A: Sorry I'm late. I thought the meeting was tomorrow.

B: What happened?

A: I'm ashamed to say I just forgot to put it on my calendar.

B: Don't worry. That can happen to anyone.

A: Well, if I had written it down, I wouldn't have forgotten.

B: No harm done. We were just getting started.

B ▶4:26 **RHYTHM AND INTONATION** Listen again and repeat.
Then practice the Conversation Model with a partner.

GRAMMAR *The past unreal conditional*

The past unreal conditional describes past unreal or untrue conditions and results. Use the past
perfect in the <u>if</u> clause. Use <u>would have</u> or <u>could have</u> + a past participle in the result clause.
 If she **had rented** a more economical car, she **wouldn't have spent** so much money on gas.
  (But she *didn't* rent a more economical car.)
 If Jonas Salk **hadn't invented** a vaccine to protect people against polio, many more people
  would have gotten the disease. (But he *did* invent a vaccine.)

Questions and answers
 Could they **have prevented** the accident if they **had known** the tires were so old?
  (Yes, they could have. / No, they couldn't have.)
 What **would** you **have done** if you **hadn't had** your phone with you?
  (I would have borrowed one.)

> **Be careful!**
> Don't use <u>would</u> or
> <u>could</u> in the <u>if</u> clause.
> Don't say: "If Jonas
> Salk ~~wouldn't have~~
> invented . . ."

> **GRAMMAR BOOSTER** p. 140
> • The unreal conditional:
> variety of forms

A **UNDERSTAND THE GRAMMAR** Choose the meaning of each past unreal conditional sentence.

1 I wouldn't have gone to class if I had known I had the flu.
  a I went to class.   **b** I didn't go to class.

2 If we had used our GPS, we wouldn't have gotten lost.
  a We got lost.   **b** We didn't get lost.

3 If they hadn't planted that new variety of tomatoes, they would have lost this year's crop.
  a They lost this year's crop.   **b** They didn't lose this year's crop.

4 The airline wouldn't have canceled the flight if the weather had been better.
  a They canceled the flight.   **b** They didn't cancel the flight.

B **GRAMMAR PRACTICE** Complete the sentences in the past unreal conditional. Use <u>would</u>.

1 What .... you .... if you .... the train?
                                                    do   miss
2 We .... this digital video conference if an Internet connection .... available.
      not / have   not / be
3 If our huge old camcorder .... , we .... this smaller one.
                                        not / break   not / buy
4 If she .... her smart phone, she .... they canceled her flight.
             not / take   not / know
5 If they .... good weather, they .... in Alaska this morning.
              not / have   not / land
6 If the weather .... better, we .... to the beach.
                            be   go

C **PAIR WORK** Read each case study and complete the statements with your own ideas and the past unreal conditional.

1 On Monday you bought a new Blendini sports car because its advertising said it was very economical. However, on Friday you read this headline in the newspaper: "Blendini Company fined for lying about statistics. Car uses more fuel than all others of its class."

If I had seen ....

....

2 You forgot to close the windows in your house before a weekend trip. There was a terrible rainstorm. When you got home, some of your furniture was damaged by the water. Your family blamed you because you were the last to leave the house.

If I hadn't forgotten ....

....

3 There was a big sale at the Morton Street Mall. Everything in every store was half-price. You didn't know, and you went shopping somewhere else. When you got home, a friend called to tell you about all the bargains she got.

If I ....

....

4 You bought some insect repellent for a trip to the mountains. When you got there, the mosquitoes were brutal. Before you sprayed the repellent on yourself and your children, you looked at the label. It said, "Caution. Not for use on children under 12."

If I ....

....

D **APPLY THE GRAMMAR** Reread the Photo Story on page 87. Complete this statement:

If .... , Leslie and Ben wouldn't have gotten eaten alive by mosquitoes.

PRONUNCIATION *Contractions with 'd in spoken English*

A ▶4:27 Notice the pronunciation of the spoken contractions of <u>had</u>, <u>would</u>, and <u>did</u>. Read and listen. Then listen again and repeat.

1 Where did you go? → /wɛrd/ Where'd you go?

2 Who did you see? → /hud/ Who'd you see?

3 It would be OK. → /ɪtəd/ It'd be OK.

4 If we had had a map, we wouldn't have gotten lost. → /wid/ If we'd had a map, we wouldn't have gotten lost.

Note: <u>Where'd</u>, <u>Who'd</u>, and <u>It'd</u> are contracted in speech, but not in writing.

B ▶4:28 **LISTENING COMPREHENSION** Write the sentences you hear. Write full, not contracted, forms.

1 ....   4 ....
2 ....   5 ....
3 ....   6 ....

NOW YOU CAN Take responsibility for a mistake

A **CONVERSATION ACTIVATOR** Role-play a new conversation with a partner, taking responsibility for a different mistake. Use the Ideas (OR your own ideas) and the past unreal conditional. Then change roles.

A: Sorry I ....
B: What happened?
A: I'm ashamed to say I just ....
B: Don't worry. That can happen to anyone.
A: Well, if I .... , I .... have ....
B: No harm done. ....

DON'T STOP!

Continue the conversation.

Ideas

Some mistakes you can make
• You were late for something.
• You forgot to do something.
• You missed a meeting.
• You missed someone's birthday.
• You didn't call someone.
• You didn't return someone's call.
• Another mistake: __

Some reasons for a mistake
• You accidentally deleted an e-mail.
• You forgot to write something down.
• You wrote down the wrong date or time.
• You just got too busy, and it slipped your mind.
• Someone stole your [phone / purse / date book].
• Another reason: __

B **CHANGE PARTNERS** Take responsibility for another mistake.

91

GOAL Describe new inventions

BEFORE YOU LISTEN

A ▶4:29 **VOCABULARY** • *More descriptive adjectives* Read and listen. Then listen again and repeat.

low-tech / high-tech

wacky

unique

efficient / inefficient

B Complete the chart with the correct adjective and one product or invention you know.

Definition	Adjective	A product or invention
the only one of its kind		
pretty silly		
doesn't use modern technology		
uses modern technology		
doesn't waste time, money, or energy		
wastes time, money, or energy		

LISTENING COMPREHENSION

A ▶4:30 **LISTEN TO DRAW CONCLUSIONS** Listen and write the number of the conversation next to the invention each person should have had.

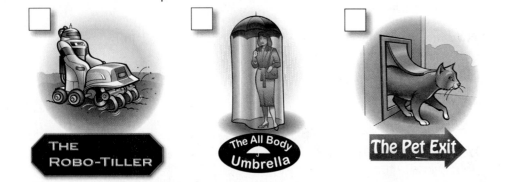

THE ROBO-TILLER

The All Body Umbrella

The Pet Exit

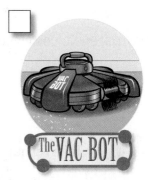

The VAC-BOT

B ▶4:31 **LISTEN TO SUMMARIZE** Listen again and then write each problem in your own words.

1 ....
2 ....
3 ....
4 ....

C **DISCUSSION** Describe each of the inventions. Use one or more of the adjectives from the Vocabulary above and from page 88. Listen again if necessary.

❝ It's not a novel idea, but the Pet Exit is both low-tech and efficient. It doesn't need electronics or machinery. ❞

A FRAME YOUR IDEAS Read the checklist and check the boxes of at least five categories where you think new inventions are needed.

WHAT DO WE NEED NEW INVENTIONS FOR?

- ☐ for safety in the car
- ☐ for safety at home
- ☐ for organizing things at home
- ☐ for cooking and preparing food
- ☐ for eating or snacking
- ☐ for getting into shape
- ☐ for raising children
- ☐ for taking care of pets
- ☐ for relaxing at home

- ☐ for reading faster
- ☐ for preparing for a natural disaster
- ☐ for writing at the office
- ☐ for training office staff
- ☐ for communicating with colleagues
- ☐ for learning new English words and grammar
- ☐ for preparing for tests
- ☐ (your own idea) _____

B NOTEPADDING Imagine an invention for five situations you checked. On the notepad, write a description and benefit of each invention.

Descriptions of your inventions	Benefits
a wake-up alarm in the car	so you don't fall asleep while driving

	Descriptions of your inventions	Benefits
1		
2		
3		
4		
5		

C PROJECT Work in small groups. Choose one invention from someone's chart. Give it a name, draw a picture of it, and write an advertisement for it. Include real and unreal conditional sentences in your ad. (For fun, the invention can be low-tech, high-tech, wacky, or even impossible! The name can be funny.)

If I were you, I'd get the new revolutionary "Drive Awake" alarm. You'll never have to worry about falling asleep while driving your car. Be safe. Stay awake with the Drive Awake Alarm.

BEEP!!!

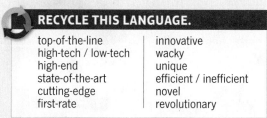

🔄 **RECYCLE THIS LANGUAGE.**

top-of-the-line	innovative
high-tech / low-tech	wacky
high-end	unique
state-of-the-art	efficient / inefficient
cutting-edge	novel
first-rate	revolutionary

D GROUP WORK Present your ads to the class.

If she had bought the state-of-the-art "EAR-RINGS," she would have gotten your phone call. Very practical!

Hello?

R-r-ring

BEFORE YOU READ

WARM-UP In your opinion, what has been the most important medical discovery in history? Explain your reason(s).

READING ▶ 4:32

Antibiotics

Today, vaccines can prevent some of the infectious diseases that in the past resulted in serious illness and death. Fortunately, for diseases caused by bacteria (tiny organisms that can only be seen by microscope), vaccines can make the difference between life and death.

What are antibiotics?

Antibiotics are substances that work in one of two ways. Some antibiotics, such as penicillin, kill disease-causing bacteria. Others, such as tetracycline, stop them from multiplying.

History

In 1675, Dutch scientist Antonie Van Leeuwenhoek, using a microscope, discovered the existence of microorganisms. However, it wasn't known that they could cause disease until French scientist

Fleming examines the behavior of penicillium in a petri dish.

Louis Pasteur confirmed that approximately 200 years later. Finally, in 1928, British scientist Alexander Fleming noticed that a mold, penicillium, growing in one of his petri dishes, was capable of killing bacteria, and the development of antibiotics became possible. Fleming named the active agent in the mold "penicillin" but was unable to create a drug from it.

In 1940, during the Second World War, two scientists working at Oxford University, Ernst Chain and Howard Florey, were able to make an antibacterial powder from penicillin that was safe to use on humans. Penicillin was mass-produced for use on soldiers in the war. If there had been no penicillin, many would have died from bacterial

infections caused by their injuries and wounds. Soon penicillin was used for serious diseases such as pneumonia and tuberculosis, which had always caused many deaths. Fleming, Florey, and Chain received the Nobel Prize in 1945. Antibiotics changed medicine and continue today to enable people to survive conditions that would have killed them before the antibiotic age.

Overuse of antibiotics

Since their discovery and widespread use, antibiotics have been considered a wonder drug. Many common diseases, however, are caused by viruses, not bacteria, and antibiotics are not effective against them. Nevertheless, too many people use antibiotics regularly, believing they will cure viral illnesses such as common upper respiratory infections, colds, and sore throats. Why is this a problem?

First, it is a waste of money to use antibiotics to treat viruses. Our body's immune system eventually combats most viruses, and we recover without treatment. But more importantly, bacteria exposed to an antibiotic can become resistant to it, making the antibiotic less effective, or even useless. If antibiotics no longer work against infections and diseases, people will begin to die from them again.

If scientists had recognized that bacteria could develop resistance, perhaps they would have warned doctors not to use antibiotics unless a patient has a bacterial infection. Hopefully, worldwide awareness of this threat to an important class of drugs will convince us to avoid using them for conditions that don't require them.

Van Leeuwenhoek used a microscope to observe microorganisms.

Some diseases caused by bacteria	Some diseases caused by viruses
Tuberculosis	Influenza (or "the flu")
Plague	Polio
Pertussis	AIDS
Streptococcal sore throat (or "strep throat")	The common cold
	Hepatitis

A FIND SUPPORTING DETAILS Answer the questions in your own words. Explain your answers, based on information in the Reading.

1 What is the benefit of antibiotics?

2 Why are antibiotics not effective against the common cold?

3 Why are antibiotics effective against strep throat?

4 What problem has overuse of antibiotics caused?

B UNDERSTAND FROM CONTEXT Choose the correct word to complete the sentence.

1 (An antibiotic / A vaccine) prevents diseases from occurring.

2 (Bacteria / Tetracycline) can cause infectious diseases.

3 Bacteria are small organisms that can only be seen (in a petri dish / with a microscope).

4 (Penicillium / Penicillin) is a drug that kills bacteria.

5 The common cold and influenza are common (bacterial / upper respiratory) infections.

6 Some antibiotics are no longer effective because certain bacteria have developed (overuse / resistance) to antibiotics.

DIGITAL
MORE
EXERCISES

NOW YOU CAN Discuss the impact of inventions / discoveries

A FRAME YOUR IDEAS Look at some key inventions and discoveries and how they changed people's lives.

2000 BCE: The plow loosens and turns the soil so crops can be planted efficiently.

15th Century: Johannes Gutenberg invents typecasting, resulting in the printing press, which could print more than one copy of a book.

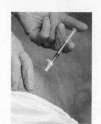

1796: The discovery by Edward Jenner of the process of vaccination made the first successful vaccine possible.

1914: The modern zipper permits the opening and closing of clothes without buttons and buttonholes.

1940–1945: The first electronic computers, the size of a large room, enabled users to organize and examine information. The computer opened a new era of communications and research technology.

B NOTEPADDING Write your ideas about how life was before and after each invention or discovery.

	What was life like before?	What was life like after?
the plow		
the printing press		
vaccination		
the zipper		
the computer		

Text-mining (optional)
Find and underline three words or phrases in the Reading that were new to you. Use them in your Group Report. For example: "infections."

C GROUP REPORT Present a report about an invention or a discovery to your class. Describe its impact in history. Use the past unreal conditional.

❝ After the plow was invented, farmers could plant large areas. If it hadn't been invented, they couldn't have planted enough food to sell. ❞

A ▶4:33 Listen to people talking about new products. Match the name of each product with the best adjective to describe it.

Name of product	Adjective
___ 1 The Ultraphone	a top-of-the-line
___ 2 Dinner-from-a-distance	b unique
___ 3 Kinder-TV	c efficient
___ 4 Ten Years Off	d cutting-edge

B Check the statement that is true for each situation.

1 We wouldn't have gotten lost if we had remembered to bring our portable GPS device.

☐ We brought it, and we got lost.

☐ We brought it, and we didn't get lost.

☐ We didn't bring it, and we got lost.

☐ We didn't bring it, and we didn't get lost.

2 If the salesclerk were here, she would explain how the Omni works.

☐ The salesclerk is here, so she will explain how the Omni works.

☐ The salesclerk is here, but she won't explain how the Omni works.

☐ The salesclerk isn't here, but she will explain how the Omni works.

☐ The salesclerk isn't here, so she won't explain how the Omni works.

3 If Ron had brought the Ultraphone with him, he would have already sent those e-mails.

☐ Ron brought the Ultraphone, and he has already sent those e-mails.

☐ Ron brought the Ultraphone, but he hasn't sent those e-mails yet.

☐ Ron didn't bring the Ultraphone, but he has already sent those e-mails.

☐ Ron didn't bring the Ultraphone, so he hasn't sent those e-mails yet.

C Complete each conditional sentence with your own ideas.

1 If the computer hadn't been invented, ...

2 If I had to decide what the most important scientific discovery in history was, ...

....

3 If most people cared about the environment, ...

4 Would new cars be less expensive if .... ?

5 If Ella had known that being a teacher was so hard, ... ?

WRITING

Choose one of the inventions or discoveries on pages 86, 94, or 95, or another invention or discovery. Describe the advantages, disadvantages, and historical impact of the invention or discovery you chose.

For additional language practice...

♫ TOP NOTCH POP • Lyrics p. 155
"Reinvent the Wheel"

DIGITAL SONG   DIGITAL KARAOKE

WRITING BOOSTER p. 152
• Summary statements
• Guidance for this writing exercise

① Uses of the WHEEL

the wagon wheel

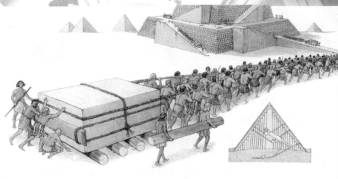

logs used as wheels

ORAL REVIEW

CONTEST Look at the pictures about the uses of the wheel for one minute. Then close your books and try to remember all the uses of the wheel in the pictures. You get a bonus point for thinking of another use.

PAIR WORK

1 Choose one use of the wheel. Discuss how it changed history and people's lives. Present your ideas. For example:

> The log helped people move heavy objects over great distances. They could build more easily with stone.

2 The family in the picture below is late. Create a conversation for the two women. For example:

> A: Hello, Mom. I'm sorry. We're going to be late. If we hadn't...

the horse-drawn chariot

the potter's wheel

the two-wheeled cart

the automobile

②

✔ NOW I CAN

- ☐ Describe technology.
- ☐ Take responsibility for a mistake.
- ☐ Describe new inventions.
- ☐ Discuss the impact of inventions / discoveries.

Controversial Issues

COMMUNICATION GOALS
1 Talk about politics.
2 Discuss controversial issues politely.
3 Propose solutions to global problems.
4 Debate the pros and cons of issues.

PREVIEW

How politically literate are you? Test yourself to find out.

Choose the correct term for each definition. Then look at the answers to see how you did.

1 A group of people who govern a country or state
☐ a government ☐ a constitution

2 The art or science of government or governing
☐ a constitution ☐ politics

3 A set of basic laws and principles that a country is governed by, which cannot easily be changed by the political party in power
☐ a constitution ☐ a democracy

4 An occasion when people vote to choose someone for an official position
☐ a government ☐ an election

5 Show, by marking a paper or using a machine, etc., which person you want in a government position
☐ govern ☐ vote

6 Lead or take part in a series of actions intended to win an election for a government position
☐ campaign ☐ vote

7 A system of government in which every citizen in the country can vote to elect its government officials
☐ a monarchy ☐ a democracy

8 A system in which a country is ruled by a king or queen
☐ a dictatorship ☐ a monarchy

9 Government by a ruler who has complete power
☐ a democracy ☐ a dictatorship

10 A country ruled by a king or a queen whose power is limited by a constitution
☐ a dictatorship ☐ a constitutional monarchy

ANSWERS: 1 a government 2 politics 3 a constitution 4 an election 5 vote 6 campaign 7 a democracy 8 a monarchy 9 a dictatorship 10 a constitutional monarchy

A ▶5:02 **VOCABULARY • *Political terminology*** Read and listen. Then listen again and repeat.

| a government | politics | a constitution | an election | vote |
| campaign | a democracy | a monarchy | a dictatorship | a constitutional monarchy |

B **PAIR WORK** How much do you know about world politics? On the chart, discuss and write the name of at least one country for each type of government. Then compare charts with other classmates.

A democracy	A monarchy	A constitutional monarchy	A dictatorship

ENGLISH FOR TODAY'S WORLD
Understand English speakers from
different language backgrounds.
Carlo = Italian speaker

C ▶5:03 **PHOTO STORY** Read and listen to a conversation about discussing politics.

Paul: What a coincidence! I was just thinking about calling you. It's been such a long time.

Carlo: It sure has. Let's sit down and catch up. . . . What are you up to these days?

Paul: Busy, busy. The office has been crazy, with the election coming up next month. You can imagine.

Carlo: But I'll bet working at a TV station is exciting. . . . Hey, Paul, do you mind if I ask you a political question? I hope it's not inappropriate. I'm not sure it's polite to ask about politics here in the U.S.

Paul: That's funny. They always say not to talk about religion or politics, but everyone does. Shoot.

Carlo: OK. Who are you planning to vote for in the election?

Paul: Well, because we're friends, I'll answer. But I should warn you that it might not be a good idea to ask just anyone that question. Some people might find it a little personal.

Carlo: Oops.

Paul: No worries. Actually, I haven't made up my mind. I'm leaning toward Clancy, though. I think he's better than the other guy.

D **PARAPHRASE** Restate each of the following sentences from the Photo Story in your own words.

1 "Let's sit down and catch up."

2 "What are you up to these days?"

3 "Some people might find it a little personal."

4 "No worries."

5 "Actually, I haven't made up my mind."

6 "I'm leaning toward Clancy . . . "

E **THINK AND EXPLAIN** Answer the questions, based on your understanding of the Photo Story.

1 Why does Paul say "What a coincidence!" when he sees Carlo?

2 What does Paul mean when he says, "Busy, busy. The office has been crazy."

3 Why does Carlo ask whether Paul minds if he asks him a political question?

4 Why does Paul warn Carlo not to ask some people about their political opinions?

SPEAKING *Discussion topics*

1 Do you like to talk about politics? Do you think politics is a good topic for discussion with "just anybody"? Or is politics always "a little too personal"? Explain.

2 Review the types of government from page 98. Do you think every country should have the same form of government? Why don't all countries have the same form of government? In your opinion, is there a "best" form of government? Explain.

Do you like to discuss politics at the dinner table?

GOAL Talk about politics

GRAMMAR *Non-count nouns that represent abstract ideas*

Nouns that represent abstract ideas are always non-count nouns.

Education is an important issue.
NOT: ~~The~~ education is an important issue.
NOT: ~~Educations are~~ an important issue.

News about politics is always interesting.
NOT: News about ~~the~~ politics is always interesting.
NOT: News about politics ~~are~~ always interesting.

Nouns for abstract ideas		
advice	justice	progress
crime	life	proof
education	news	success
health	patience	time
help	peace	work
information	politics	
investment	poverty	

GRAMMAR BOOSTER p. 141
• Count and non-count nouns: review and extension

A   GRAMMAR PRACTICE   Choose the correct form of the nouns and verbs.

1 Our (advice / advices) to you (is / are) to avoid discussing politics.

2 (Poverty / The poverty) (was / were) the topic of the international conference.

3 Both candidates have programs for (the health / health) and (educations / education).

4 Making (peace / the peace) takes a lot of (work / works) and a long time.

5 Good news (is / are) hard to find in the newspaper these days.

B   GRAMMAR PRACTICE   Correct the errors.

                      information
Here's some political ~~informations~~ about the election. The good news are that both candidates
have programs for the education. The liberal candidate, Bill Slate, says financial helps for the schools
are a question of the justice. The poverty has affected the quality of the schools, and students from
schools in poor areas don't have a success. Joanna Clark, the conservative candidate, disagrees. She
believes a progress has been made by investing in the teacher education. Her advices are to keep
the old policy. "Creating better schools takes the time and a patience," she says.

DIGITAL
MORE EXERCISES

DIGITAL
FLASH CARDS

VOCABULARY *A continuum of political and social beliefs*

A   ▶5:04 Read and listen. Then listen again and repeat.

radical *adj.*   supporting complete political or social change —**a radical** *n.*

liberal *adj.*   supporting changes in political, social, or religious systems that respect the different beliefs, ideas, etc., of other people —**a liberal** *n.*

moderate *adj.*   having opinions or beliefs, especially about politics, that are not extreme and that most people consider reasonable or sensible —**a moderate** *n.*

conservative *adj.*   preferring to continue to do things as they have been done in the past rather than risking changes —**a conservative** *n.*

reactionary *adj.*   strongly opposed to political or social change —**a reactionary** *n.*

B   ▶5:05 **LISTEN TO INFER AND ACTIVATE VOCABULARY**   Listen to each conversation. Then, with a partner, complete the chart. Listen again, if necessary, to check your work or settle any disagreements.

	radical	liberal	moderate	conservative	reactionary
1 He's	○	○	○	○	○
2 She's	○	○	○	○	○
3 He's	○	○	○	○	○
4 She's	○	○	○	○	○
5 He's	○	○	○	○	○

CONVERSATION MODEL

A ▶5:06 Read and listen to a conversation about politics.

A: Do you mind if I ask you a political question?

B: No problem. What would you like to know?

A: Well, are you a liberal or a conservative?

B: Actually, I'm neither. I like to make up my mind based on the issue.

A: So, would you say you're an independent?

B: I guess you could say that.

If you don't want to answer . . .

B: No offense, but I feel a little uncomfortable talking about that. I hope you don't mind.

A: Absolutely not. It's a good thing I asked.

B ▶5:07 **RHYTHM AND INTONATION** Listen again and repeat. Then practice the Conversation Model with a partner.

PRONUNCIATION *Stress to emphasize meaning*

A ▶5:08 Listen to the different intonations of the same sentence. Then listen again and repeat.

1 Are you a conservative? (normal stress—no special meaning)

2 Are you a conSERVative? (I'm surprised that you would have such a belief.)

3 Are YOU a conservative? (I'm surprised that you, among all people, would be a conservative.)

4 ARE you a conservative? (I think you might be a conservative, and I'd like to be sure.)

B **PAIR WORK** Practice varying the stress in this statement: "Would you say you're an independent?" Discuss the different meanings.

NOW YOU CAN Talk about politics

A **PAIR WORK** Which political questions do you think would be too personal or controversial to ask?

- [ ] What advice would you like to give the president / prime minister / king / queen?
- [ ] What do you think about the president / prime minister / king / queen?
- [ ] What do you think about our government's policies?
- [ ] Are you liberal or conservative?
- [ ] Who are you voting for in the election?

B **CONVERSATION ACTIVATOR** With a partner, change the Conversation Model to bring up a topic that might be controversial. Partner B can answer or decline to discuss the question. Then change roles.

A: Do you mind if I ask you a political question?

B: No problem. What would you like to know?

A: Well, ... ?

B: Actually, ...

DON'T STOP!
Ask other political questions.

C **CHANGE PARTNERS** Discuss another political subject.

GOAL Discuss controversial issues politely

CONVERSATION MODEL

A ▶5:09 Read and listen to a polite conversation about a controversial issue.

A: How do you feel about capital punishment?

B: I'm in favor of it. I believe if you kill someone, you deserve to be killed. What about you?

A: Actually, I'm against the death penalty. I think it's wrong to take a life, no matter what.

B: Well, I guess we'll have to agree to disagree!

B ▶5:10 **RHYTHM AND INTONATION** Listen again and repeat. Then practice the Conversation Model with a partner.

C **DISCUSSION** Are you in favor of capital punishment? Explain.

▶5:11 **Disagreement**
I guess we'll have to agree to disagree.
Really? I have to disagree with you there.
Do you think so? I'm not sure I agree.
Well, I'm afraid I don't agree.
No offense, but I just can't agree.

▶5:12 **Agreement**
I agree with you on that one.
I couldn't agree more.
I couldn't have said it better myself.
That's exactly what I think.

VOCABULARY *Some controversial issues*

DIGITAL FLASH CARDS

A ▶5:13 Read and listen. Then listen again and repeat.

censorship of books and movies

compulsory military service

lowering the driving age

raising the voting age

prohibiting smoking indoors

B ▶5:14 **LISTEN TO ACTIVATE VOCABULARY** Listen to people's opinions about controversial issues. Complete the chart with each issue they discuss. Use the Vocabulary.

C ▶5:15 **LISTEN TO INFER** Now listen again and check <u>For</u> or <u>Against</u> in the chart, according to what the person says.

	The issues they discuss	For	Against
1			
2			
3			
4			
5			

GRAMMAR *Verbs followed by objects and infinitives*

Certain verbs can be followed by infinitives, but some verbs must be followed by an object before an infinitive.

> The newspaper reminded all eighteen-year-olds <u>to vote</u>.
> We urged them <u>to write</u> letters against the death penalty.

These verbs cannot be followed by an object. However, they can be followed directly by an infinitive.

agree	can't wait	hope	need	pretend
appear	decide	learn	offer	refuse
can't afford	deserve	manage	plan	seem

Verbs followed by an object before an infinitive:

advise	encourage	remind	urge
allow	invite	request	warn
cause	permit	require	
convince	persuade	tell	

GRAMMAR BOOSTER p. 141
Gerunds and infinitives: review of
• form and usage
• usage after certain verbs

A **GRAMMAR PRACTICE** Complete each statement or question with an object and an infinitive.

1 The newspaper advised ....._all voters to register_..... early for the next election.
all voters / register

2 Did you remind .... her voter registration card?
your daughter / complete

3 We persuaded .... for our candidate.
our friends / vote

4 Our teacher always encourages .... every night, not just the day before the exam.
students / study

5 Can't we convince .... taxes on property?
legislators / lower

B **GRAMMAR PRACTICE** Write two sentences using verbs that can be followed directly by an infinitive and two sentences with verbs that must have an object before an infinitive.

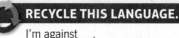
NOW YOU CAN Discuss controversial issues politely

A **CONVERSATION ACTIVATOR** With a partner, change the Conversation Model, giving a reason for your point of view. Use the Vocabulary and expressions of Agreement and Disagreement from page 102. Then change roles and issues.

A: How do you feel about .... ?
B: .... I .... What about you?
A: Actually, I .... I think ....
B: ....

DON'T STOP!

Ask your partner's opinion of other issues.

 RECYCLE THIS LANGUAGE.

I'm against __.
I'm in favor of __.
I think / believe / feel:
   it's wrong.
   it's right.
   it's wrong, no matter what.
   it depends.

B **CHANGE PARTNERS** Discuss another issue, giving reasons to support your opinion.

GOAL Propose solutions to global problems

BEFORE YOU READ

EXPLORE YOUR IDEAS What is the difference between a problem and a global problem? Do you think your generation faces more serious global problems than the generation of your parents or grandparents? Explain.

READING ▶ 5:16

The following issues were most frequently mentioned in a global survey about current world problems.

CORRUPTION People all over the world complain about the corruption of police, government officials, and business leaders. Two examples of corruption are:

- A police officer takes money (a "bribe") from a driver so he doesn't give the driver a ticket for speeding.
- A company that wants to do business with a government agency offers a public official money or a gift to choose that company for the job.

Some people feel that power promotes corruption and that corruption is unavoidable. But an independent media—for example, non-government-backed newspapers, television stations, and Internet blogs—can also play an important role in exposing corruption.

POVERTY Approximately one-fifth of the world's population, over 1 billion people, earns less than US $1 a day. Each day, over a billion people in the world lack basic food supplies. And according to UNICEF, each day, 25,000 children under the age of five die of starvation or preventable infectious disease.

There are many causes of poverty, ranging from catastrophic natural events to bad economic and agricultural policies, so there's no one solution to poverty worldwide. Some people feel that wealthy nations must send aid to poorer nations, while others are concerned that nothing will help unless local corruption is reduced and bad government policies are changed.

TERRORISM Every day, we see or hear about suicide bombings and other violent acts committed against innocent people for religious or political reasons. Many ask why terrorism is on the rise.

Some social scientists believe that television and movies may contribute to growing anger. They claim that some people may feel frustrated and powerless when they measure their lives against the lives of extremely wealthy people they see in the media.

However, views about what causes terrorism can be very controversial, and many people disagree about its causes or possible solutions. While some feel that terrorism can be met with military force, others believe

that people's extreme poverty and powerlessness must be reduced to make a difference.

RACISM AND DISCRIMINATION Racism (the belief that one's own race or ethnic group is superior to others) and racial and ethnic discrimination (treating members of other groups unfairly) exist in many places. These two common problems cause human rights violations all over the world. In some cases a more powerful ethnic or racial group justifies the domination and, horribly, even the complete destruction of ethnic or racial minorities they consider to be inferior. When taken to this extreme, genocides such as the European Holocaust and the massacre in Sudan have threatened to wipe out entire peoples.

Can racism and discrimination be eliminated—or are these simply unfortunate features of human nature? Many people believe that education can help build tolerance of the "other" and may contribute to creating a more peaceful world.

A UNDERSTAND FROM CONTEXT Match each definition with a word from the box.

.... **1** a lack of necessary money to survive

.... **2** the attempt to destroy all members of a racial or ethnic group

.... **3** judging or harming people because of their racial or ethnic heritage

.... **4** money paid or some other reward given to a person to perform a dishonest or unethical act or to provide a favor

.... **5** the abuse of power by people in government or business

.... **6** the belief that other racial or ethnic groups are inferior to one's own

a a bribe
b genocide
c poverty
d corruption
e discrimination
f racism

B **ACTIVATE LANGUAGE FROM A TEXT** Based on the information in the Reading, cross out the one word or phrase in each row that is unrelated to the others. Explain your reasoning.

1	people	politics	ethnic groups	races
2	money	property	income	racism
3	bribe	corruption	discrimination	money
4	hunger	starvation	domination	lack of food
5	racism	business	discrimination	prejudice

C **CRITICAL THINKING** Discuss each of the following.

1 Reread the section on corruption in the Reading. What do all acts of corruption have in common? Do you think it is possible to end corruption, or do you feel that it is a part of human nature? Use specific examples in your discussion.

2 What are some of the causes of poverty, and what are its effects?

3 In your opinion, why do people engage in acts of terrorism? Is terrorism an expression of power or powerlessness and frustration? Provide examples to support your opinion.

4 What reasons do people have to hate other groups? Is hatred of another group ever understandable, appropriate, or justified? Explain the reasons for your opinion.

5 Do you see a single problem connecting all four issues in the Reading? If so, what is it?

DIGITAL
MORE
EXERCISES

NOW YOU CAN Propose solutions to global problems

A **FRAME YOUR IDEAS** On a scale of 1 to 6, put the goals in order of importance and difficulty to accomplish (1 = most important or most difficult).

ORDER OF IMPORTANCE	GOAL	ORDER OF DIFFICULTY TO ACCOMPLISH
☐	reducing poverty and hunger	☐
☐	preventing terrorism	☐
☐	avoiding war	☐
☐	ending or reducing corruption	☐
☐	wiping out racism and ethnic discrimination	☐
☐	protecting human rights	☐

B **NOTEPADDING** Write some possible solutions to global problems.

Problem	Possible solutions

C **DISCUSSION** Discuss the solutions to the global problems you proposed. Do you all have the same concerns?

Text-mining (optional)
Find and underline three words or phrases in the Reading that were new to you. Use them in your Discussion.
For example: "a bribe."

BEFORE YOU LISTEN

A ▶5:17 **VOCABULARY** • *How to debate an issue politely*   Read and listen. Then listen again and repeat.

1

" I think smoking is a disgusting habit. "

" **That may be true, but** if you only smoke in your own house, you're not hurting anyone but yourself. "

2

" I think more people should be active in politics. That way, we would have better governments. "

" **I see what you mean, but** it's not realistic to expect everyone to care. "

3

" I think our president is doing an excellent job. "

" **Well, on the one hand,** he's not corrupt. **But on the other hand,** he hasn't done much to improve the country. "

4

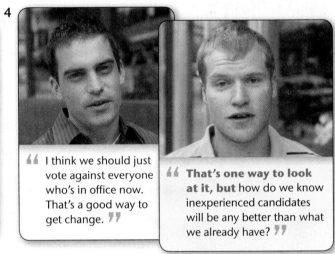

" I think we should just vote against everyone who's in office now. That's a good way to get change. "

" **That's one way to look at it, but** how do we know inexperienced candidates will be any better than what we already have? "

B   **PAIR WORK**   Take turns saying and responding to each opinion. Use the Vocabulary above to disagree politely. Or, if you agree with the opinion, use the language of agreement from page 102. For example:

1 "In some countries, dictatorship has helped stop corruption."

" I couldn't agree more. Countries with dictatorships are better off. "   **OR**   " That may be true, but no one should have to live under a dictatorship. "

2 "There is no real democracy. All governments are controlled by a few powerful people."

3 "I think moderates are the only people you can trust in government."

4 "I'm not going to vote. All the candidates are corrupt."

5 "Terrorism is getting worse and worse all over the world."

6 "I don't think it's important to vote. Nothing ever changes."

LISTENING COMPREHENSION

▶ 5:18 **LISTEN TO SUMMARIZE** Listen to three conversations about dictatorship, democracy, and monarchy. Then listen again and, on a separate sheet of paper, take notes about the arguments in favor of and against each system of government. Then work in pairs. Partner A: Summarize the arguments in favor. Partner B: Summarize the arguments against.

NOW YOU CAN Debate the pros and cons of issues

A GROUP WORK Choose an issue that you'd like to debate.

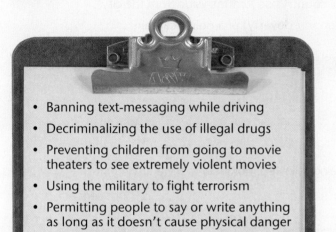

- Banning text-messaging while driving
- Decriminalizing the use of illegal drugs
- Preventing children from going to movie theaters to see extremely violent movies
- Using the military to fight terrorism
- Permitting people to say or write anything as long as it doesn't cause physical danger
- Your own local or political issue:

_____

_____

B NOTEPADDING On your notepad, write arguments in favor and against.

Issue:
Arguments in favor:
Arguments against:

C DEBATE Divide the group into two teams, with one team in favor and the other team against. Take turns presenting your views. Use the Vocabulary from page 106. Take turns and disagree politely. Then continue the discussion.

 RECYCLE THIS LANGUAGE.

Discuss controversies	Express agreement	Express disagreement
Are you in favor of __?	I agree with you on that one.	I guess we'll have to agree to disagree!
I'm against / in favor of __.	I couldn't agree more.	I have to disagree with you there.
I think / believe / feel:	I couldn't have said it better myself.	I'm not sure I agree.
it's wrong.	That's exactly what I think.	I'm afraid I don't agree.
it's right.		No offense, but I can't agree.
it's wrong, no matter what.		
it depends.		

A ▶5:19 Listen to the news report about four news stories. Then listen again and circle the correct word or phrase.

1 Sorindians and Ramays are two (ethnic groups / governments) that occupy land areas next to each other.

2 (Sorindians / Ramays) want to be able to observe their dietary laws and traditional clothing customs.

3 The problem between the Sorindians and the Ramays is an example of (corruption / ethnic discrimination).

4 A package left in the bathroom at the central post office raised fears of (terrorism / corruption).

5 Poor people are migrating into the (city from the countryside / countryside from the city).

6 Another story in the news is the reported (corruption / poverty) of a police captain.

B Complete the paragraph about an election, using verbs and count and non-count nouns correctly.

Many .... running for election make .... about
1 candidate / candidates   2 promise / promises
.... But .... comes slowly, and ....
3 education / the education   4 progress / the progress   5 information / informations
.... hard to get. Voters would like to see .... that their
6 is / are   7 proof / proofs
.... being followed. For instance, we are just now
8 advice / advices   9 is / are
receiving .... of education statistics and .... not very good.
10 news / the news   11 it's / they're
.... is needed, and .... is necessary to improve our schools.
12 Help / The help   13 the time / time

C Complete each sentence.

1 The law doesn't allow .... the Constitution.
  a the president change   **b** the president to change   **c** change

2 Our friends advised .... disappointed about the election.
  a not to be   **b** us not to be   **c** us to be not

3 The Constitution requires .... office after two terms.
  a to leave   **b** senators to leave   **c** senators leave

4 The election committee permitted .... about their educational policies.
  a the candidates to speak   **b** the candidates speak   **c** to speak

D Disagree politely with each statement, using a different way to disagree each time. Then add a reason why you disagree with each statement.

> 1. That's one way to look at it, but...

1 Monarchies are dictatorships.
  YOU ....

2 There's no such thing as a real democracy anywhere in the world.
  YOU ....

3 All people with power are corrupt.
  YOU ....

For additional language practice . . .

♫ TOP NOTCH POP • Lyrics p. 155
"We Can Agree to Disagree"

DIGITAL SONG   DIGITAL KARAOKE

WRITING

Write at least two paragraphs about one of these issues: compulsory military service, capital punishment, or censorship of books and movies. Include both the pros and cons of the issue.

WRITING BOOSTER p. 152
• Contrasting ideas
• Guidance for this writing exercise

ORAL REVIEW

CONTEST Look at the pictures for one minute. Then close your books and name the three issues depicted in the news.

PAIR WORK Create conversations.

1 Create a conversation between the man and woman in Picture 1. Continue the conversation, discussing corruption in general. Start like this:

Look at this article about the judge who was taking bribes in court.

2 Create a conversation between the two women in Picture 2. Start like this and continue the conversation, discussing terrorism in general:

A: Look! Another terrorist bombing.
B: Terrible! What do you think causes this?

3 Create a conversation between the two men discussing the election in Senegal in Picture 3. Start like this and continue the conversation:

Do you mind if I ask you a question about the elections in Senegal?

CITY POST
Judge goes to prison for taking bribes.

Daily Gazette
Car bomb explodes near open-air market.
Numerous casualties. Unknown group claims responsibility.

ELECTION IN SENEGAL

✓ NOW I CAN

☐ Talk about politics.
☐ Discuss controversial issues politely.
☐ Propose solutions to global problems.
☐ Debate the pros and cons of issues.

Beautiful World

COMMUNICATION GOALS
1 Describe a geographical location.
2 Warn about a possible risk.
3 Describe a natural setting.
4 Discuss solutions to global warming.

PREVIEW

The Arenal Volcano

CENTRAL AMERICA

COSTA RICA

Lake Nicaragua

NICARAGUA

Liberia

Lake Arenal

Arenal Volcano

La Fortuna

Caribbean Sea

COSTA RICA

Puntarenas

San José

Irazu Volcano

Puerto Limón

Gulf of Nicoya

Pacific Ocean

Quepos

Coronado Bay

PANAMA

Gulf of Dulce

Mountain Ranges
1 Guanacaste Range
2 Central Volcanic Range
3 Talamanca Range
▲ = Volcano
● = City
★ = Capital City

National Parks
4 Santa Rosa
5 Braulio Carrillo
6 Tortuguero
7 Chirripó
8 La Amistad
9 Corcovado

| 0 | 50 | 100 kilometers |
| 0 | 31 | 62 miles |

The waterfall at La Fortuna

A ▶ 5:22 **VOCABULARY • *Geographical features*** Read and listen. Then listen again and repeat. Find these features on the map.

a gulf	an ocean	a mountain range
a bay	a sea	a national park
a lake	a volcano	

B Use the map to answer the questions about Costa Rica.

1 What two countries share a border with Costa Rica?

2 In what mountain range is Costa Rica's capital located?

3 What is Costa Rica's largest national park?

4 What is Costa Rica's largest lake?

5 Approximately how far is Puntarenas from San José?

6 What bodies of water are on Costa Rica's two coasts?

C ▶5:23 **PHOTO STORY** Read and listen to two tourists talking about Costa Rica.

Max: Have you folks been here long?

Frank: A little over a week. Unfortunately, we've only got two days left. You?

Max: We just got here yesterday, actually.

Frank: I'm Frank, by the way. Frank Lew. From Hong Kong.

Max: Max Belli. From Labro, Italy. Have you heard of it?

Frank: I can't say I have.

Max: It's a very small town about 20 kilometers north of Rome.

Max: Hey, you wouldn't happen to know anything about the La Fortuna waterfall, would you? We plan on driving up there this weekend.

Frank: Actually, we just got back from there yesterday.

Max: What a coincidence! Was it worth seeing?

Frank: Spectacular. You don't want to miss it.

Frank: But be sure to take it slow on the path down to the bottom of the falls. It can get pretty wet and slippery.

Max: Thanks for the warning. What if we want to get a look at the Arenal Volcano, too? Do you think that's doable in two days?

Frank: No problem. The volcano's only about twenty minutes west of La Fortuna by car. So I'm sure you could handle them both.

D **FOCUS ON LANGUAGE** Write each of the following statements from the Photo Story in your *own* way. Use the context of the story to help you restate each one.

1 "I can't say I have." ....

2 "What a coincidence!" ....

3 "Was it worth seeing?" ....

4 "You don't want to miss it." ....

5 ". . . be sure to take it slow." ....

6 "Do you think that's doable in two days?" ....

7 ". . . I'm sure you could handle them both." ....

SPEAKING

A **PAIR WORK** Brainstorm and write the names of places you know for each of the following geographical features.

an ocean or sea		a national park	
a bay or gulf		a lake	
a mountain or volcano		a waterfall	
a mountain range		a capital	

B **GUESSING GAME** Describe a geographical feature of your country. Your classmates guess what place it is.

66 It's a beautiful lake. It's between . . . 99

66 It's a volcano. It's near . . . 99

GOAL **Describe a geographical location**

GRAMMAR *Prepositional phrases of geographical place*

Look at the map and study the examples.

Mexico is **north of** (OR **to the north of**) Guatemala.
Honduras and El Salvador are located **to the south**.

Tikal is **in the north**. Guatemala City is **in the south**.
Cobán is located **in the central part** of Guatemala.

El Rancho is located **on** the Motagua River.
Champerico is **on the west coast** of Guatemala.
Flores is **on the south shore** of Lake Petén Itzá.

> **GRAMMAR BOOSTER** p. 143
> • Prepositions of place: more usage
> • Proper nouns: capitalization
> • Proper nouns: use of <u>the</u>

A **GRAMMAR PRACTICE** Complete the sentences with the correct prepositions.

1 Vladivostok is located .... the eastern coast .... Russia.

2 Barranquilla is .... the northern part .... Colombia.

3 Haikou is .... the northern coast .... Hainan Island in China.

4 Machu Picchu is located about 100 kilometers northwest .... Cuzco.

5 Vietnam is located south .... China.

6 Kota Kinabalu is .... the north coast of Borneo, a part of Malaysia.

7 Manaus is located .... the Amazon River in Brazil.

8 Canada is .... the north .... the United States.

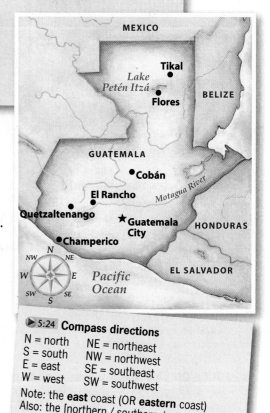

▶ 5:24 **Compass directions**

N = north   NE = northeast
S = south   NW = northwest
E = east   SE = southeast
W = west   SW = southwest

Note: the **east** coast (OR **eastern** coast)
Also: the [northern / southern / western] coast

B **PAIR WORK** With a partner, choose five places you know in or near your country. Then describe and write where they are, using prepositional phrases of geographical location.

DIGITAL
MORE
EXERCISES

DIGITAL
VIDEO
COACH

PRONUNCIATION *Voiced and voiceless <u>th</u>*

A ▶ 5:25 Read and listen. Then listen again and repeat.

Voiced <u>th</u>	Voiceless <u>th</u>
1 there	thanks
2 this	think
3 northern	north
4 southern	south
5 the west	southwest

B **PAIR WORK** Take turns reading the sentences you wrote in Exercise B above, paying attention to voiced and voiceless <u>th</u> sounds.

CONVERSATION MODEL

A ▶5:26 Read and listen to someone describing a geographical location.

A: Where exactly is the temple located?

B: About 15 kilometers north of Kyoto. Are you planning to go there?

A: I've been thinking about it.

B: It's a must-see. Be sure to take pictures!

> ▶5:28 **Recommendations**
> It's a must-see.
> You don't want to miss it.

> ▶5:29 **Criticisms**
> It's overrated.
> It's a waste of time.

B ▶5:27 **RHYTHM AND INTONATION** Listen again and repeat. Then practice the Conversation Model with a partner.

NOW YOU CAN Describe a geographical location

DIGITAL VIDEO

A **CONVERSATION ACTIVATOR** With a partner, change the Conversation Model to talk about the location of an interesting place. Use the map and the pictures or a map of your own country. Then change roles.

A: Where exactly .... located?

B: .... Are you planning to go there?

A: I've been thinking about it.

B: ....

DON'T STOP!

- Ask more questions about the place.
  [Is it / Are they] worth seeing?
  Is [it / the trip] doable in [one day]?
- Ask about other places.

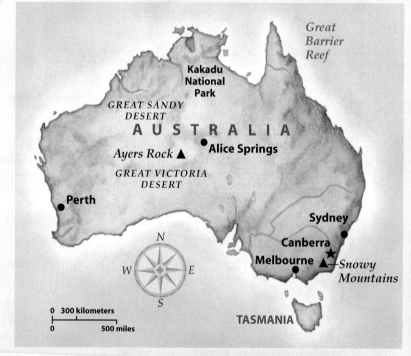

AYERS ROCK

THE GREAT BARRIER REEF

KAKADU NATIONAL PARK

THE SNOWY MOUNTAINS

B **CHANGE PARTNERS** Describe other places.

VOCABULARY *Describe risks*

A ▶5:30 Read and listen. Then listen again and repeat.

It can be quite **dangerous**.

It can be very **rocky**.

It can be extremely **steep**.

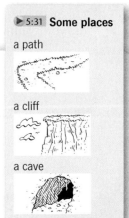

It can be so **slippery**.

It can be pretty **dark**.

It can be terribly **exhausting**.

It can be really **foggy**.

▶5:32 Dangerous animals and insects

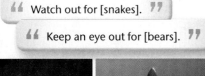

" Watch out for [snakes]. "

" Keep an eye out for [bears]. "

a snake   a shark

a jellyfish   a bear

a scorpion   a mosquito

B ▶5:33 **LISTEN TO INFER** Listen to the conversations. Check if the speaker thinks the place is risky or not.

	risky	not risky
1 He thinks hiking around the waterfall is . . .	☐	☐
2 She thinks climbing the mountain is . . .	☐	☐
3 She thinks swimming in the bay is . . .	☐	☐
4 He thinks walking on the cliffs is . . .	☐	☐

C ▶5:34 **LISTEN TO ACTIVATE VOCABULARY** Listen again. Complete each statement with the risks.

1 He warns that the path is sometimes .... and there may be ....

2 She warns that there may be .... and that the path can be ....

3 He's worried that there will be a lot of .... and there may be ....

4 He warns that the cliffs are .... and there may be ....

GRAMMAR *Too* + adjective and infinitive

> **Use <u>too</u> + an adjective and an infinitive to give a warning or an explanation.**
> It's **too dark to go** hiking now. = Don't go hiking now because it's dark.
> Those cliffs are **too steep to climb**. = You shouldn't climb those cliffs because they're very steep.
>
> **Use a <u>for</u> phrase to further clarify a warning or explanation.**
> It's too dangerous **for children** to go swimming there. (Only adults should swim there.)

GRAMMAR BOOSTER p. 145
• Infinitives with <u>enough</u>

GRAMMAR PRACTICE   Complete the sentences, using <u>too</u> + an adjective
and a <u>for</u> phrase + an infinitive.

1 It's .... to that neighborhood alone.
              dangerous / you / go

2 The pyramid at Teotihuacán is ....
                               steep / older tourists / climb

3 It's .... the last train to the capital.
         late / your friends / catch

4 The path is .... safely.
            rocky / your children / walk on

5 It's really .... hiking to the waterfall today.
              hot / us / go

6 Don't you think this map is .... ?
                    confusing / them / understand

CONVERSATION MODEL

A ▶5:35 Read and listen to someone warning about a risk.

A: Excuse me. Can you tell me the way to the beach?

B: That way. It's not very far.

A: Thanks. Is it safe to go swimming there?

B: Sure, but be careful. There's sometimes an undertow.

A: Really?

B: Well, it's too dangerous for children to go swimming there. But I'm sure you'll be fine.

A: Thanks for the warning.

B ▶5:36 **RHYTHM AND INTONATION**   Listen again and repeat. Then practice the Conversation Model with a partner.

undertow

NOW YOU CAN   Warn about a possible risk

A **CONVERSATION ACTIVATOR**   With a partner, change the Conversation Model. Ask for directions to another place. Warn about possible risks. Then change roles.

A: Excuse me. Can you tell me the way to .... ?
B: ....
A: Thanks. Is it safe to .... there?
B: ....

B **CHANGE PARTNERS**   Warn about another place.

Places to go
a waterfall
a path
a cave
a beach
cliffs
a volcano
a national park

Things to do
go swimming
go hiking
go climbing
go biking
go skiing

DON'T STOP!
• **Ask for more information.**
Do I need to watch out for [jellyfish / sharks]?
Are there a lot of [snakes / bears]?
Is the path very [steep / rocky / slippery]?
[Is it / Are they] worth seeing?

• **Warn about other risks.**
Watch out for [scorpions].
It's too [dangerous / dark] [for __] to __ there.

BEFORE YOU LISTEN

DIGITAL FLASH CARDS

A ▶5:37 **VOCABULARY • *Describing natural features*** Read and listen. Then listen again and repeat.

▶5:38 **Strong positive adjectives**
The scenery was **breathtaking**.
The views were **spectacular**.
The sights were **extraordinary**.

Geographic nouns

a forest a jungle a valley a canyon an island a glacier

Geographic adjectives

mountainous hilly flat dry / arid lush / green

B PAIR WORK Talk about places you know, using the nouns and adjectives from the Vocabulary.

" The north of this country is pretty flat and arid, but in the south it's really mountainous. The green valleys and forests are spectacular. "

LISTENING COMPREHENSION

A ▶5:39 **LISTEN FOR MAIN IDEAS** Read the questions. Listen to a description of a memorable trip and answer the questions.

1 What country did Mr. Yamagichi visit?
   a the U.S. **b** Australia **c** Canada **d** the U.K.

2 What kind of place did he visit?
   a a park **b** a beach **c** an island **d** a jungle

3 What activity did he and his wife do the most?
   a go skiing **b** go swimming **c** go hiking **d** go hang gliding

4 What geographical adjective best describes this place?
   a flat **b** arid **c** hilly **d** mountainous

Mitsuhiko Yamagichi

B ▶5:40 **LISTEN FOR DETAILS** Listen again and pay attention to how Mr. Yamagichi describes what he saw on his trip. Complete each phrase with a word from the box.

air	lake
canyon	mountains
cliffs	path
forests	views
glacier	water
hotel	waterfalls

1 amazing ....

2 breathtaking ....

3 extraordinary ....

4 famous ....

5 fantastic ....

6 fresh, clean ....

7 slippery ....

8 spectacular ....

C **PAIR WORK** With a partner, summarize Mr. Yamagichi's trip in your own words by restating key details. Listen again if necessary.

NOW YOU CAN Describe a natural setting

A **FRAME YOUR IDEAS** Choose a photo. Describe the place and what a person could do there. Your partner guesses which place you chose.

Tahiti

❝ It's a lush island in a beautiful ocean. You can lie on the beach and do nothing or go snorkeling. ❞

Yellow Mountain, China

The Galapagos Islands, Ecuador

Iguazu Falls, Brazil and Argentina

Alaska

B **NOTEPADDING** On your notepad, write about a spectacular place you know or a place you'd like to visit. What does it look like? What can you do there?

Name of place:	Things you can do there:
Description:	

C **PAIR WORK** Tell your partner about the place you wrote about on your notepad. Use the Vocabulary.

RECYCLE THIS LANGUAGE.

It's in the [north] / on the [coast].
It's located on the [Orinoco River].
It's located on the [shore / east coast] of [Lake Victoria].
It's south of ___.
It's in the central part of ___.
It's a must-see.

You don't want to miss it.
[Bash Bish Falls] is overrated, but [Niagara Falls] is breathtaking.
[Saw Valley] is a waste of time, but [Pine Valley] is extraordinary.
It's very [rocky / steep / slippery].

GOAL Discuss solutions to global warming

BEFORE YOU READ

A ▶ 5:41 **VOCABULARY** • *Energy and the environment* Read and listen. Then listen again and repeat.

the environment *n.* the air, water, and land in which people, animals, and plants live

pollution *n.* the act of causing air, water, or land to become dirty and unhealthy for people, animals, and plants

climate change *n.* a long-term change in the Earth's temperatures and weather patterns

power *n.* electricity or other force that can be used to make machines, cars, etc., work

renewable energy *n.* power from natural resources, such as wind power or solar power (from the sun), that is continually available for human use

energy-efficient *adj.* using as little power as possible

> ▶ 5:42 **Stress in verbs and nouns**
> **increase** *v.* to become larger in amount
>   **an increase** in [temperature] *n.*
> **decrease** *v.* to become smaller in amount
>   **a decrease** in [pollution] *n.*

B **DISCUSSION** What do you already know about global warming? What causes it? What effect is it having on the environment?

READING ▶ 5:43

Choose Clean Energy and Help Curb Global Warming

Fossil fuels such as oil, coal, and natural gas provide energy for our cars and homes, but increase the amount of carbon dioxide (CO_2) in the air, contributing to climate change in the form of global warming. However, there are choices we can make that can lessen their negative impact on the environment.

Get moving—Take good care of your car and keep your tires properly inflated with air. You will use less gasoline and save money. Better yet, skip the drive and walk, take public transportation, or ride a bicycle when you can.

Upgrade—Replace your old refrigerator or air conditioner with a new energy-efficient model. Not only will you save money on your electric bill, but you'll contribute to cutting back on the pollution that causes global warming.

See the light—Use new energy-saving compact fluorescent light bulbs. They produce the same amount of light as older incandescent bulbs, but they use 75% less electricity and last much longer.

Cut back—Try to reduce the amount of water you use for showers, laundry, and washing dishes. And turn the temperature on your hot water heater down.

Recycle—Use products that are recycled from old paper, glass, and metal to reduce energy waste and pollution by 70 to 90%. And before you toss things in the garbage, think about what you can reuse.

Think local—Shipping foods over long distances is a waste of energy and adds to pollution. In addition, the pesticides and chemicals used to grow them are bad for the environment. So buy locally grown fruits and vegetables instead.

Speak out—Talk to lawmakers about your interest in curbing global warming. Support their attempts to improve standards for fuel efficiency, to fund renewable and clean energy solutions, such as wind and solar power, and to protect forests.

The effects of global warming

- An increase in floods, droughts, tornadoes, and other extreme weather conditions
- A rise in sea levels, causing flooding in coastal areas
- Higher sea surface temperatures, endangering sea life
- The shrinking of glaciers, leading to a decrease in fresh water for rivers and less energy production
- A loss of tropical forests, an increase in arid lands, more forest fires, and a loss of animal and plant species
- A decrease in agricultural yields, leading to famine

Clean, renewable energy solutions like wind power can help curb global warming.

Compact fluorescent light bulbs use less electricity.

A **UNDERSTAND FROM CONTEXT** Find and underline each of the following words or phrases in the Reading. Then use your understanding of the words to write definitions.

1 fossil fuels ....

2 global warming ....

3 inflated ....

4 reduce ....

5 curbing ....

6 a rise ....

B **CRITICAL THINKING** Discuss the questions.

1 The article mentions fossil fuels as a major source of energy. What two other sources of energy are mentioned? How are they different from fossil fuels?

2 Look at the list of the effects of global warming in the Reading. What impact could they have on these aspects of your country's economy: tourism, food production, housing, and disaster relief?

DIGITAL MORE EXERCISES **C** **SUMMARIZE** Review the Reading again. Then close your book. With a partner, discuss and make a list of the ways the Reading suggests you can help curb global warming.

NOW YOU CAN Discuss solutions to global warming

A **NOTEPADDING** What do you do in your daily life that might contribute to the energy waste and pollution that causes global warming? Make a list on your notepad.

at home:
at work:
at school:
in transportation:
other:

C **DISCUSSION** Do you agree with the suggestions in the Reading? Discuss the value of trying to take personal actions to help curb global warming. Talk about:

• what you are doing now.
• what you'd like to do in the future.
• what you think is not worth doing.

RECYCLE THIS LANGUAGE.

Are you in favor of __?
I think / don't think it's a good idea to __.
I'm against __.
That's true, but __.
I see what you mean, but __.
Well, on the one hand, __. But, on the other hand, __.
That's one way to look at it, but __.
That depends.
We'll have to agree to disagree.

Text-mining (optional)
Find and underline three words or phrases in the Reading that were new to you. Use them in your Discussion.
    For example: "a waste of energy."

B **PAIR WORK** Compare notepads with a partner. Discuss what you think each of you could do to help cut down on energy waste and pollution.

❝ I don't really recycle everything I can right now, but I'd like to. I think it would be better for the environment if I did. ❞

❝ I want to buy energy-efficient light bulbs, but they're more expensive than the regular kind. ❞

GLASS

PLASTIC

PAPER

META

REVIEW

A ▶ 5:44 Listen to the conversations. Write the type of place each person is talking about, choosing words from the box. Then check whether or not the person recommends going there.

a canyon	a desert	an island	a volcano
a cave	a glacier	a valley	a waterfall

Type of place	Recommended?	Type of place	Recommended?
1	☐ yes ☐ no	3	☐ yes ☐ no
2	☐ yes ☐ no	4	☐ yes ☐ no

B Look at the pictures. Complete the warnings about each danger, using <u>too</u>.

1  2  3  4

1 That road .... to ride on if you're not careful.

2 Those steps .... climb safely after a rain.

3 .... go in the cave without a flashlight.

4 .... go swimming in the bay.

C Complete the locations, using the map.

1 The town of Saint-Pierre is .... the shore .... the island of Saint-Pierre.

2 Grand Barachois Bay .... the village of Miquelon.

3 The island of Saint-Pierre .... Langlade.

4 The village of Miquelon .... about .... from the town of Saint-Pierre.

5 The beaches .... the .... coast.

WRITING

Write a description of your country, state, or province. Include the location and description of major cities, geographical features, national parks, and other points of interest. Use adjectives to provide details that help the reader see and feel what the places are like.

quiet / noisy	humid / foggy	spectacular
crowded	dry / arid	breathtaking
hot / warm	lush / green	extraordinary
cold / cool	steep / rocky	beautiful
mountainous	high / low	gorgeous
flat / hilly	green / blue	unique

[Map showing: Village of Miquelon, Miquelon, St. Lawrence Gulf, Grand Barachois Bay, the beaches, Langlade, Island of Saint-Pierre, Town of Saint-Pierre, North Atlantic Ocean. Scale: 0 5 10 kilometers / 0 5 10 miles. Compass N S E W]

WRITING BOOSTER p. 153
- Organizing by spatial relations
- Guidance for this writing exercise

For additional language practice . . .

🎵 TOP NOTCH **POP** • Lyrics p. 155
"It's a Beautiful World"

DIGITAL SONG   DIGITAL KARAOKE

ORAL REVIEW

GAME Using the map and the pictures, describe a location or natural features. Your classmates guess the place. For example:

It's located south of Denali National Park. **OR** *It has spectacular glaciers.*

PAIR WORK Use the map and the "Explore Alaska!" chart to create conversations for the man and the woman. Start like this:

Where exactly is __? **OR** *Excuse me. Could you tell me the way to __?*

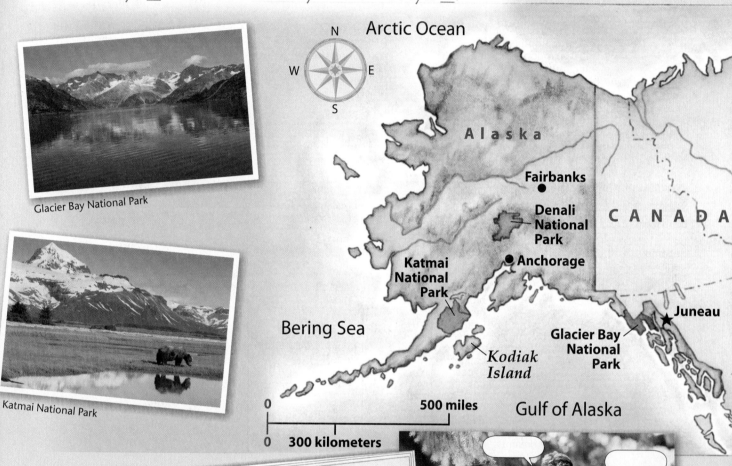

Glacier Bay National Park

Katmai National Park

Explore Alaska!

	bears	mosquitos	snakes	fog
Denali National Park	✓	✓	✗	✓
Kodiak Island	✓	✓	✗	✓
Katmai National Park	✓	✓	✗	✗
Glacier Bay National Park	✗	✗	✗	✓

✔ NOW I CAN

☐ Describe a geographical location.
☐ Warn about a possible risk.
☐ Describe a natural setting.
☐ Discuss solutions to global warming.

Reference Charts

PRONUNCIATION TABLE

Vowels			Consonants			
Symbol	**Key Words**		**Symbol**	**Key Words**	**Symbol**	**Key Words**
i	b**ea**t, f**ee**d		p	**p**ack, ha**pp**y	z	**z**ip, plea**s**e, goe**s**
ɪ	b**i**t, d**i**d		b	**b**ack, ru**bb**er	ʃ	**sh**ip, ma**ch**ine, **s**ta**ti**on,
eɪ	d**a**te, p**ai**d		t	**t**ie		**s**pe**ci**al, di**s**cu**ss**ion
ɛ	b**e**t, b**e**d		d	**d**ie	ʒ	mea**s**ure, vi**s**ion
æ	b**a**t, b**a**d		k	**c**ame, **k**ey, **q**ui**ck**	h	**h**ot, **wh**o
ɑ	b**o**x, **o**dd, f**a**ther		g	**g**ame, **g**uest	m	**m**en
ɔ	b**ou**ght, d**o**g		tʃ	**ch**urch, na**t**ure, wa**tch**	n	su**n**, **kn**ow, **pn**eumonia
oʊ	b**oa**t, r**oa**d		dʒ	**j**udge, **g**eneral, ma**j**or	ŋ	su**ng**, ri**ng**i**ng**
ʊ	b**oo**k, g**oo**d		f	**f**an, **ph**otogra**ph**	w	**w**et, **wh**ite
u	b**oo**t, f**oo**d, fl**u**		v	**v**an	l	**l**ight, **l**ong
ʌ	b**u**t, m**u**d, m**o**ther		θ	**th**ing, brea**th**	r	**r**ight, **wr**ong
ə	b**a**n**a**n**a**, **a**mong		ð	**th**en, brea**the**	y	**y**es
ɚ	sh**ir**t, m**ur**der		s	**s**ip, **c**ity, p**s**ychology		
aɪ	b**i**te, cr**y**, b**uy**, **eye**		ṭ	bu**tt**er, bo**tt**le		
aʊ	**a**bout, h**ow**		tˀ	bu**tt**on		
ɔɪ	v**oi**ce, b**oy**					
ɪr	d**eer**					
ɛr	b**are**					
ɑr	b**ar**					
ɔr	d**oor**					
ʊr	t**our**					

IRREGULAR VERBS

base form	simple past	past participle	base form	simple past	past participle
be	was / were	been	lend	lent	lent
become	became	become	let	let	let
begin	began	begun	lose	lost	lost
bite	bit	bit / bitten	make	made	made
bleed	bled	bled	mean	meant	meant
break	broke	broken	meet	met	met
bring	brought	brought	pay	paid	paid
build	built	built	put	put	put
burn	burned / burnt	burned / burnt	quit	quit	quit
buy	bought	bought	read /rid/	read /rɛd/	read /rɛd/
catch	caught	caught	ride	rode	ridden
choose	chose	chosen	ring	rang	rung
come	came	come	rise	rose	risen
cost	cost	cost	run	ran	run
cut	cut	cut	say	said	said
do	did	done	see	saw	seen
draw	drew	drawn	sell	sold	sold
dream	dreamed / dreamt	dreamed / dreamt	send	sent	sent
drink	drank	drunk	sew	sewed	sewn
drive	drove	driven	shake	shook	shaken
eat	ate	eaten	sing	sang	sung
fall	fell	fallen	sit	sat	sat
feed	fed	fed	sleep	slept	slept
feel	felt	felt	speak	spoke	spoken
fight	fought	fought	spend	spent	spent
find	found	found	spread	spread	spread
fit	fit	fit	stand	stood	stood
flee	fled	fled	steal	stole	stolen
fly	flew	flown	stick	stuck	stuck
forbid	forbade	forbidden	sting	stung	stung
forget	forgot	forgotten	strike	struck	struck
get	got	gotten	swim	swam	swum
give	gave	given	take	took	taken
go	went	gone	teach	taught	taught
grow	grew	grown	tell	told	told
have	had	had	think	thought	thought
hear	heard	heard	throw	threw	thrown
hit	hit	hit	understand	understood	understood
hold	held	held	wake up	woke up	woken up
hurt	hurt	hurt	wear	wore	worn
keep	kept	kept	win	won	won
know	knew	known	write	wrote	written
leave	left	left			

1 THE PRESENT OF <u>BE</u>

Statements

I	am / am not	
You We They	are / aren't	late.
He She It	is / isn't	

2 THE SIMPLE PRESENT TENSE

Statements

I You We They	speak / don't speak	English.
He She	speaks / doesn't speak	English.

Yes / no questions

Do / Don't	I you we they	know	them?
Does / Doesn't	he she	eat	meat?

Short answers

Yes,	I you we they	do.
	he she it	does.

No,	I you we they	don't.
	he she it	doesn't.

Information questions

What	do	I you we they	need?
When	does	he she it	start?
Who	does	she	like?
Who		wants needs likes	this book?

3 THE PRESENT CONTINUOUS

Statements

I	am	watching TV.
You We They	are	studying English.
He She It	is	arriving now.

Yes / no questions

Am	I	
Are	you we they	going too fast?
Is	he she it	

Short answers

Yes,	I	am.
	you	are.
	he she it	is.
	you we they	are.

No,	I'm not.
	you aren't / you're not.
	he isn't / he's not.
	she isn't / she's not.
	it isn't / it's not.
	you aren't / you're not.
	we aren't / we're not.
	they aren't / they're not.

Information questions

What	are	you we they	doing?
When	is	he she it	leaving?
Where	am	I	staying tonight?
Who	is		driving?

4 THE PAST CONTINUOUS

Statements

I	was / wasn't	singing that song.
You We They	were / weren't	playing the piano.
He She It	was /wasn't	leaving from Central Station.

Yes / no questions

Was	I he she it	
Were	we you they	landing in Sydney when the storm began?

(The past continuous–continued)

Short answers

Yes,	I he she it	was.		No,	I he she it	wasn't.
	we you they	were.			we you they	weren't.

Information questions

When	was	I he she	speeding?
Where	were	we you they	going?
Who	was		arriving?

5 THE PAST OF <u>BE</u>

Statements

I He She It	was	late.
We You They	were	early.

<u>Yes</u> / <u>no</u> questions

Was	I he she it	on time?
Were	we you they	in the same class?

Short answers

Yes,	I he she it	was.		No,	I he she it	wasn't.
	we you they	were.			we you they	weren't.

Information questions

Where	were	we? you? they?	
When	was	he she it	here?
Who	were	they?	
Who	was	he? she? it?	

6 THE SIMPLE PAST TENSE

Many verbs are irregular in the simple past tense.
See the list of irregular verbs on page 122.

Statements

I You He She It We They	stopped / didn't stop	working.

<u>Yes</u> / <u>no</u> questions

Did	I you he she we they	make a good dinner?

Short answers

Yes,	I you he she it we they	did.
No,		didn't

Information questions

When	did	I you he she we they	read that?
Who	did	they	see?
Who			called?

7 THE FUTURE WITH <u>WILL</u>

Affirmative and negative statements

I You He She It We They	will / won't	stop at five o-clock.

<u>Yes</u> / <u>no</u> questions

Will	I you he she It we they	be on time?

Affirmative and negative short answers

Yes,	I you he	will.
No,	she it we they	won't

Information questions

What will	I you he she it we they	do?
Who will		be there?

8   THE FUTURE WITH <u>BE GOING TO</u>

Statements

I'm You're He's She's It's We're They're	going to / not going to	be here soon.

Yes / <u>no</u> questions

Are	you we they	going to	want coffee?
Am	I	going to	be late?
Is	he she it	going to	arrive on time?

Short answers

Yes	I	am.
	you	are.
	he she it	is.
	you we they	are.

No,	I'm not.
	you aren't / you're not.
	he isn't / he's not. she isn't / she's not. it isn't / it's not.
	you aren't / you're not we aren't / we're not. they aren't / they're not.

Information questions

What	are	you we they	going to	see?
When	is	he she it	going to	stop?
Where	am	I	going to	stay tomorrow?
Who	is		going to	call?

9   THE PRESENT PERFECT

Affirmative and negative short answers

I You We They	have / haven't	left.
He She It	has / hasn't	

<u>Yes</u> / <u>no</u> questions

Have	I you we they	said enough?
Has	he she it	already started?

Affirmative and negative short answers

Yes,	I you	have.
No,	we they	haven't.
Yes,	he	has.
No,	she it	hasn't.

Information questions

Where	have	I you we they	seen the book?
How	has	he she it	been?
Who	has		read it?

10   THE PASSIVE VOICE

Form the passive voice with a form of <u>be</u> and the past participle of the verb		
	ACTIVE VOICE	**PASSIVE VOICE**
simple present	Art collectors **buy** famous paintings	Famous paintings **are bought** by art collectors.
present continous	The Cineplex **is showing** that film.	That film **is being shown** by the Cineplex.
present perfect	All the critic **have reviewed** that book.	That book **has been reviewed** by all the critics.
simple past	Vera Wang **designed** this dress.	This dress **was designed** by Vera Wang.
past continous	Last year, World Air **was** still **selling** tours to the Ivory Coast.	Last year, tours to the Ivory Coast **were** still **being sold**.
future with <u>will</u>	The children **will return** the books tomorrow.	The books **will be returned** tomorrow.
<u>be going to</u>	Bar's Garage **is going to repair** my car this afternoon.	My car **is going to be repaired** by Bart's Garage this afternoon.

GERUNDS AND INFINITIVES

Verbs followed by a gerund

acknowledge	delay	escape	keep	propose	risk
admit	deny	explain	mention	quit	suggest
advise	detest	feel like	mind	recall	support
appreciate	discontinue	finish	miss	recommend	tolerate
avoid	discuss	forgive	postpone	report	understand
can't help	dislike	give up	practice	resent	
celebrate	endure	imagine	prevent	resist	
consider	enjoy	justify	prohibit		

Verbs followed directly by an infinitive

afford	choose	hesitate	need	promise	volunteer
agree	consent	hope	neglect	refuse	wait
appear	decide	hurry	offer	request	want
arrange	deserve	intend	pay	seem	wish
ask	expect	learn	plan	struggle	would like
attempt	fail	manage	prepare	swear	yearn
can't wait	grow	mean	pretend		

Verbs followed by an object before an infinitive*

advise	convince	get*	order	remind	urge
allow	enable	help*	pay	request	warn
ask*	encourage	hire	permit	require	want*
cause	expect*	invite	persuade	teach	wish*
challenge	forbid	need*	promise*	tell	would like*
choose*	force				

* In the active voice, these verbs can also be followed by the infinitive without an object (example: *want to speak* or *want someone to speak*).

Verbs followed by either a gerund or an infinitive

begin	hate	remember*
can't stand	like	start
continue	love	stop*
forget*	prefer	try*
	regret	

* There is a complete difference in meaning when these verbs are followed by a gerund or an infinitive.
I forgot **closing** the window. (= I forgot that I did it.)
I forgot **to close** the window. (= I didn't do it because I forgot.)

I remembered **locking** the door. (= I have a memory of having locked it.)
I remembered **to lock** the door. (= I didn't forget to lock it.)

I stopped **smoking**. (= I stopped the habit.)
I stopped **to smoke**. (= I stopped what I was doing in order to smoke.)

Adjectives followed by an infinitive*

afraid	curious	disturbed	fortunate	pleased	shocked
alarmed	delighted	eager	glad	proud	sorry
amazed	depressed	easy	happy	ready	surprised
angry	determined	embarrassed	hesitant	relieved	touched
anxious	disappointed	encouraged	likely	reluctant	upset
ashamed	distressed	excited	lucky	sad	willing

* EXAMPLE: I'm willing **to accept** that.

Grammar Booster

The Grammar Booster is optional. It offers more information and extra practice. Sometimes it further explains or expands the unit grammar and points out common errors. In other cases, it reviews and practices previously learned grammar that would be helpful when learning new grammar concepts. If you use the Grammar Booster, you will find extra exercises in the Workbook in a separate section labeled Grammar Booster. The Grammar Booster content is not tested on any *Top Notch* tests.

UNIT 1   Lesson 1

Tag questions: short answers

Tag questions are <u>yes</u> / <u>no</u> questions and they can be answered with short answers. The short answers to tag questions, like the short answers to all <u>yes</u> / <u>no</u> questions, use the same tense or modal as the question. Following are the short answers to the tag questions from page 4.

	Short answers
You're Lee, **aren't you?**	Yes, I am. / No, I'm not.
You're not Amy, **are you?**	Yes, I am. / No, I'm not.
She speaks Thai, **doesn't she?**	Yes, she does. / No, she doesn't.
I don't know you, **do I?**	Yes, you do. / No, you don't.
He's going to drive, **isn't he?**	Yes, he is. / No, he isn't.
We're not going to eat here, **are we?**	Yes, we are. / No, we aren't.
They'll be here later, **won't they?**	Yes, they will. / No, they won't.
It won't be long, **will it?**	Yes, it will. / No, it won't.
There are a lot of rules, **aren't there?**	Yes, there are. / No, there aren't.
He wasn't driving, **was he?**	Yes, he was. / No, he wasn't.
There isn't any sugar, **is there?**	Yes, there is. / No, there isn't.
We didn't know, **did we?**	Yes, you did. / No, you didn't.
You were there, **weren't you?**	Yes, I was. / No, I wasn't.
She hasn't been here long, **has she?**	Yes, she has. / No, she hasn't.
They left, **didn't they?**	Yes, they did. / No, they didn't.
You wouldn't do that, **would you?**	Yes, I would. / No, I wouldn't.
It's been a great day, **hasn't it?**	Yes, it has. / No, it hasn't.
He can't speak Japanese, **can he?**	Yes, he can. / No, he can't.
Ann would like Quito, **wouldn't she?**	Yes, she would. / No, she wouldn't.
They can hear me, **can't they?**	Yes, they can. / No, they can't.

A Complete each conversation by circling the correct tag question and completing the short answer.

1 A: Mary would like to study foreign cultures, (would / wouldn't) she?

    B: Yes, ...

2 A: It's a long time until dinner, (is / isn't) it?

    B: No, ...

3 A: We met last summer, (did / didn't) we?

    B: Yes, ...

4 A: They're starting the meeting really late, (haven't / aren't) they?

    B: No, ...

5 A: There weren't too many delays in the meeting, (wasn't it / were there)?

    B: No, ...

6 A: You don't know what to do, (do / don't) you?

    B: No, ...

7 A: There isn't any reason to call, (is / isn't) there?

    B: No, ...

8 A: It's awful to not have time for lunch, (isn't it / aren't you)?

    B: Yes, ...

9 A: When you know etiquette, you can feel comfortable anywhere, (can / can't) you?

    B: Yes, ...

10 A: It's really getting late, (is it / isn't it)?

    B: No, ...

B Correct the error in each item.

1 They'd both like to study abroad, ~~would~~ they? *(handwritten: wouldn't)*
2 It's only a six-month course, is it?
3 Clark met his wife on a rafting trip, didn't Clark?
4 Marian made three trips to Japan last year, hasn't she?
5 There were a lot of English-speaking people on the tour, wasn't it?
6 The students don't know anything about that, don't they?
7 There isn't any problem with my student visa, isn't there?
8 It's always interesting to travel with people from other countries, aren't they?
9 With English, you can travel to most parts of the world, can you?
10 I'm next, don't I?

UNIT 1 *Lesson 2*

Verb usage: present and past (overview)

Use the simple present tense (but NOT the present continuous):
- **for facts and regular occurrences**
  I study English. Class meets every day. Water boils at 100 degrees Celsius.
- **with frequency adverbs and time expressions**
  They never eat before 6:00 on weekdays.
- **with stative ("non-action") verbs**
  I remember her now.
- **for future actions, especially those indicating schedules**
  Flight 100 usually leaves at 2:00, but tomorrow it leaves at 1:30.

Use the present continuous (but NOT the simple present tense):
- **for actions happening now (but NOT with stative or non-action verbs)**
  They're talking on the phone.
- **for actions occurring during a time period in the present**
  This year I'm studying English.
- **for some future actions, especially those already planned**
  Thursday I'm going to the theater.

Use the present perfect or the present perfect continuous:
- **for unfinished or continuous actions**
  I've lived here since 2012. OR I've been living here since 2012.
  We've lived here for five years. OR We've been living here for five years.

Use the present perfect (but NOT the present perfect continuous):
- **for completed or non-continuing actions**
  I've eaten there three times.
  I've never read that book.
  I've already seen him.

Use the simple past tense:
- **for actions completed at a specified time in the past**
  I ate there in 2010. NOT ~~I've eaten~~ there in 2010.

Use the past continuous:
- **for one or more actions in progress at a time in the past**
  At 7:00, we were eating dinner.
  They were swimming, and we were sitting on the beach.

Use the past continuous and the simple past tense:
- **for a continuing action in the past that was interrupted**
  I was eating when my sister called.

Use <u>use to</u> / <u>used to</u>:
- **for past situations and habits that no longer exist**
  I used to smoke, but I stopped.
  They didn't use to require a visa, but now they do.

Use the past perfect:
- **to indicate that one past action preceded another past action.**
  When I arrived, they had finished lunch.

Stative (non-action) verbs

appear	notice
be	own
believe	possess
belong	prefer
contain	remember
cost	see
feel	seem
hate	smell
have	sound
hear	suppose
know	taste
like	think
look	understand
love	want
need	weigh

A Correct the verbs in the sentences.

1 I talk on the phone with my fiancé right now.
2 She's usually avoiding sweets.
3 They eat dinner now and can't talk on the phone.
4 Every Friday I'm going to the gym at 7:00.
5 Burt is wanting to go home early.

6 Today we all study in the library.
7 The train is never leaving before 8:00.
8 Water is freezing when the temperature goes down.
9 We're liking coffee.
10 On most days I'm staying home.

B Complete each sentence with the present perfect continuous.

1 We .... to this spa for two years.
　　　　　come

2 *Life of Pi* .... at the Classic Cinema since last Saturday.
　　　　　　　　play

3 Robert .... for an admissions letter from the language school for a week.
　　　　　wait

4 The tour operators .... weather conditions for the rafting trip.
　　　　　　　　worry about

5 He .... that tour with everyone.
　　　　talk about

C Check the sentences and questions that express unfinished or continuing actions. Then, on a separate sheet of paper, change the verb phrase in those sentences to the present perfect continuous.

The Averys have lived in New York since the late nineties.

The Averys have been living in New York since the late nineties.

☐ 1 Their relatives have already called them.
☐ 2 We have waited to see them for six months.
☐ 3 I haven't seen the Berlin Philharmonic yet.
☐ 4 This is the first time I've visited Dubai.
☐ 5 We have eaten at that old Peruvian restaurant for years.

☐ 6 Has he ever met your father?
☐ 7 How long have they studied Arabic?
☐ 8 My husband still hasn't bought a car.
☐ 9 The kids have just come back from the soccer game.

UNIT 2 *Lesson 1*

Draw conclusions with *probably* and *most likely*

You can draw conclusions with less certainty than *must* by using *probably* or *most likely*.

Probably and *most likely* frequently occur after the verb *be* or when *be* is part of a verb phrase.
　They're probably (OR They're most likely) at the dentist's office.
　It's probably (OR It's most likely) going to rain.

> **Be careful!** Don't use *probably* or *most likely* after verbs other than *be*.
> Don't say: He ~~forgot probably~~ about the appointment.
> Don't say: He ~~forgot most likely~~ about the appointment.

Use *probably* or *most likely* before *isn't* or *aren't*. With *is not* or *are not*, use *probably* before *not*.
　She probably (OR They're most likely) isn't feeling well.
　She's probably (OR It's most likely) not feeling well.

Use *probably* or *most likely* before other verbs.
　He probably (OR most likely) forgot about the appointment.
　The dentist probably (OR most likely) doesn't have time to see a new patient.

You can also use *Probably* or *Most likely* at the beginning of a sentence to draw a conclusion.
　Probably (OR Most likely) she's a teacher.
　Probably (OR Most likely) he forgot about the appointment.

On a separate sheet of paper, rewrite each sentence with *probably* or *most likely*.

1 He must have a terrible cold.
2 She must be feeling very nauseous.
3 They must not like going to the dentist.

4 The dentist must not be in her office today.
5 Acupuncture must be very popular in Asia.
6 A conventional doctor must have to study for a long time.

Expressing possibility with *maybe*

Maybe most frequently occurs at the beginning of a sentence.
> **Maybe** he'll need an X-ray. (= He may need an X-ray.)

> **Be careful!** **Don't confuse** <u>maybe</u> and <u>may be</u>.
> She **may be** a doctor.
> NOT She ~~maybe~~ a doctor.
> **Maybe** she's a doctor.
> NOT ~~May be~~ she's a doctor.

On a separate sheet of paper, rewrite each sentence with <u>maybe</u>.

1 His doctor may use herbal therapy.

2 Conventional medicine may be the best choice.

3 The doctor may want to take a blood test.

4 She may prefer to wait until tomorrow.

5 They may be afraid to see a dentist.

Causative *make* to indicate obligation

The causative <u>make</u> is used to express the idea that one person forces another to do something. Use a form of <u>make</u> + an object and the base form of a verb.

	object	base form	
They **make**	their kids	finish	their homework before dinner.
She **made**	him	sign	the form.

A Complete the statements and questions, using the causative <u>make</u>. Use the correct form of <u>make</u>.

1 Yesterday, ... (Nick's mother / make / apologize / him) for his mistake.

2 .... (you / be going to / make / tell / your friends) the truth?

3 .... (our teacher / might / make / turn off / us) our phones.

4 .... (we / should / make / pay / your sister) for dinner?

5 .... (no one / not can / make / come / Gail) to the meeting if she doesn't want to.

6 If you go to that restaurant, ... (they / will / your husband / make / wear) a tie.

7 The movie was awful! .... (we / can / make / give / the theater) our money back?

Let to indicate permission

Use an object and the base form of a verb with <u>let</u>.
>   object   base form
> She **let** her sister **wear** her favorite skirt.

<u>Let</u> has the same meaning as <u>permit</u>. Use <u>let</u> to indicate that permission is being given to do something.
> My boss **let** me **take** the day off.
> I **don't let** my children **stay** out after 9:00 P.M.

> **Be careful!**
> Don't say: She let her sister ~~to wear~~
>   her favorite skirt
> Don't use an infinitive after <u>let</u>.

B On a separate sheet of paper, rewrite each sentence, using <u>let</u>.

1 Don't permit your younger brother to open the oven door.

2 You should permit your little sister to go to the store with you.

3 We don't permit our daughter to eat a lot of candy.

4 I wouldn't permit my youngest son to go to the mall alone.

5 Will you permit your children to see that movie?

6 You should permit them to make their own decision.

7 We always permit him to stay out late.

Causative *have*: common errors

Be careful! Don't confuse the simple past tense causative <u>have</u> with the past perfect auxiliary have.
I **had** them **call** me before 10:00.   (They called me.)
I **had called** them before 10:00.   (I called them.)

C Who did what? Read each sentence. Complete each statement. Follow the example.

We had them fix the car before our trip.   ....*They*.. fixed .*the car*..
We had fixed the car before our trip.   ...*We*.... fixed .*the car*..

1 Janet had already called her mother.   .... called ....
   Janet had her mother call the train station.   .... called ....

2 Mark had his friends help him with moving.   .... helped ....
   Mark had helped his friends with moving.   .... helped ....

3 My father had signed the check for his boss.   .... signed ....
   My father had his boss sign the check.   .... signed ....

4 Mr. Gates had them open the bank early.   .... opened ....
   Mr. Gates had opened the bank early.   .... opened ....

UNIT 3 Lesson 2

The passive causative: the *by* phrase

Use a <u>by</u> phrase to add specific or important information. If knowing who performed the action is not important, you don't need to include a <u>by</u> phrase.
I had my dress shortened **by someone** at the shop next to the train station. (not necessary)
I had my luggage delivered to my room **by someone at the hotel front desk.** (specific information)

On a separate sheet of paper, use the cues to write advice about services, using <u>You should</u> and the passive causative <u>get</u> or <u>have</u>. Use a <u>by</u> phrase if the information is specific or important.

   shoe / repair / Mr. B / at the Boot Stop
   You should get your shoes repaired by Mr. B at the Boot Stop.

1 picture / frame / Lydia / at Austin Custom Framing
2 hair / cut / one of the great hairdressers / at the Curl Up Hair Salon
3 photos / print / someone / at the mall
4 a suit / make / Luigi / at Top Notch Tailors
5 sweaters / dry-clean / someone / at Midtown Dry Cleaners

UNIT 4 Lesson 1

Verbs that can be followed by noun clauses with *that*

The following verbs often have noun clauses as their direct objects. Notice that each verb expresses a kind of "mental activity." In each case, it is optional to include <u>that</u>.

She	agrees thinks believes feels	(that) the students should work harder.	I	assume suppose doubt guess	(that) they made reservations.
We	hear see understand hope	(that) the government has a new plan.	He	forgot noticed realized remembered knew	(that) the stores weren't open.
They	decided discovered dreamed hoped learned	(that) everyone could pass the test.			

Adjectives that can be followed by clauses with *that*

Use a clause with *that* after a predicate adjective of emotion to futher explain its meaning.

I'm	afraid angry	(that) we'll have to leave early.		He's	sorry unhappy	(that) the flight was canceled.
We're	worried ashamed	(that) we won't be on time to the event.		She's	surprised disappointed	(that) the news spread so fast.
They're	happy sad	(that) the teacher is leaving.				

On a separate sheet of paper, complete each sentence in your own way. Use clauses with *that*.

1 When I was young, I couldn't believe . . .
2 Last year, I decided . . .
3 This year, I was surprised to discover . . .
4 I'm really happy . . .
5 Last week, I forgot . . .
6 Recently, I heard . . .
7 In the future, I hope . . .

8 Now that I study English, I know . . .
9 In the last year, I learned . . .
10 Not long ago, I remembered . . .
11 Sometimes I'm worried . . .
12 Recently, I dreamed . . .
13 (Your own idea)
14 (Your own idea)

UNIT 4 Lesson 2

Embedded questions with *whether*

You can also use *whether* to begin embedded *yes* / *no* questions. *Whether* has the same meaning as *if*.
Tell me if that magazine is interesting. = Tell me whether that magazine is interesting.
I'd like to know if he liked the article. = I'd like to know whether he liked the article.
Could you tell me if you've finished that newspaper? = Could you tell me whether you've finished that newspaper?

A   On a separate sheet of paper, rewrite each embedded question, using *whether*.

1 I can't remember if there's a test today.
2 We're not sure if the restaurant is still open at 10:00 P.M.
3 Could you tell me if the movie has started yet?
4 I wonder if this hotel has 24-hour room service.
5 Would she like to know if there's an express train?
6 Do you know if this book has a happy ending?

Embedded questions: usage and common errors

You can use an embedded question to ask for information more politely.
Are we late? → Can you tell me if we're late?
What time is it? → Can you tell me what time it is?
Why isn't it working? → Could you explain why it isn't working?
Where's the bathroom? → Do you know where the bathroom is?
How do I get to the bank? → Would you mind telling me how I get to the bank?

Be careful! Do not invert the subject and verb in embedded questions. Use regular statement word order.
Do you know why she won't read the newspaper?
Don't say: Do you know why ~~won't she~~ read the newspaper?

Can you tell me whether this bus runs express?
Don't say: Can you tell me ~~does this bus run~~ express?

Phrases that are often followed by embedded questions	
I don't know . . .	Do you know . . . ?
I'd like to know . . .	Can you tell me . . . ?
Let me know . . .	Can you remember . . . ?
I can't remember . . .	Could you explain . . . ?
Let's ask . . .	Would you mind telling me . . . ?
I wonder . . .	
I'm not sure . . .	

Sentences with embedded questions are punctuated according to the meaning of the whole sentence.

If an embedded question is in a statement, use a period.
I don't know (something). → I don't know who she is.

If an embedded question is in a question, use a question mark.
Can you tell me (something)? → Can you tell me who she is?

B On a separate sheet of paper, combine each phrase and question to write a statement or question with an embedded question.

1 Please let me know (When does the movie start?)
2 I wonder (Where is the subway station?)
3 Can you tell me (How do you know that?)
4 We're not sure (What should we bring for dinner?)
5 They'd like to understand (Why doesn't Pat want to come to the meeting?)
6 Please tell the class (Who painted this picture?)

C On a separate sheet of paper, rewrite each question more politely, using noun clauses with embedded questions. Begin each one with a different phrase. Follow the example.

Where's the airport? *Can you tell me where the airport is?*

1 What time does the concert start?
2 How does this new e-reader work?
3 Why is the express train late?
4 Where is the nearest bathroom?
5 Who speaks English at that hotel?
6 When does Flight 18 arrive from Paris?

D Correct the wording and punctuation errors in each item.

1 Could you please tell me does this train go to Nagoya.
2 I was wondering can I get your phone number?
3 I'd like to know what time does the next bus arrive?
4 Can you tell me how much does this magazine cost.
5 Do you remember where did he use to live?
6 I'm not sure why do they keep calling me.
7 I wonder will she come on time?

UNIT 5 | *Lesson 1*

Direct speech: punctuation rules

When writing direct speech, use quotation marks to indicate the words the speaker actually said.
Put final punctuation marks before the second quotation mark.
Jeremy said, "Don't answer the phone."

Use a comma after the verb or verb phrase that introduces the quoted speech.
They said, "Call me after the storm."

Begin the quoted speech with a capital letter.
I said, "Please come to dinner at nine."

A On a separate sheet of paper, write and punctuate each of the statements in direct speech. Follow the example.

They said tell us when you will be home

They said, "Tell us when you will be home."

1 Martin told me don't get a flu shot
2 My daughter said please pick me up after school
3 The English teacher said read the newspaper tonight and bring in a story about the weather
4 We said please don't forget to listen to the news
5 They said don't buy milk
6 We told them please call us in the morning
7 She said please tell your parents I'm sorry I can't talk right now

B On a separate sheet of paper, change each statement in indirect speech to direct speech.

They told us to be home before midnight.

They told us, "Be home before midnight."

1 The sign downtown said to pack emergency supplies before the storm.
2 Your daughter called and told me to turn on the radio and listen to the news about the flood.
3 Your parents said not to call them before 9 A.M.
4 Mr. Rossi phoned to tell me not to go downtown this afternoon.

 *Lesson 2*

Indirect speech: optional tense changes

When the reporting verbs <u>say</u> or <u>tell</u> are in the simple past tense, it is not always necessary to use a different tense in indirect speech from the one the speaker used. These are three times when it's optional:

When the statement refers to something JUST said:
I just heard the news. They said a storm is coming. OR
I just heard the news. They said a storm was coming.

When the quoted speech refers to something that's still true:
May told us she wants to get a flu shot tomorrow. OR
May told us she wanted to get a flu shot tomorrow.

When the quoted speech refers to a scientific or general truth:
They said that English is an international language. OR
They said that English was an international language.

Be careful! Remember that when the reporting verb is in the present tense, the verb tense in indirect speech does not change.
They say a big storm is expected to arrive tomorrow morning. OR
Don't say: They say a big storm ~~was~~ expected to arrive tomorrow morning.

On a separate sheet of paper, write each direct speech statement in indirect speech. Change the verb in the indirect speech only if necessary.

1 Last Friday my husband said, "I'm going to pick up some things at the pharmacy before the storm." (The storm hit on Saturday.)
2 My next-door neighbors said, "We're going to Spain on vacation this year."
3 She told them, "This year's flu shot is not entirely protective against the flu."
4 He just said, "The danger of a flood is over."
5 We always say, "It's easier to take the train than drive."
6 When I was a child, my parents told me, "It's really important to get a good education." (They still believe that today.)
7 The National Weather Service is saying, "Tonight's weather is terrible."
8 Your parents just told me, "We want to leave for the shelter immediately." (The storm is almost here.)

Expressing the future: review

These forms can express or imply the future:

The present continuous

My tooth has been killing me all week. I'm calling the dentist tomorrow.

What are you doing this afternoon? I'm going to the beach.

The simple present tense

The office is usually open until 9:00, but it closes at 6:00 tomorrow.

Although should, could, ought to, may, might, can, and have to are not future forms, they often imply a future action.

You could catch the next bus.   We should call her next week.

A   Read each sentence. Check the sentences that have future meaning.

☐ 1 Hannah is studying English this month.

☐ 2 Nancy studies English in the evening.

☐ 3 You should call me tomorrow.

☐ 4 He might have time to see you later.

☐ 5 My parents are arriving at 10:00.

☐ 6 I'm taking my daughter out for dinner tonight.

☐ 7 I'm eating dinner with my daughter. Can I call you back?

☐ 8 The class always starts at 2:00 and finishes at 4:00.

☐ 9 We may stay another week in Paris.

The future with will and be going to: review

Use will or be going to to make a prediction or to indicate that something in the future will be true. There is no difference in meaning.

Getting a new car will cost a lot of money. = Getting a new car is going to cost a lot of money.

Use be going to to express a plan.

My tooth has been killing me all week. I'm going to call a dentist. NOT I will call a dentist.

Be careful! Will is also used for willingness. This use of will doesn't have a future meaning. Be going to cannot be used for willingness.

A: Is it true that you won't go to the dentist?

B: I'll go to the dentist, but I don't like fillings. NOT I'm going to go to the dentist, but . . .

B   Complete the conversations, using will or be going to.

1 A: Would you like to go running in the park? I .... in about half an hour.
   B: That sounds great. I .... you there. ^{leave}
                        meet

2 A: It's midnight. Why are you still reading?
   B: We .... a test tomorrow.
                     have

3 A: Do you have plans for tomorrow?
   B: Yes. I .... a chiropractor for the first time.
                        see

4 A: I hope you can come tomorrow night. We'd really like you to be there.
   B: OK. I ....
                  come

5 A: I'm thinking about getting a new laptop.
   B: Really? Well, I .... you mine. I love it.
                      show

Regrets about the past: _wish_ + the past perfect; _should have_ and _ought to have_

> <u>Wish</u> + the past perfect
> I wish I had married later in life. And I wish I hadn't married Celine!
> Do you wish you had bought that car when it was available?
>
> <u>Should have</u> and <u>ought to have</u> + past participle
> <u>Ought to have</u> has the same meaning as <u>should have</u>.
> I should have married later in life. = I ought to have married later in life.
> I shouldn't have married Celine. = I ought not to have married Celine.
>
> Note: American English speakers commonly use <u>should have</u> instead of <u>ought to have</u> in negative statements and in questions.

A On a separate sheet of paper, rewrite the statements and questions, changing <u>wish</u> + the past perfect to <u>should have</u> or <u>ought to have</u>.

She wishes she had had children. (ought to)
She ought to have had children.

1 Do you wish you had studied Swahili? (should)

2 I wish I had gone to New Zealand instead of Australia. (ought to)

3 Do you wish you had taken the job at the embassy? (should)

4 I wish I hadn't studied law. (should)

B Answer each question with a statement using <u>wish</u> + the past perfect.

1 Steven said, "I should have stopped smoking." What does Steven wish? *He wishes he had stopped smoking.*

2 Lauren said, "I shouldn't have bought this car." What does Lauren wish? ....

3 Carl's wife said, "You should have bought a convertible." What does Carl's wife wish? ....

4 Ms. Baker said, "The students should have studied more for the exam." What does Ms. Baker wish? ....

Adjective clauses: common errors

> **Remember:**
> Use the relative pronouns <u>who</u> or <u>that</u> for adjective clauses that describe people. Use <u>that</u> for adjective clauses that describe things.
> Don't say: Feijoada is a dish ~~who~~ is famous in Brazil.
>
> **Don't use a subject pronoun after the relative pronoun.**
> Don't say: Feijoada is a dish that ~~it~~ is famous in Brazil.

A On a separate sheet of paper, combine the two sentences into one, making the second sentence an adjective clause. Use <u>who</u> whenever possible. When it isn't possible, use <u>that</u>. Follow the example.

The hotel clerk was very helpful. / He recommended the restaurant.
The hotel clerk who recommended the restaurant was very helpful.

1 My cousin lives in New Zealand. / She called today.

2 We have a meeting every morning. / It begins at 9:30.

3 The celebration is exciting. / It takes place in spring.

4 The teacher is not very formal. / She teaches the grammar class.

5 Patients might prefer homeopathy. / They want to avoid strong medications.

6 The copy shop is closed on weekends. / It offers express service.

7 The hotel is very expensive. / It has three swimming pools.

8 Do you like the teacher? / He teaches advanced English.

Reflexive pronouns

A reflexive pronoun should always agree with the subject of the verb.
People really enjoy **themselves** at Brazil's Carnaval celebrations.
My sister made **herself** sick from eating so much.

Reflexive pronouns	
myself	itself
yourself	ourselves
himself	yourselves
herself	themselves

Common expressions with reflexive pronouns

believe in oneself	If you believe in yourself, you can do anything.
enjoy oneself	We enjoyed ourselves on our vacation.
feel sorry for oneself	Don't sit around feeling sorry for yourself.
help oneself (to something)	Please help yourselves to dessert.
hurt oneself	Paul hurt himself when he tried to move the fridge.
give oneself (something)	I wanted to give myself a gift, so I got a massage.
introduce oneself	Why don't you introduce yourselves to your new neighbors?
be proud of oneself	She was proud of herself for getting the job.
take care of oneself	You should take better care of yourself.
talk to oneself	I sometimes talk to myself when I feel nervous.
teach oneself (to do something)	Nick taught himself to use a computer.
tell oneself (something)	I always tell myself I'm not going to eat dessert, but I do.
work for oneself	Oscar left the company and now he works for himself.

B Complete the sentences with reflexive pronouns.

1 My brother and his wife really enjoyed .... on their vacation.

2 My uncle has been teaching .... how to cook.

3 The food was so terrific that I helped .... to some more.

4 Instead of staying at home and feeling sorry for .... after the accident, I stayed in touch with all my friends.

5 I hope your sister's been taking good care of ....

6 I was too shy to introduce .... to anyone at the party.

7 Mr. Yu hurt .... while lighting firecrackers for the Chinese New Year.

C Complete each sentence with one of the common expressions with reflexive pronouns. Then add two more sentences of your own.

1 When did your brother .... how to play the guitar?

2 You'd better tell your daughter to stop playing near the stove or she'll ....

3 I really hope you .... when you're on vacation.

4 ....

5 ....

By + reflexive pronouns

Use by with a reflexive pronoun to mean "alone."
You cannot put on a kimono **by yourself**. You need help.
Students cannot learn to speak English **by themselves**. They need practice with others in English.

D Complete each sentence with by and a reflexive pronoun.

1 Very young children shouldn't be allowed to play outside ....

2 Did your father go to the store .... ?

3 How old were you when you learned to make breakfast .... ?

4 We got tired of waiting for a table at the restaurant, so we found one ....

Reciprocal pronouns: _each other_ and _one another_

Each other and **one another** have the same meaning, but **one another** is more formal.

People give each other (or one another) gifts.
Friends send each other (or one another) cards.

> **Be careful!**
> **Reciprocal pronouns don't have the same meaning as reflexive pronouns.**
>
> They looked at themselves. (Each person looked in a mirror or at a photo.)
> They looked at each other. (Each person looked at the other person.)

E On a separate sheet of paper, rewrite each underlined phrase, using a reciprocal pronoun. Then add one sentence of your own. Follow the example.

On Christmas, in many places in the world, people give and receive presents.

On Christmas, in many places in the world, people give each other presents.

1 On New Year's Eve in New York City, people wait in Times Square for midnight to come so they can kiss other people and wish other people a happy new year.

2 During the Thai holiday Songkran, people throw water at other people on the street.

3 During the Tomato Festival in Buñol, Spain, people have a lot of fun throwing tomatoes at other people for about two hours.

4 After a day of fasting during Ramadan, Muslims around the world invite other people home to have something to eat that evening.

5 (Your own sentence)

UNIT 7 Lesson 2

Adjective clauses: _who_ and _whom_ in formal English

In formal written or spoken English, use **who** for subject relative pronouns and **whom** for object relative pronouns.

	subject
The singer was terrible.	+ **He** sang in the restaurant.
The singer	**who sang in the restaurant** was terrible.

	object
The singer was terrible.	+ We heard **him** last night.
The singer	**whom we heard last night** was terrible.

> **Remember:** An object relative pronoun can be omitted.
> The singer we heard last night was terrible.

Complete each formal sentence with **who** or **whom**.

1 The front desk clerk .... works at that hotel is very helpful.

2 The man .... I met on the plane has invited us to lunch.

3 The manager .... lives in Singapore may apply for the job.

4 I'm very satisfied with the dentist .... you recommended.

5 The guests .... we invited to the dinner were an hour late.

6 The sales representative .... you are going to call speaks English.

7 The singer .... you told me about is performing tonight.

8 My friend .... works at the bank can help you.

9 Is your colleague someone .... I can ask to help me?

Real and unreal conditionals: review

• Real (or "factual") conditionals express the present or future results of real conditions.

  Present or everlasting results: Use the present of <u>be</u> or the simple present tense in both clauses.
  If I speak slowly, people understand me.
  If the temperature of water rises above 100 degrees Celsius, it turns to steam.

  Future results: Use the present of <u>be</u> or the simple present tense in the <u>if</u> clause. Use a future form (future with <u>will</u> or present continuous for the future) in the result clause.
  If I'm late, I'll disturb the others at the meeting.

• Unreal conditionals express the results of conditions that don't exist. Use the simple past tense or <u>were</u> in the <u>if</u> clause. Use <u>would</u> + a base form in the result clause. The order of the clauses can be reversed.
  If I bought a more economical car, I wouldn't worry so much about the price of gasoline.
  If he were here, he would tell us about his trip.

  Remember: The order of the clauses in conditional sentences can be reversed. It's customary to use a comma after the <u>if</u> clause when it comes first.
  If you buy a food processor, you won't need to buy a blender.
  You won't need to buy a blender if you buy a food processor.

> **Remember: Conditional sentences have two clauses: an <u>if</u> clause and a result clause.**
>
> • Don't use a future form in an <u>if</u> clause. Don't say: If I ~~will be~~ late, I'll disturb the others at the meeting.
> • Don't use <u>would</u> in an <u>if</u> clause. Don't say: If he ~~would be~~ here, he would tell us about his trip.

A Correct the errors in the conditional sentences. More than one correct answer may be possible.

1 If you will take a good picture, it can preserve memories of times you might forget.

2 If I was you, I would send them an e-mail right away.

3 If you would go out today, you'll need an umbrella.

4 Most people would eat healthy food if they understand the consequences of eating too much junk food.

5 These speakers will be OK if you used them in a smaller room.

6 If the weather will be better, I'd go for a swim.

7 If I would have a chance, I would work shorter hours.

8 Will you ride a bicycle to work if your car broke down?

9 What would you do if I would ask you to make dinner?

10 He won't eat at that restaurant if they would tell him he had to wear formal clothes.

Clauses after <u>wish</u>

Use <u>were</u> or the simple past tense after <u>wish</u> to express a regret about something that's not true now.
  I wish my laptop were top-of-the-line. (But it's not top-of-the-line.)
  I wish I had a Brew Rite digital coffeemaker. (But I don't have one.)

Remember: Use the past perfect after <u>wish</u> to express a regret about something that was not true in the past.
  Sean wishes he hadn't sold his car. (But he did sell it.)
  Sean wished he hadn't sold his car. (But he did.)

Use the conditional (<u>would</u> + a base form) after <u>wish</u> to express a desire in the present that something will occur in the future or on an ongoing basis.
  I wish it would rain. (a desire for a future occurrence)
  I wish it would rain more often. (a desire for something to occur on an ongoing basis)

Use <u>would</u> and a base form after <u>wished</u> to express a wish one had in the past for a future occurrence.
  Yesterday I wished it would rain, but it didn't. (a past wish for a future occurrence)

B Complete each statement or question with the correct form of the verb.

1 I wish my favorite author .... a new book. I've read all her old books so many times.
   write

2 Pat wished she .... more time test-driving cars before she bought that SUV.
   spend

3 Most people wish they .... rich.
be

4 I wish it .... possible for me to get a better camera when I bought this one.
be

5 They wished they .... sooner that their computer was a lemon.
know

6 When I was a child, my parents wished I .... a doctor.
become

7 Do you wish you .... a more comfortable car for the trip tomorrow?
have

8 Marie and her boyfriend are going to Germany tomorrow. Does she wish her boyfriend .... German?
study

9 I wish you .... to bed earlier when you have to get up for work.
go

Unless in conditional sentences

You can use unless instead of if + not.

Unless they buy a freezer, they'll have to go shopping every day. (= If they don't buy a freezer, . . .)

She wouldn't go for a long drive unless she had a phone with her. (= ...if she didn't have a phone with her.)

Martin doesn't buy electronics unless they're state-of-the-art. (= . . . if they're not state-of-the-art.)

C On a separate sheet of paper, rewrite the sentences, changing if + not statements to unless and making any necessary changes. Follow the example.

> If you don't buy the Brew Rite coffeemaker, you'll have to spend a lot more money on another brand.
>
> *Unless you buy the Brew Rite coffeemaker, you'll have to spend a lot more money on another brand.*

1 If you aren't in a hurry, you should walk.

2 If you don't care about special features, you shouldn't consider getting the top-of-the-line model.

3 She won't go running in the park if her friends don't go with her.

4 Claire won't buy a car if it doesn't have a high-tech sound system.

UNIT 8 Lesson 2

The unreal conditional: variety of forms

Unreal conditional sentences can have a variety of active and passive forms in either clause.

If she had worn a seat belt, she wouldn't have been hurt.

If the car had been badly damaged, he would have bought a new one.

If the automobile hadn't been invented, we would still be using horses.

If horses were still being used, our high-speed highway system would never have been created.

If Marie Claire were getting married today, she wouldn't marry Joe.

If Ellie had married Tom, she would have children today.

On a separate sheet of paper, complete the unreal conditional sentences in your own way, using active and passive forms. Refer to the presentation above for some possibilities.

1 If I were elected ruler of a country, . . .

2 The car would have been invented earlier if . . .

3 If I were looking for a high-tech smart phone, . . .

4 If this laptop had been available when I was looking for one, . . .

5 . . . , I wouldn't be studying English now.

6 If I were going to take a commercial space flight today, . . .

Count and non-count nouns: review and extension

Count nouns name things that can be counted individually. They have singular and plural forms.

a president / presidents   a liberal / liberals   a candidate / candidates
a government / governments   an election / elections   a monarchy / monarchies

Non-count nouns name things that are not counted individually. They don't have singular or plural forms and they are not preceded by <u>a</u> or <u>an</u>. To express a specific quantity of a non-count noun, use unit expressions.

a piece of news   a cup of tea   2 kilos of rice   a time of peace   an act of justice

Many nouns can be used as count or non-count nouns, but the meaning is different.

She studied government at the university. (= an academic subject)
That country has had four governments in ten years. (= a group of people who rule the country)

Democracy is the best form of government. (= a type of government)
After the revolution, the country became a democracy. (= a country with a democratic system)

I love chicken. (the food, in general)
I bought a chicken. (one actual bird)

She has blond hair. (in general = all of her hair)
She got a hair in her eye. (= one individual strand of hair)

Complete each sentence with the correct form of each noun.

1 The government has made .... with the economic situation.
                          progress

2 They've given a lot of .... to making the banks stable.
                 importance

3 Unfortunately, ... changed the law.
              radical

4 .... can only come if people stop making war.
      peace

5 .... don't favor extreme change.
        moderate

6 He's .... who would like to outlaw freedom of speech.
          reactionary

7 If I could give you one piece of ...., it would be to vote.
                  advice

8 If more people don't find ...., people will elect a different president.
                work

9 Some .... are more liberal than others.
         government

10 It's impossible to end all ....
             poverty

Gerunds and infinitives: review of form and usage

Form

Gerunds: A gerund is a noun formed from a verb. All gerunds end in -<u>ing</u>. To form a gerund, add -<u>ing</u> to the base form of a verb.

discuss → discussing

If the base form ends in a silent -<u>e</u>, drop the -<u>e</u> and add -<u>ing</u>.

vote → voting

In verbs of one syllable, if the last three letters are a consonant-vowel-consonant* (CVC) sequence, double the last consonant and then add -<u>ing</u> to the base form.

C V C
s i t → sitting

> * Vowels = a, e, i, o, u
> * Consonants = b, c, d, f, g, h, j, k, l, m, n, p, q, r, s, t, v, w, x, y, z

BUT: If the base form of the verb ends in -<u>w</u>, -<u>x</u>, or -<u>y</u>, don't double the final consonant.

blow → blowing   fix → fixing   say → saying

If a base form has more than one syllable and ends in a consonant-vowel-consonant sequence, double the last consonant only if the spoken stress is on the last syllable.

permit → permitting   BUT   order → ordering

Infinitives: An infinitive is also a verbal noun. It is formed with <u>to</u> + the base form of a verb.

elect → to elect   persuade → to persuade

Usage

Gerunds can be subjects, objects, and subject complements within sentences.

Discussing politics is my favorite activity. (subject)

I love reading about government. (direct object of verb <u>love</u>)

I read a book about voting. (object of preposition <u>about</u>)

My favorite pastime is watching TV news. (subject complement after <u>be</u>)

Infinitives function as subjects, direct objects, and subject complements.

To hang out all day discussing politics would be my favorite weekend activity. (subject)

I love to guess who's going to win elections. (direct object of verb <u>love</u>)

My greatest dream for the future is to work in the government. (subject complement after <u>be</u>)

A   Using the sentences in the grammar presentation above as a model, write pairs of sentences on a separate sheet of paper, using the gerunds and infinitives in the two ways shown.

1 voting
  a (as the subject of a sentence)
  b (as a direct object)

2 smoking
  a (as a direct object)
  b (as an object of the preposition <u>to</u>)

3 censoring
  a (as the object of the preposition <u>of</u>)
  b (as a subject complement)

4 to permit
  a (as the subject of a sentence)
  b (as a direct object)

5 to lower
  a (as a direct object)
  b (as the subject of a sentence)

Gerunds and infinitives: review of usage after certain verbs

Certain verbs are followed by gerunds:

avoid, can't stand, discuss, dislike, enjoy, feel like, (don't) mind, practice, quit, sick of, suggest

Other verbs are followed by infinitives:

agree, choose, decide, expect, hope, learn, need, plan, seem, want, wish, would like

Other verbs can be followed by either a gerund or an infinitive:

begin, continue, hate, like, love, prefer

> For a review of gerunds and infinitives, see the Reference Charts on page 126.

B   Complete the paragraph with gerunds or infinitives. When either a gerund or an infinitive would be correct, fill in the blank with both forms.

I hope .... some positive changes in my life, and I would like .... right away. I have
                    1 make   2 start

observed that a lot of people enjoy .... about the political situation, but they don't like
                                              3 complain

.... anything about it. They love .... the news and .... they care about all
     4 do   5 watch   6 say

the poor people who don't have enough to eat, but they don't feel like .... anything to change the
                                                                                  7 do

situation. They worry about poverty, but they don't mind .... money on stupid things they don't need
                                                                      8 waste

.... Well, I'm sick of .... about how people are suffering, and I've agreed
     9 have   10 read

.... a political action group. I simply hate .... anything!
     11 join   12 not do

Prepositions of place: more usage

It's in	Cheju Province. the Rocky Mountains. the Central Valley. the Sahara Desert. the Atlantic Ocean. the state of Jalisco.	It's on	the Nicoya Peninsula. Easter Island. the Hudson River. Coronado Bay. the coast. Lake Placid. the Gulf of Aqaba.	It's in the central part It's southwest It's about 50 kilometers north	of Madrid.

A Write the correct prepositions of place, using <u>in</u>, <u>on</u>, or <u>of</u>.

1 Pisco is .... the Pacific coast of Peru.

2 Tianjin, in China, is .... Hebei Province.

3 Desaguadero is .... Lake Titicaca in Bolivia.

4 The island of Bahrain is .... the Persian Gulf.

5 Cabimas is .... Lake Maracaibo in Venezuela.

6 Sapporo is .... Hokkaido Island in Japan.

7 Riobamba is .... the Pastaza River in Ecuador.

8 Taiwan's Jade Mountain National Park is east .... the city of Alishan.

9 Fengkang is .... the southern part .... Taiwan.

10 The city of Budapest, Hungary, is .... the Danube River.

11 Denmark is north .... Germany.

12 The capital of Chile, Santiago, is located .... the Central Valley.

Proper nouns: capitalization

Capitalize names of:

places	Bolivia, the United Kingdom, Kyoto
languages / nationalities	French, Korean, Arabic
buildings and public places	the Paramount Theater, the Tower of London, the Golden Gate Bridge
organizations	the U.N., the World Bank, the European Union
names and titles	Mary, Mary Smith, Dr. Mary Smith
days / months / holidays	Monday, January, the Moon Festival
religions	Islam, Buddhism, Christianity
historic times or events	the Cold War, the Middle Ages, the Edo Period

When a proper noun has more than one word, each word is capitalized, except for articles (<u>the</u>) and prepositions (<u>of</u>).

Panama City	the Gulf of Aqaba	Mount Fuji
the University of Buenos Aires	Niagara Falls	the Bay of Biscayne

Capitalize all the words of a title, except for articles and prepositions that have fewer than four letters. If an article or a preposition is the first word of a title, capitalize it.

The Story of English	*Looking Back on My Life*
The Financial Times	*I Know Why the Caged Bird Sings*

B On a separate sheet of paper, rewrite each sentence with correct capitalization. Follow the example.

i'm reading *one hundred years of solitude*.

I'm reading One Hundred Years of Solitude.

1 my cousins are studying french.

2 the leaning tower of pisa is in northern italy.

3 it's on the southern coast of australia.

4 i visit the city museum of art every saturday.

5 my uncle jack works for the united nations.

6 the channel tunnel between england and france was completed in 1994.

7 she graduated from the university of washington.

8 we liked the movie about the great wall of china.

9 my son is in the college of sciences.

10 his father speaks korean and japanese fluently.

11 their grandson was born last march.

When a proper noun includes the word <u>of</u>, use <u>the</u>.

with <u>the</u>	without <u>the</u>
the Republic of Korea	Korea
the Gulf of Mexico	Mexico City
the Kingdom of Thailand	Thailand

When a proper noun uses a political word such as <u>republic</u>, <u>empire</u>, or <u>kingdom</u>, use <u>the</u>.

the United Kingdom   the British Empire   the Malagasy Republic

When a proper noun is plural, use <u>the</u>.

the Philippines	the United States
the Netherlands	the Andes Mountains

When a proper noun includes a geographical word such as <u>ocean</u>, <u>desert</u>, or <u>river</u>, use <u>the</u>. BUT do not use <u>the</u> with these geographical words: <u>lake</u>, <u>bay</u>, <u>mountain</u>, <u>island</u>, or <u>park</u>.

with <u>the</u>	without <u>the</u>
the Atlantic Ocean	Crystal Lake
the Atacama Desert	Hudson Bay
the Persian Gulf	Yellow Mountain
the Yangtze River	Hainan Island
the Iberian Peninsula	Ueno Park

When words like <u>east</u> or <u>southwest</u> are used as the name of a geographical area, use <u>the</u>. Do not use <u>the</u> when they are used as adjectives.

with <u>the</u>	without <u>the</u>
the Middle East	Western Europe
the Far East	East Timor
the West	Northern Ireland

When a proper noun includes a word that is a kind of organization or educational group, use <u>the</u>. Do not use <u>the</u> with a university or college (unless the name uses <u>of</u>).

with <u>the</u>	without <u>the</u>
the International Language Institute	Columbia College
the United Nations	Chubu University
the World Health Organization	
the University of Adelaide	

Do not use <u>the</u> with acronyms.

U.C.L.A. (the University of California, Los Angeles)
NATO (the North Atlantic Treaty Organization)
OPEC (the Organization of Petroleum Exporting Countries)

C   Correct the errors in the sentences. Explain your answers.

1   When she went to the Malaysia, she brought her husband with her.

2   A lot of people from United States teach English here.

3   The Haiti is the closest neighbor to Dominican Republic.

4   When we arrived in the Berlin, I was very excited.

5   The Jordan is a country in Middle East.

6   I introduced our visitors to University of Riyadh.

7   I lived in People's Republic of China for about two years.

8   Mr. Yan is a student at College of Arts and Sciences.

9   She is the director of English Language Institute.

10   She's the most famous actress in Netherlands.

11   He's interested in cultures in Far East.

12   The Poland was one of the first countries in the Eastern Europe to change to democracy.

Infinitives with <u>enough</u>

You can use an infinitive after an adjective + <u>enough</u> to give an explanation.
She's **old enough** to vote.   He's not **busy enough** to complain.

Be careful! <u>Too</u> comes before an adjective, but <u>enough</u> comes after an adjective.
It's **too far** to walk.
It isn't **close enough** to walk. NOT It isn't ~~enough close~~ to walk.

A On a separate sheet of paper, complete each statement in your own way, using an infinitive.

1 He's tall enough . . .
2 He isn't strong enough . . .
3 She's thirsty enough . . .

4 She isn't hungry enough . . .
5 The movie was interesting enough . . .
6 The movie wasn't exciting enough . . .

B On a separate sheet of paper, write ten sentences, using your choice of adjectives from the box. Write five using <u>too</u> and an infinitive and five using <u>enough</u> and an infinitive.

early	heavy	important	old	young	long
expensive	high	loud	sick	scary	short

Writing Booster

The Writing Booster is optional. It is intended to orient students to the conventions of written English. Each unit's Writing Booster is focused both on a skill and its application to the Writing exercise from the Unit Review page.

UNIT 1   Formal e-mail etiquette

Social e-mails between friends are informal and have almost no rules. Friends use "emoticons" and abbreviations and don't mind seeing spelling or grammar errors.

Emoticons	Abbreviations
☺ = I'm smiling.	LOL = "Laughing out loud"
☹ = I'm not happy.	LMK = "Let me know"
	BTW = "By the way"
	IMHO = "In my humble opinion"

However, e-mail is also commonly used in business communication between people who have a more formal relationship. When writing a more formal e-mail, it is not acceptable to use the same informal style you would use when communicating with a friend.

For formal e-mails . . .

Do:
- Use title and last name and a colon in the salutation, unless you are already on a first-name basis:
    Dear Mr. Samuelson:
    Dear Dr. Kent:
  If you are on a first-name basis, it's appropriate to address the person with his or her first name:
    Dear Marian:
- Write in complete sentences, not fragments or run-on sentences.
- Check and correct your spelling.
- Use capital and lowercase letters correctly.
- Use correct punctuation.
- Use a complimentary close as in a formal letter, such as:
    Sincerely, Cordially, Thank you, Thanks so much,
- End with your name, even though it's already in the e-mail message bar.

Don't:
- Use emoticons.
- Use abbreviations such as "LOL" or "u" for "you."
- Use all lowercase or uppercase letters.
- Date the e-mail the way you would a written letter. (The date is already in the headings bar.)

A   Circle all the formal e-mail etiquette errors in the e-mail to a business associate. Then explain your reasons.

> Glenn, it was nice to see u yesterday at the meeting. I was wondering if we could continue the meeting sometime next week. Maybe on Tuesday at your place? There's still a lot we need 2 discus. I know you love long meetings LMK if u wanna change the time.

B   **Guidance for the Writing Exercise (on page 12)** Use the do's and don'ts for formal e-mails to check the two e-mail messages you wrote.

UNIT 2   Comparisons and contrasts

COMPARISONS: Use this language to compare two things:

To introduce similarities

- **be alike**
  Herbal medicine and homeopathy are alike in some ways.
- **be similar to**
  Homeopathy is similar to conventional medicine in some ways.

To provide details

- **both**
  Both herbal medicine and homeopathy are based on plants. / Herbal medicine and homeopathy are both based on plants.
- **and . . . too**
  Herbal medicine is based on plants, and homeopathy is too.

- **and . . . (not) either**
  Herbal medicine doesn't use medications, and homeopathy doesn't either.
- **also**
  Many of the medications in conventional medicine also come from plants.
- **as well**
  Many of the medications in conventional medicine come from plants as well.
- **Likewise,**
  Herbs offer an alternative to conventional medications. Likewise, homeopathy offers a different approach.
- **Similarly,**
  Similarly, homeopathy offers a different approach.

CONTRASTS: Use this language to contrast two things: To introduce differences
- **be different from**
  Conventional medicine is different from acupuncture in a number of ways.

To provide details
- **but**
  Herbal medicine treats illness with herbs, but acupuncture mainly treats illness with needles.
- **while / whereas**
  Herbal medicine treats illness with herbs while (or whereas) acupuncture treats illness with needles. OR While (or Whereas) herbal medicine treats illness with herbs, acupuncture treats illness with needles.
- **unlike**
  Spiritual healing involves taking responsibility for one's own healing, unlike conventional medicine. OR Unlike conventional medicine, spiritual healing involves taking responsibility for one's own healing.
- **However,**
  Conventional doctors routinely treat heart disease with bypass surgery. However, acupuncturists take a different approach.
- **In contrast,**
  Herbal doctors treat illnesses with teas made from plants. In contrast, conventional doctors use medicines and surgery.
- **On the other hand,**
  Conventional medicine is based on modern scientific research. On the other hand, herbal therapy is based on centuries of common knowledge.

A On a separate sheet of paper, make comparisons, using the cues in parentheses.

1 There's nothing scarier than having a toothache while traveling. Feeling short of breath while on the road can be a frightening experience. (likewise)
2 Many painkillers can be bought without a prescription. Many antihistamines can be bought without a prescription. (both)
3 A broken tooth requires a visit to the dentist. A lost filling requires a visit to the dentist. (and . . . too)
4 You may have to wait for the results of an X-ray. The results of a blood test may not be ready for several days. (similarly)
5 An X-ray doesn't take much time to do. A blood test doesn't take much time to do. (and . . . not / either)

B On a separate sheet of paper, make contrasts, using the cues in parentheses.

1 If you feel pain in your back, you can try taking a painkiller. If you have pain in your chest, you should see a doctor. (on the other hand)
2 Homeopathy is fairly common in Europe. It is not as popular in the United States. (while)
3 Spiritual healing uses the mind or religious faith to treat illnesses. Other types of treatments do not. (unlike)
4 Conventional medicine and acupuncture have been used for thousands of years. Homeopathy was only introduced in the late eighteenth century. (whereas)
5 Many people choose conventional medicine first when they need medical help. About 80% of the world's population uses some form of herbal therapy for their regular health care. (however)

C **Guidance for the Writing Exercise (on page 24)** Write three statements that show similarities in the two medical treatments you chose to write about and three statements that contrast them. Use the language of comparison and contrast in each statement. Use these statements in your writing.

Use these expressions to state your opinions. Follow the punctuation style in the examples.

- **In my opinion,**
  In my opinion, there's nothing wrong with being a procrastinator. People just have different personalities.

- **To me,**
  To me, it's better to be well organized. Being a procrastinator keeps a person from getting things done.

- **From my point of view,**
  From my point of view, if you aren't well organized, you're going to have a lot of problems in life.

- **I believe**
  I believe that people who are procrastinators have other strengths, such as creativity.

- **I find**
  I find being well organized helps a person get more done.

Use personal examples to make your opinions clear and interesting to readers.

- **For example,**
  I'm usually on time in everything I do. For example, I always pay my bills on time.

- **For instance,**
  My brother is usually on time in everything he does, but sometimes he isn't. For instance, last week he completely forgot to get our mother a birthday gift.

- **. . . , such as . . .**
  There are a few things I tend to put off, such as paying bills and studying for tests.

- **Whenever**
  Some people have a hard time paying their bills on time. Whenever my husband receives a bill, he puts it on the shelf and forgets about it.

- **Every time**
  Every time I forget to pay a bill, I feel terrible.

- **When I was . . .**
  I had to learn how to be well organized. When I was a child, my parents did everything for me.

> **Note:** All of these expressions for stating your opinion can be used either at the beginning of a sentence or at the end. Use a comma before the expression when you use it at the end of a sentence.
> There's nothing wrong with being a procrastinator, **in my opinion**.
> Being well-organized helps a person get more done, **I find**.

> **Be careful!**
> Do not use <u>for example</u> or <u>for instance</u> to combine sentences.
> Don't write: I'm usually on time for everything I do, ~~for example~~, I always pay my bills on time.

> **Remember:**
> Use a comma before <u>such as</u> when it introduces a dependent clause.

A On a separate sheet of paper, write a sentence expressing your personal opinion in response to each of the questions.

1 Do you think children should study the arts in school?

2 Do you think extroverts are better people than introverts?

3 Do you think it's OK to wear casual clothes in an office?

B On a separate sheet of paper, provide a personal example for each of the statements.

1 I'm (I'm not) a very well-organized person.

2 Some (None) of the people I know procrastinate.

3 I always (I don't always) pay my bills on time.

4 I've always (I've never) had a hard time doing things on time.

C **Guidance for the Writing Exercise (on page 36)** State your opinion on the topic. Then list at least five personal examples to support your view. Use the examples in your writing.

A good summary provides only the main ideas of a much longer reading, movie, or event. It should not include lots of details. Here are two effective ways to write a summary:

1 **Answer basic information questions:** For a longer reading, one approach to writing a summary is to think about the answers to the basic questions of: Who?, What?, When?, Where?, Why?, and How?

2 **Focus on main ideas instead of details:** For a shorter reading, identify the main ideas. Sentences that are main ideas provide enough information to tell the story. After you have identified the sentences that express the main ideas, rewrite them in your own words.

> **Some basic information questions:**
> **Who is the book about?**
> The book I read is about Benito Juárez.
> **Who was Juárez?**
> Juárez was the president of Mexico from 1861 to 1872.
> **Why was he important?**
> He restored the Republic and modernized the country.

A Practice answering basic information questions. Think of a movie you really like. On a separate sheet of paper, write any answers you can to the questions.

1 Who is the movie about?

2 When does the movie take place?

3 Where does the movie take place?

4 In three to five sentences, what is the movie about?

5 What actors are in the movie? Who is the director?

6 (Add your own information question.)

B Practice focusing on main ideas. In the article, underline any sentences you think are main ideas. Cross out any sentences you think are details.

Thirty years ago, most people in the United States, Canada, and Europe didn't think about what to wear to work in an office. Men always wore suits and ties. Women wore suits or conservative skirt outfits. But in the 1990s, that started to change.

It began with "casual Fridays." During the summer, some companies invited their employees to "dress down," or wear more casual clothes to work on Fridays. The policy quickly became popular with employees. After this, it didn't take long for employees to start dressing more casually every day of the week.

Many employees welcomed the new dress policy and the more comfortable work environment that came with it. Etiquette had definitely changed, and suits and ties were rarely seen in many offices. Some employees went as far as wearing jeans, T-shirts, and sneakers to the office.

Then some people began to change their minds about casual dress at work. Many managers felt that casual dress had led to casual attitudes toward work. Now the etiquette for dress in many companies is beginning to change back again.

> After you have completed Exercise B, read this summary of the article. How does it compare with the sentences you underlined in the article?
>
> Thirty years ago, most people in the United States, Canada, and Europe didn't think about what to wear to work in an office. But in the 1990s, that started to change. During the summer, some companies invited their employees to "dress down," or wear more casual clothes to work on Fridays. Then some people began to change their minds about casual dress at work. Now the etiquette for dress in many companies is beginning to change back again.

C **Guidance for the Writing Exercise (on page 48)** Answer each question if you can. If you cannot answer a question, answer the next one. Then use your answers to write the summary within your review.

1 What is the title of the reading material you chose?

2 Who is the writer?

3 Who is it about?

4 What is it about?

5 Where does it take place?

6 When does it take place?

7 Why was it written?

8 Why is it important?

9 Did you like it? Why or why not?

10 Would you recommend it to others? Why or why not?

One way to organize supporting details within a paragraph is by **order of importance**, usually beginning with the most important and ending with the least important. Or, if you wish, it is possible to reverse the order, beginning with the least important and building to the most important.

Imagine you are writing an essay about how to prepare for a trip. Use words and expressions that indicate the relative importance of details to the reader.

First, [OR First and most important,] make sure your passport is up-to-date. Nothing can be worse than arriving at the airport and not being able to get on the plane.

Second, [OR Next, OR Following that,] check the weather for your destination. This will ensure that you bring the right clothes. It's terrible to arrive somewhere and find out that the weather is unusually cold for this time of year. The last thing you want to do is to have to go shopping!

Last, [OR Finally,] write a list of important phone numbers and e-mail addresses of people you have to contact. It can be hard to get that information if you are out of your own country.

Following are two ways to construct the paragraph:

1 Write a topic sentence stating the main idea of the paragraph and then begin describing the details in order of importance.

The severity of an earthquake is determined by several factors. First and most important, the magnitude of the quake can make a huge difference. Really strong earthquakes cause lots of damage, even to well-constructed buildings, no matter where or when they occur. Earthquakes with a Richter reading of 9 or over are uniformly catastrophic. The second most important factor is location, . . . etc.

2 Write a topic sentence that states the details in the order of importance.

The severity of an earthquake is determined by four factors, in order of importance: magnitude, location, quality of construction, and timing. The magnitude of an earthquake is by far the most significant factor in its destructive power . . . etc.

A On a separate sheet of paper, rewrite the paragraph, inserting words to indicate the relative importance of each item.

Here are some things not to forget when preparing for an emergency. Call your relatives who live in other places, telling them where you are so they don't worry. Have a discussion with all family members about the importance of listening to emergency broadcasts. Keep a supply of blankets and warm jackets in case of power outages or flooding. Be sure to follow all emergency instructions carefully: Your life and the life of your family could depend on it.

B **Guidance for the Writing Exercise (on page 60)**
Look at the list of supplies and resources. Number them in order of their importance for the emergency you chose. Write notes about why each one is important. Use your notes to help you write about how to prepare for your emergency.

Type of emergency: _____

Supplies and resources	Notes
non-perishable food	
bottled water	
batteries	
smart phones	
GPS devices	
medications	
phone numbers	

Look at the picture in the Oral Review on page 73. The picture tells the story of the lives of Michael and Carlota. It is divided into three topics, each with a date and a topic heading. The headings help the viewer see at a glance how the story will be organized.

Similarly, if a piece of writing contains more than one section or topic, it is sometimes helpful to include **topic headings** each time a new section begins. Each topic heading signals the topic of the paragraph or section in the way a table of contents in a book tells a reader what the sections will be about.

A Read the short biography of famous Dutch painter Vincent Van Gogh. Write your own topic headings to divide the biography into sections.

> Early Life
>
> Vincent Van Gogh was born in a small village in Holland on March 30, 1853. He was an introverted child, and he didn't have many friends. But his younger brother, Theo, was one of them. As he grew up, Vincent became interested in drawing—and he was very good at it.
>
> [   ]
>
> In 1886, Vincent Van Gogh moved to Paris to live with Theo, who collected and sold paintings. In Paris, he met other artists and was influenced by their work. He also became interested in Japanese art and collected woodblock prints.
>
> [   ]
>
> In 1888, he moved to Arles, a town in southern France. The artist Paul Gauguin moved there, too, and they became good friends. But they didn't have much money. Van Gogh often became sad and could not paint.
>
> [   ]
>
> After a while, Van Gogh recovered and began to paint again. He sent some paintings to Paris, but he could not sell them. Then, in 1890, early on a Sunday evening, Van Gogh went out to the countryside with his paints. He took out a gun and shot himself in the chest. In his short, sad life, Van Gogh painted 200 paintings. He sold only one of them.

B **Guidance for the Writing Exercise (on page 72)** Use headings like these to organize your autobiography by topic. Under each heading, write notes of facts that belong in that section. Then refer to those notes as you write your autobiography.

Some headings:
My parents   My birth   My childhood
My studies   (other)

UNIT 7   Descriptive details

To describe an event, be sure to provide descriptive details that express these four senses:

sight   The fireworks are like beautiful red and yellow flowers in the sky.
There is a huge parade with thousands of people, and everyone is smiling.

sound   As you walk down the street, you can hear music and people singing.
The fireworks are as loud as thunder, and you have to cover your ears.

smell   You can smell the meat grilling on the street.
Everything smells delicious, and you can't wait to eat!

taste   The pastries are as sweet as honey, and you can't stop eating them.
The dish has the sour taste of lemon.

> Try using these patterns in some of your details.
> **like**
> This traditional dessert looks **like** a beautiful white cloud.
> **as . . . as**
> When it is in season, this local fruit is **as sweet as** sugar.
> **so . . . that**
> The decorations in the street are **so colorful that** you feel like a child seeing them for the first time.

A On a separate sheet of paper, write a sentence that expresses one of the four senses for each of the topics. Try to use like, as . . . as, and so . . . that in some of your sentences.

1 Describe a smell in someone's kitchen.
2 Describe a sound in your classroom.
3 Describe the taste of your favorite food.
4 Describe the taste of something you liked as a child.

5 Describe something you see early in the morning.
6 Describe something you hear at a park.
7 Describe something you see at a park.

B **Guidance for the Writing Exercise (on page 84)** Write the names of the two holidays you chose. Then, under the name of each holiday, make a list of sights, sounds, smells, and tastes associated with it. Use these details in your writing.

When a piece of writing contains several paragraphs, the ideas are often summarized in a paragraph at the end. Including a final **summary statement** reminds the reader of the main ideas that were presented. Read the short essay to the right. Notice the summary statement at the end.

After a problem or a breakdown, many drivers say, "If I had only had a spare tire, I would have been able to fix it and be on my way in a few minutes." Here are the things responsible drivers should never forget. First, a flashlight with working batteries can help you repair your car in the dark. Second, a spare tire can save you hours of waiting for help. You can't change that tire without a jack. If your car breaks down at night, flares can warn oncoming traffic that you are stopped. And if your battery dies, jumper cables can help you start the car again.

No matter how high-tech a car you have, breakdowns can happen at a moment's notice. However, we can plan ahead and be equipped with some simple technology to prevent a problem from becoming worse.

A   Read the paragraphs and underline the main ideas. Then write your own summary statement.

There are a number of excellent presentation graphics technologies available today. Two well-known ones are Microsoft Office's PowerPoint™ and Macintosh's Keynote™. No matter which technology you use, here are some do's and don'ts that will make your presentation more successful.

First, the do's: Keep your slides concise. Keep the amount of text to a minimum because it's hard for the audience to focus on your main points if there's too much text. Use large letters (from 18 to 48 points) and simple, easy-to-read fonts. Use bullets to separate items in a list. Use just a few colors and keep that color scheme consistent throughout the presentation. If you project your slides in a bright room, light-colored text on dark backgrounds will be easiest to read.

What should a presenter avoid? Don't use all capital letters. They are hard to read. Never use dark letters on a dark background. The presentation will be hard to see. Don't use sound effects that are unrelated to the meaning of your presentation and avoid distracting transitions.

When presenting from a PowerPoint or Keynote presentation, look at your computer screen or handheld notes, not the screen the audience is looking at—to do that you would have to turn away from your audience and you would lose contact with the people you are presenting to.

Your summary statement:

_____

_____

_____

B   **Guidance for the Writing Exercise (on page 96)** After you have completed writing about the advantages, disadvantages, and historical impact of your invention or discovery, circle the main ideas in each paragraph. Use the main ideas to write a summary statement for your final paragraph.

The following language helps organize information by contrasting it. It signals to the reader that a contrasting idea will follow.

in contrast
on the one hand / on the other hand
however
nevertheless
even though

A technique to help organize contrasting ideas is to make two lists: **pros** (arguments in favor) and **cons** (arguments against).

To the right are handwritten notes a student made to prepare an essay that presents arguments for and against the mandatory use of a motorcycle helmet. The actual essay can be organized in two ways:

Pros	Cons
—injuries will be less serious in case of accidents	—it limits a person's freedom
—lives will be saved	—people should drive carefully to prevent most accidents
—medical costs will be lower in case of accidents	—if people think they are protected and safe from injury when they use a helmet, they might not drive carefully
—people don't have good judgment, so the government has to make decisions for them	
—looks cool	—the government shouldn't interfere in the decisions of adults
	—messes up your hair

1   the pros and cons are presented together in contrasting sentences in each paragraph, or
2   as two paragraphs with the ideas in favor in one paragraph and the ideas against in another.

A The essay is organized into two paragraphs. Read the essay and write the main idea of each paragraph.

Should motorcycle drivers be required to wear helmets?

Main idea:

Many cities and countries have laws requiring motorcycle drivers to wear a helmet. In some ways, these laws are good and effective. For example, it is well known that motorcycle driving is very dangerous. If a motorcycle collides with another vehicle, the driver of the motorcycle has no protection and is often injured or killed. Most fatal injuries are caused by the driver's head hitting the pavement. On the one hand, such injuries are often not survivable. But on the other hand, if a driver is wearing a helmet, the chance of fatal head injury is reduced. Unfortunately, even though drivers know that helmet use could save their lives, many think an accident won't happen to them. However, if there is a law requiring drivers to wear helmets, a lack of judgment won't matter. Drivers will have no choice but to wear the helmet.

Main idea:

Nevertheless, there are arguments against compulsory helmet-use laws. Some people feel that wearing a helmet causes drivers to have a false sense of security. In other words, drivers may feel that when they are wearing a helmet, they don't have to drive carefully. With a helmet, they feel they have a justification for reckless driving. In contrast, other people object to helmet laws because they feel that the government shouldn't interfere with the decisions of adults. They argue that if they get hurt, it's their own responsibility, and if they die, it doesn't hurt anyone but themselves. People who have this opinion often complain about government intrusion in personal freedom.

B **Guidance for the Writing Exercise (on page 108)** Write the issue you chose and make a list of pros and cons. Use your notes to organize and write your essay.

UNIT 10   Organizing by spatial relations

To describe a place, organize details according to spatial relations. Choose a starting point (for example, the capital city or the largest city). Describe its location.
Lima is the capital of Peru. It is located **on** the west coast, **on** the Pacific Ocean.
The largest city in China is Shanghai. It is located **in** the southeast, **along** the East China Sea.

Describe where things are located in relation to that point. Choose a logical order to follow, such as north to south or west to east, so it is easy for the reader to understand.

- **To the [north] of**
  To the north of São Paulo is the city of Campinas.

- **In the [south] of**
  In the south of the island is the city of Kaosiung.

- **[East] of**
  East of Tokyo is the city of Chiba.

- **Next to**
  Next to Washington, D.C., is the city of Baltimore.

- **In the middle / center of**
  In the center of the country is the city of Madrid.

- **Along the [coast / river]**
  Along the coast, and west of the capital, are the cities of Valparaíso and Viña del Mar.

- **At the start of**
  At the start of the Pan-American Highway is the city of Fairbanks, Alaska.

- **At the end of**
  At the end of the Volga River is the Caspian Sea.

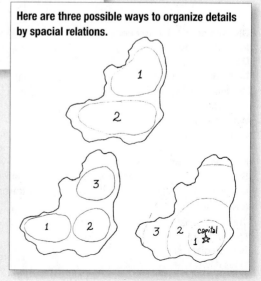

Here are three possible ways to organize details by spacial relations.

A On a separate sheet of paper, write a description for each of these places, using the language above. (Use the map on the page shown.)

  1 Cobán (page 112)   4 Mexico (page 112)
  2 Denali National Park (page 121)   5 Alice Springs (page 113)
  3 Sydney (page 113)   6 Juneau (page 121)

B **Guidance for the Writing Exercise (on page 120)** Draw a simple map of the place you chose. Write numbers on your map for at least two important places, beginning with 1 for the location you will start from, 2 for the next location, and so on. Then use your map to help you write your descriptions, using the language of spatial relations.

Top Notch Pop Lyrics

▶ 1:16–1:17 **It's a Great Day for Love**
[Unit 1]

Wherever you go,
there are things you should know,
so be aware
of the customs and views—
all the do's and taboos—
of people there.
You were just a stranger in a sea of new faces.
Now we're making small talk on a
first-name basis.

(CHORUS)
It's a great day for love, isn't it?
Aren't you the one I was hoping to find?
It's a great day for love, isn't it?
By the time you said hello,
I had already made up my mind.

Wherever you stay
be sure to obey
the golden rules,
and before you relax,
brush up on the facts
you learned at school.
Try to be polite and always be sure to get
some friendly advice on proper etiquette.

(CHORUS)

And when you smiled at me
and I fell in love,
the sun had just appeared
in the sky above.
You know how much I care, don't you?
And you'll always be there, won't you?

(CHORUS)

▶ 1:33–1:34 **X-ray of My Heart** **[Unit 2]**

Thanks for fitting me in.
This heart is killing me.
Oh, that must hurt.
Are you in a lot of pain?
Yes, I thought I'd better
see someone right away.
It might be an emergency—
could you try to explain?

(CHORUS)
Give me something to keep me
from falling apart.
Doctor, won't you please
take an X-ray of my heart.

You know, I'm here on business,
and today I saw a guy …
Why don't you have a seat
while I do some simple tests?
Thanks. As I was saying,
he walked by without a word.
So that's what's bothering you—
just go home and get some rest!

(CHORUS)
The minute that I saw him
I felt weak in the knees.
Are you dizzy, short of breath?
Does it hurt when you sneeze?

Yes, I have all those symptoms—
and a pain in my chest.
Well, love at first sight
can have painful side effects.
Now, I might not be able
to go to work today.
Could I get a prescription
for some kind of medicine?
Well, let's have a look now.
You might have to heal yourself,
or try another treatment
for the kind of pain you're in.

(CHORUS)

▶ 2:17–2:18 **I'll Get Back to You** **[Unit 3]**

Your camera isn't working right.
It needs a few repairs.
You make me ship it overnight.
Nothing else compares.
You had to lengthen your new skirt,
and now you want to get
someone to wash your fancy shirts
and dry them when they're wet.
Come a little closer—
let me whisper in your ear.
Is my message getting across
to you loud and clear?

(CHORUS)
You're always making plans.
I'll tell you what I'll do:
let me think it over and
I'll get back to you.

You want to get your suit dry-cleaned.
You want to get someone
to shorten your new pair of jeans
and call you when they're done.
I guess I'll have them print a sign
and hang it on your shelf,
with four small words in one big line:
"Just do it yourself."
Let me tell you what this song
is really all about.
I'm getting tired of waiting while you
figure it out.
I've heard all your demands,
but I have a life, too.
Let me think it over and
I'll get back to you.
I'm really reliable,
incredibly fast,
extremely helpful
from first to last.
Let me see what I can do.
Day after day,
everybody knows
I always do what I say.

(CHORUS)

▶ 2:31–2:32 **A True Life Story** **[Unit 4]**

The story of our lives
is a real page-turner,
and we both know

what it's all about.
It's a fast read,
but I'm a slow learner,
and I want to see
how it all turns out.

(CHORUS)
It's a true life story.
I can't put it down.
If you want to know who's in it,
just look around.

The story of our lives
is a real cliffhanger.
It's hard to follow,
but boy, does it pack a thrill—
a rollercoaster ride
of love and anger,
and if you don't write it,
baby, then I will.

(CHORUS)
You can't judge a book by its cover.
I wonder what you're going to discover.
When you read between the lines,
you never know what you might find.
It's not a poem or a romance novel.
It's not a memoir or a self-help book.
If that's what you like, baby, please
don't bother.
If you want the truth, take another look.

(CHORUS)

▶ 3:17–3:18 **Lucky to Be Alive** **[Unit 5]**

(CHORUS)
Thank you for helping me to survive.
I'm really lucky to be alive.

When I was caught in a freezing snowstorm,
you taught me how to stay warm.
When I was running from a landslide
with no place to hide,
you protected me from injury.
Even the world's biggest tsunami
has got nothing on me,
because you can go faster.
You keep me safe from disaster.
You're like some kind of hero—
you're the best friend that I know.

(CHORUS)
When the big flood came with the
pouring rain,
they were saying that a natural
disaster loomed.
You just opened your umbrella.
You were the only fellow who kept calm
and prepared.
You found us shelter.
I never felt like anybody cared
the way that you did when you said,
"I will always be there—
you can bet your life on it."
And when the cyclone turned the day
into night,
you held a flashlight and showed me the safe
way home.

You called for help on your cell phone.
You said you'd never leave me.
You said, "Believe me,
in times of trouble you will never be alone."
They said it wasn't such a bad situation.
It was beyond imagination.
I'm just glad to be alive—
and that is no exaggeration.

(CHORUS)

▶ 3:31–3:32 **I Should Have Married Her** [Unit 6]

She was born with talents
in both literature and art.
It must have been her love of books
that first captured my heart.
We both had experience
with unhappiness before.
I thought we would be together
for rich or for poor.

(CHORUS)
I should have married her.
She was the love of my life,
but now she's someone else's wife.
I thought we would be happy.
I thought our love was so strong.
I must have got it all wrong.

It's hard to make a living
when you're living in the past.
I wish we could have worked it out,
but some things just don't last.
I wonder what she's doing
or if she thinks of me.
One day she just changed her mind.
The rest is history.

(CHORUS)

It's too late for regrets.
She's gone forever now.
We make our plans,
but people change,
and life goes on somehow.

(CHORUS)

▶ 4:18–4:19 **Endless Holiday** [Unit 7]

Day after day,
all my thoughts drift away
before they've begun.
I sit in my room
in the darkness and gloom
just waiting for someone
to take me to a tourist town,
with parties in the street and people dancing
to a joyful sound.

(CHORUS)
It's a song that people sing.
It's the laughter that you bring
on an endless holiday.
It's the happiness inside.
It's a roller coaster ride
on an endless holiday.

I try and I try
to work hard, but I
get lost in a daze,
and I think about
how sad life is without

a few good holidays.
I close my eyes, pull down the shade,
and in my imagination I am dancing in a
big parade,
and the music is loud.
I get lost in the crowd
on an endless holiday.
It's a picnic at noon.
It's a trip to the moon
on an endless holiday,
with flags and confetti,
wild costumes and a great big
marching band,
as we wish each other well
in a language we all understand.
The sky above fills with the light
of fireworks exploding, as we dance along
the street tonight.

(CHORUS)

▶ 4:34–4:35 **Reinvent the Wheel** [Unit 8]

You've got your digi-camera with
the Powershot,
Four mega pixels and a memory slot.
You've got your e-mail and your Internet.
You send me pictures of your digi-pet.
I got the digi-dog and the digi-cat,
the "digi" this and the "digi" that.
I hate to be the one to break the news,
but you're giving me the "digi" blues,

(CHORUS)
And you don't know
the way I really feel.
Why'd you have to go and
reinvent the wheel?

You've got your cordless phone and
your microwave,
and your Reflex Plus for the perfect shave.
It's super special, top of the line,
with the latest new, cutting-edge design.
You've got your SLR and your LCD,
your PS2 and your USB.
I've seen the future and it's pretty grim:
They've used up all the acronyms.

(CHORUS)

I keep waiting for a breakthrough innovation:
Something to help our poor communication.
Hey, where'd you get all of that high-tech taste?
Your faith in progress is such a waste.
Your life may be state of the art,
but you don't understand the human heart.

(CHORUS)

▶ 5:20–5:21 **We Can Agree to Disagree** [Unit 9]

I believe that dogs should be
allowed to wander free.
That may be true, but don't you think
that people have rights, too?
I believe that time has come
for true dog liberty.
I see what you mean, but I don't
share your point of view.

(CHORUS)
We can agree to disagree
about what's wrong and right.
It wouldn't be cool for you and me
to fight when we don't see eye to eye.

I think my cat deserves to eat
a treat, no matter what.
Well, on the one hand, yes,
but on the other hand, well, no.
Don't you feel that every meal
should be shared with a pet?
That's one way to look at it,
but I don't think so.

(CHORUS)

You can be a radical.
You can be conservative.
My dog doesn't care, and he won't ask you
to leave.
You can be a moderate.
You can be a liberal.
You can believe what you want to believe.
I urge you to think it over
before you decide.
That your dog is very nice,
I couldn't agree more.
I believe that you and I
should be the best of friends.
That's exactly what I think.
Why weren't we friends before?

(CHORUS)

▶ 5:45–5:46 **It's a Beautiful World** [Unit 10]

The path is located
half an hour west of here.
I heard it's a must-see,
and that it goes pretty near
to a breathtaking beach
a little farther up the coast.
That's the one that everybody
seems to like the most.

(CHORUS)
It's a beautiful world.
Be careful as you go.
The road is dark and dangerous.
Be sure to take it slow.
Yes, it's a beautiful world,
from the mountains to the seas.
Through life's lonesome valleys,
won't you come with me?

Are you planning on going
to see the waterfall?
I've been thinking about it,
and I want to do it all!
Would you happen to know
anything about Rocky Cave?
How do you get there?
Can you show me the way?

(CHORUS)
I can't wait.
I don't want to miss it.
There isn't a place worth seeing
that I don't want to visit.

(CHORUS)